ty

es

DATE DUE

THE 10 BEST-EVER ANXIETY MANAGEMENT TECHNIQUES

Understanding How Your Brain Makes You Anxious

and What You Can Do to Change It

SECOND EDITION

MARGARET WEHRENBERG

W. W. NORTON

Independent Publishers since 1923

New York • London

All rights reserved
Printed in the United States of America
Second Edition

For information about special discounts for bulk purchases, please contact
W. W. Norton Special Sales at specialsales@wwnorton.com or 800-233-4830

Manufacturing by LSC Harrisonburg
Production Manager: Christine Critelli

Library of Congress Cataloging-in-Publication Data

Names: Wehrenberg, Margaret, author.
Title: The 10 best-ever anxiety management techniques : understanding how your brain makes you anxious and what you can do to change it / Margaret Wehrenberg.
Other titles: Ten best-ever anxiety management techniques
Description: Second edition. | New York : W.W. Norton & Company, [2018] |
Series: A Norton professional book | Includes bibliographical references and index.
Identifiers: LCCN 2017050780 | ISBN 9780393712148 (pbk.)
Subjects: LCSH: Anxiety. | Brain.
Classification: LCC BF575.A6 W44 2018 | DDC 152.4/6—dc23
LC record available at https://lccn.loc.gov/2017050780

W. W. Norton & Company, Inc., 500 Fifth Avenue, New York, N. Y. 10110
www.wwnorton.com

W. W. Norton & Company Ltd., 15 Carlisle Street, London W1D 3BS

1 2 3 4 5 6 7 8 9 0

For Ellie and Hal

Contents

Acknowledgments

If I could, I would acknowledge every client I have had who taught me through our therapy interactions how to understand anxiety and to resolve the symptoms. Although naming any of them, much less all of them, is not possible, I remember those who shared so much with me and appreciate the trust they showed. The techniques in this volume have all been used in the consulting room and reflect the experiences that I have had with those whose identities are not revealed but whose stories made this book possible.

The 10 Best-Ever Anxiety
Management Techniques

Preface

———

Continuity gives us roots. Change gives us branches,
letting us stretch and grow and reach new heights.
———Pauline R. Kezer

How does it happen that the *10 Best-Ever Anxiety Management Techniques* need revision? If they were the best ever, then maybe they should remain the same. I believe, however, that Pauline Kezer got it right: there are times when change is necessary if we're going to grow. As I teach the seminar based on this book, I am constantly changing and adapting it based on the latest neuroscientific research about how therapy works and how we can most effectively manage anxiety. This edition of the book reflects new information that makes anxiety easier to alleviate.

In fact, all the methods I included in the first edition of this book are still included, but some have taken a backseat as other, more significant methods have been highlighted. Some tried-and-true methods are truer than ever before, as research has provided increasing support for how important they are. In many cases, I have clarified how to use the techniques, again based on the continuing stream of research about anxiety and its treatment.

If you benefited from the first edition of this book, this revised edition will add to that. If you didn't read the first edition, this is the resource that will help you to take charge of anxiety and get free from crippling panic, worry, or social anxiety.

It is a blessing in my life to have this forum to share such life-altering knowledge.

Margaret Wehrenberg
March 2017

PART I

UNDERSTANDING
YOUR BRAIN

When it comes right down to it, you can understand your brain only by using your brain. Every thought, image, and perception you have and every action you make begins with activity in your brain. And that's good news, because—as this book is going to demonstrate—you can use your brain to change your anxious brain. And you can't separate your brain activity from your body. If you think of your brain and body as distinct from each other, you set up a false dichotomy. Our brains are organs in our bodies, and every thought, image, and perception is linked to how it is affected and interpreted through sensory and visceral sensations. This brain–body interconnectedness is a major focus of this discussion about how your brain creates anxiety and can change anxiety.

Now, you can manage anxiety effectively whether or not you know about the brain. You could skip Chapter 1 and use the rest of the book very well. The 10 techniques outlined in this book work, but their effectiveness doesn't rely on understanding *how* they work. Nevertheless, an understanding of *why* these techniques are effective from a neurobiological standpoint can maximize how well they work. It will be easier for you to exert the effort needed to manage anxiety, even when it seems hard to do, if you know you're changing your brain every time you control the symptoms. You automatically gain a certain measure of control over anxiety when you say to yourself, "This is my brain doing this. Anxiety is not *me*, and I can control it." Chapter 1 is intended to give you enough brain basics to understand why these 10 techniques will work.

MEDICATION CONTROLS THE BRAIN BUT DOESN'T TEACH TECHNIQUE

It's important to understand what medications do for anxiety and how they work so that when you make decisions about whether to add medication to anxiety management, you have clarity about the benefits and limits of drug therapy. What you may not have been told if you've started using meds for anxiety symptoms is that by relying solely on pills, you won't learn how to control or eliminate your symptoms *without* medication. You'll never develop the tools for managing the anxiety, which, in all likelihood, will turn up again whenever you feel undue stress or go through significant life changes. What you should be told when getting medication is that in many cases, the right management techniques can offer relief from anxiety in a matter of weeks—about the same amount of time it might take for anxiety medications to become effective. It is often best to have a therapist and a physician working with you to integrate an initial medication protocol with techniques you can use for effective anxiety management even after your meds are discontinued.

ONE

How Your Brain Makes You Anxious

My goal in this chapter is simple: to sketch out basic aspects of brain structure and function to clarify why the anxiety management techniques outlined in this book work. Although you don't need to become an expert in brain chemistry, I want to give you just enough knowledge to use the techniques successfully. Of course, as I indicated in the introduction to Part I, they work even if you don't know why they work, but you will be able to apply these techniques more effectively if you understand how doing them will change your brain in ways that will make you less anxious for life.

Neuroscientists have learned so much about the brain in recent years that it is now possible to describe how some parts of the brain and neurotransmitter function contribute to feelings of anxiety. (If you want the detailed research for this chapter, I refer you to the tome *The Neurobiology of Mental Illness*, edited by Dennis Charney, Pamela Sklar, Joseph Buxbaum and Eric Nestler, published in 2013. See Section IV on mood disorders, edited by Helen S. Myberg, and Section V on anxiety disorders, edited by Kerry J. Ressler.) This research has made quite a difference in the way those of us in the mental health profession view the treatment of anxiety. Although many techniques we have used for years remain effective, we now know more about why those techniques work so well and when and how you can use those techniques for your benefit. And we also know now that you can get some relief from anxiety symptoms even before you complete psychotherapy for other problems. Remember that you can *use* your brain to *change* your brain.

SYSTEMS AND FEEDBACK

Just about all of your brain-body workings occur in *systems* that start and stop the thoughts and sensations you experience. The systems that are important to understanding the psychology of anxiety and its treatment are the central nervous system, the peripheral nervous system, and the stress response system. Those systems determine how you sense anxiety and influence how you think about it and how you act. The *central* nervous system is made up of the brain and spinal cord. The *peripheral* nervous system includes all the nerves that go to and from the spinal cord, and it branches into two subsystems: the autonomic nervous system and the somatic nervous system.

The brain directs the whole show via the spinal cord. The various structures of this organ, working in concert, are responsible for receiving input, organizing and creating emotional and physical responses, developing cognition (such as thinking and remembering), and planning motor responses. The spinal cord carries nerve impulses and receives impulses from the peripheral nervous system. The *somatic* branch of the nervous system includes the voluntary movements of muscles and joints. The *autonomic* system, which is responsible for involuntary movement, gets most of the attention in our discussion about how your brain makes you anxious.

The autonomic nervous system has three branches: the sympathetic and

Table 1.1 The Nervous System

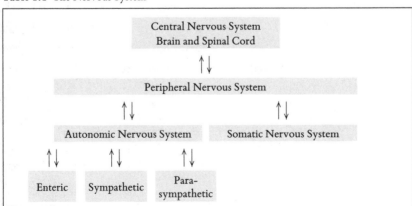

the parasympathetic systems, which are responsible for getting things going in your body and calming things down, respectively, and the *enteric* system for digestive processes. The *sympathetic* system initiates arousal in the heart, lungs, and other organs. The *parasympathetic* system communicates via the vagus nerve to calm activity in the cardiovascular, respiratory, and other systems. The digestive system is reactive to the action in the sympathetic and parasympathetic systems. The skin and glands also react to autonomic nervous system activity.

These systems communicate in feedback loops, i.e., when neurotransmitters initiate activity in the brain or body, the action generates a message that it is complete. When activity starts, it has to stop again. Every cell has to rest and recharge so it can go again later. How do the various parts of your body receive communication about what to do when?

HOW YOUR BRAIN COMMUNICATES

Your brain is a complicated network of brain cells called *neurons*. You have 10 billion neurons, and each of them can connect with as many as 10,000 other neurons. The possibilities for how those cells connect and network are virtually endless. There is more to know about how the brain works than we will learn in our lifetimes. But what we know so far is that every function in your body, every thought you have, and every emotion you feel is the result of activity in the brain. If your brain is dead, then even with healthy bodily organs, nothing will work. And just as you don't feel your best if you have an organ in your body that's malfunctioning, your thoughts and emotions can be troubled unless every part of your brain is working well.

All of those 10 billion neurons have to communicate with each other to create your thoughts, behaviors, and emotions (among many other tasks that we're not going to discuss here). So how do they do it? Neurons communicate by sending messengers back and forth in the space between brain cells, called the *synapse*. These messengers of the brain are called *neurotransmitters*. There are many types of neurotransmitters, and where they are released can determine the message they communicate.

We all know that the meaning of a message being sent is determined by who's reading it. For example, let's say you send an email that communicates your love for a coworker. If you send it to the object of your affections, it may be readily received and induce a feeling of warmth and happiness, but what if you accidentally send it to the person you just broke up with? The same message in the wrong mailbox causes agitation for the heartbroken person who reads it. And what if your boss gets that same note and starts to fret about what you're doing on your work time? Same message, different result, depending on the receiver.

In a way, this happens with neurotransmitters. Take dopamine, for example. Dopamine (DA) is a neurotransmitter that is received in one part of your brain as "I feel good." (And not just ho-hum good, but the James Brown version, "I *fee-eel* good!") But, if the DA is received in the thinking part of your brain, it will hold your attention to what's going on. In yet another part of your brain, DA helps you have smooth motor functioning—it is depleted in people with Parkinson's disease. So, as you can see, DA produces different results depending on where in the brain it is received.

When you learn about DA as it relates to anxiety, you will be interested in that first function—pleasure—because it's what helps people feel motivated to overcome anxiety. And when you want to learn how to decrease your reactions to scary incidents, you might want to know how dopamine causes you to pay extra attention when you're very scared. Certain therapy methods help you unlearn the scariness of situations by taking charge of what you pay attention to.

What can go wrong with neurotransmitters? For messages to get sent from one neuron to another in the first place, there must be enough neurotransmitters available to get the message across. One reason people with anxiety might use medication is to increase the number of neurotransmitters that will help get the message sent.

It is also possible that there are problems with transmission. Maybe there are enough neurotransmitters to send the message, but they can't get from one neuron to another or they don't have enough receptors (places to pick up the message.) One neurotransmitter called serotonin (SE) gets received in a lot of different places, and if it has trouble getting through, one result is worrying. One of the places in your brain where SE is needed is responsible for shifting gears in your thoughts. When you get stuck on a thought—going over and over it—you start to worry. You can use your decision-making ability to overrule worry, thus taking charge of worry on purpose (as I will describe later in the worry management techniques). This can help make up for the effect of serotonin not getting through to where it's needed. Of course, I will also discuss how to make sure that serotonin has the best chance of getting through so that worry is less of a problem to begin with.

Alternatively, there may be too *many* messages being sent. Excessive amounts of neurotransmitters may cause you to make a big deal over nothing. It will FEEL LIKE A BIG DEAL, but that's only because the flurry of neurotransmitters that are released is excessive. This happens to people who have too many stress response neurotransmitters or too many neurotransmitters that respond to the stress hormone. The phrase "making a mountain out of a molehill" is exactly what your brain may do—send out too many messages that communicate, "This is stressful!" Your brain and your body will overreact with lots of stress because the extra neurotransmitters make the situation seem urgent. You can use techniques to help you calm down on purpose for this kind of problem.

Receiving Messages

Even if the number of neurotransmitters and their transmission are fine, anxiety can occur if the message has problems at the receiving end. The neurons that are supposed to pick up messages may not do so easily. If that's the case, a neurotransmitter may not be received, and thus the message (such as to calm down or feel good) won't go through. In particular, a neurotransmitter called GABA is responsible for slowing down activity in the brain so that you can stop your brain cells from firing off anxiety-producing messages. But the networks of communication have to get cleared for new messages to be sent. So, if GABA is not being received very well, you may end up feeling very anxious or even panicky, depending on where in the brain the GABA is working (or not working well, as the case may be).

You know that there are radio waves and cell phone signals in the air all around you, but you need to have your equipment tuned in to make sense of the message. Once the signal is received, your equipment has to interpret and send information along. This is a metaphor for brain function. Different parts of the brain receive, send, interpret, and create responses to the signals they receive. The parts of the brain that are of most interest in discussing anxiety play those roles—receivers and relayers of information, coordinators and interpreters of signals that help to form a coherent picture of information, and parts of the brain that create new responses to information as it comes in. Different parts of the brain have different functions, but just as completing a call on a wireless phone requires the phone to receive a signal, interpret it, and then transmit back what you say, the parts of your brain all need to function smoothly for messages to be clearly received and sent.

Balance Is Necessary for Healthy Functioning

Your brain-body prefers a state called homeostasis—just enough arousal and not too much. Complex interactions between neurotransmitters occur at unbelievably fast rates. Before I discuss individual neurotransmitters and their role in creating anxiety symptoms, think for a minute about how much your brain likes everything to be in balance. You already know your brain carefully monitors everything going on in your body, trying to keep your whole body balanced. Think about what happens when you exercise. You increase the demand for oxygen, and when you start to run out of oxygen, your respiration increases and your heart rate may increase too. You can decide to direct your breathing on purpose, such as when you lift weights or do yoga or martial arts, but even if you don't think about it, your brain will make sure you get the right balance of oxygen by directing your body to breathe faster and telling your heart rate to pick up.

Similarly, your brain monitors the balance of neurotransmitters. If an imbalance occurs, your brain initiates activity to achieve balance. It functions best when only minor imbalances between levels of neurotransmitters exist. Just as a deficiency of oxygen is felt as shortness of breath, excesses and deficiencies of neurotransmitters produce symptoms too, and what kinds of symptoms you experience depends on which neurotransmitter in which part of the brain is having a problem. Insufficient or excessive amounts of neurotransmitters show up as problems in your mood, behavior, or think-ing. The techniques presented in this book can help your brain to rebalance itself. When your brain can't achieve balance because you're sick, not eat-ing right, not sleeping, or have some other physical problem, then you will probably also have to make changes in your eating or sleeping or get some medical help.

Neurotransmitters and Their Activities

The neurotransmitters all have multiple roles that interact in complex ways. Here I will briefly mention the ones most implicated in anxiety. All of them can be affected by or stimulated by medications for anxiety and depression, but you can improve the abundance and quality of your neurotransmitters by improving your exercise, sleep, and nutrition. Check out Chapter 3, "Change Your Intake," for thoughts on these and other factors that initi-ates neuronal activity, Briefly, the function of each of the neurotransmitters most relevant to causing anxiety is as follows:

Glutamate. Think of glutamate as the brain's "go" signal. Glutamate signals—or excites—neurons to fire, that is, to send out their neurotrans-mitters. It is distributed through the whole brain, because all the neurons need signals to fire. When glutamate is excessive or not well controlled by GABA, a person may experience mental agitation (Harvey & Shahid, 2012; Steckler & Risbrough, 2012).

GABA. Every "go" signal needs a "stop" signal. GABA (*gamma-aminobutyric acid*) is the stop signal. It slows and stops the firing of neurons. GABA is also found throughout the brain. When GABA is not slowing things down effectively or if GABA and glutamate are not in balance with one another and glutamate is too high, you may feel agitated, which is a setup for anxiety. GABA and glutamate have a complex interaction with each other; GABA is synthesized from glutamate (Schousboe & Waagepetersen, 2009). The "excitatory" function of glutamate can cause GABA neurotransmitters to be released in enough supply to slow the release of glutamate.

Acetylcholine. Even though this excitatory neurotransmitter is more involved in the somatic nervous system, busily activating muscles and joints for voluntary movement, it has a role in anxiety. A part of your brain called the *insula* is very sensitive to acetylcholine, and when it receives too much of it, you will feel agitation called "anxiety sensitivity." You might literally say, "I can't stand feeling anxious." A scale for both adults and children called the Anxiety Sensitivity Index (copyrighted by IDS Publishing Corporation and available for purchase from their website at www.idspublishing.com/anxiety/) reflects this condition. Not everyone with anxiety is that sensitive, but if you do have this sensitivity, you are probably more prone to avoiding any situation in which you expect to feel anxious. Building tolerance for anxiety sensations and learning to think differently about your (probably) unavoidable reaction to them will be very beneficial.

NPY and galanin. Neuropeptide Y (NPY) and galanin have many roles, among them fostering appetite and sleep responses to stress, allowing for an increase in energy. In the long run, they create fat buildup as a reaction to chronic stress. However, they are important buffers against stress hormones and norepinephrine (Kim et al., 2007; Zhou et al., 2008). The role of stress management in anxiety treatment is critical, and lifestyle changes will help restore balance. Both of these neurotransmitters are involved in stimulating BDNF to promote neuron growth.

BDNF. Brain-derived neurotrophic factor (BDNF) is produced in the brain and is necessary to stimulate the growth of new neurons (*neurogenesis*). It is important for changing fear memories (Mahan & Ressler, 2012) and for resilience to chronic stress (Taliaz et al., 2011). Medications like the selective serotonin reuptake inhibitors (SSRIs) can stimulate BDNF production (Duman & Monteggia, 2006), but so can lifestyle factors. Exercise is an especially good stimulator of BDNF. When this is depleted, it is harder for the brain to replenish other necessary neurotransmitters.

NO. Nitric oxide (NO) is produced in the linings of blood vessels and functions there as a vasodilator (widener of the vessels), allowing for lowered blood pressure and relaxation. It is released in the brain, where it acts to improve connectivity between neurons (Benson and Proctor, 2004; Gulatei, Rai, & Ray, 2017). This important neurochemical is a likely target for pharmaceutical interventions (Kumar, Singh, & Bhardwaj, 2017), but it can be released by many activities available to everyone without medication, such

12

as meditation, pleasurable physical activities like touching (Northrup, 2008; West, 2017), and creative activities such as playing a musical instrument or walking in nature.

Serotonin. Serotonin neurotransmitters are few in number compared to GABA and glutamate but mighty in their effects. Insufficient serotonin (SE) was once thought to be a cause of depression and anxiety, but now it is known to have major significance in modulating many systems in the brain-body. You need serotonin to regulate your mood so you are not too negative, to keep your appetite and sleep patterns stable, to help with impulse control, and to regulate your pain perception (Drabant et al., 2012; Hariri et al., 2005; Karg, Burmeister, Shedden, & Sen, 2011; Kim, 2014). With so many functions, it is clear that if serotonin is off balance, you could have a lot of different problems. The kinds of problems you have depend on how seriously serotonin is off balance and which part of the brain doesn't have enough of it.

Norepinephrine. If your brain had an energizer bunny, norepinephrine would be it. Norepinephrine keeps you mentally alert and your body energetic in general. For example, it is important for keeping your blood pressure balanced. When you need fast energy to handle stress—as when you are suddenly scared you will miss the bus—you get a little help from norepinephrine for energy. When you have too much norepinephrine (and there are many reasons why that might be—childhood abuse, lifestyle, chronic stress), you will feel jittery, "wired," "uptight," or generally too tense (Charney, 2004; Greenwood et al., 2003; Heinz & Smolke, 2006). You may be someone who has generally high levels of norepinephrine, and when norepinephrine is called upon by your sympathetic nervous system to raise energy, it may be released in quantities that are too large for the demand, thus making you feel more tense or excited than the situation requires.

Dopamine. As in my earlier example, dopamine's message depends a lot on which part of the brain is receiving it. When it is released in the reward pathway of the brain, dopamine can send the message "mm-mmmm good," so it is responsible for your feelings of pleasure—or, more specifically, creates the sense of motivation to do whatever you were doing that made the dopamine flow. Knowing what pleasure feels like motivates you to do what felt good, so dopamine is very important in anxiety. Getting motivated to achieve your goals will help you face your fears to overcome anxiety. But if dopamine is received in the thinking part of your brain, it helps you to pay attention. Paying attention may cause anxiety by forcing you to concentrate on what is negative or frightening in a specific situation and increase the probability that you will remember those sources of fear. Because dopamine causes intense focus, the flood of dopamine that occurs to help you cope with severe psychological or physical pain functions to permanently set memories of the event. Those memories later act as triggers for panic or social anxiety.

THE STRUCTURES OF YOUR BRAIN

The messengers of the brain—the neurotransmitters—are received in different parts of the brain, and, as mentioned, where they are received affects the message. Your brain has many different structures within it, and some of those work together in systems to get a task done. Also, different systems can work together. Keeping it simple and looking only at how your brain might generate anxiety, I am going to discuss parts of these systems:

- The *central nervous system*, specifically the parts of the brain connected to generating anxiety:
    - The *limbic system*, the center of emotion and memory
    - *The basal ganglia*, which together coordinate motivation and movement
    - *The anterior cingulate cortex*, passes information between thinking and emotion
    - *The insula*, where bodily sensations are coordinated and interpreted
    - *The cortex*, which is responsible for language, thinking, and decision-making—essentially all the conscious aspects of your brain
- The *peripheral nervous system*, which, as mentioned, includes the *enteric nervous system*, for digestive processes, and the *autonomic*

nervous system, which has nerves that get your organs going and nerves that calm down the activity in your organs

- The *stress response system*, which gets hormones such as adrenaline pumping

The Central Nervous System

Let's start with a look at the central nervous system: the brain and the specific structures involved in generating anxiety. Starting at the center of the brain, the limbic system, we will look at four structures that receive signals and initiate activity without conscious thought.

The Limbic System

The emotional work of the brain is done in the parts of the brain that together are called the limbic system. The term *limbic* comes from a word that means "ring," and it refers to a location in the center of the brain where these various structures are grouped. They work together to help form emotions and memories. The parts of the limbic system I will discuss are the:

- Thalamus
- Hypothalamus
- Hippocampus
- Amygdala

Each part or structure in the limbic system plays a specific role in the creation of emotional responses, and each part is connected to other parts of the brain and the nervous systems so that some of its work can be done without your thinking about it. For example, if you're faced with an emergency, like a child running away from you into traffic, you don't want to take time to think about whether you need energy. Your body gives it to you without intentional thought. (I will discuss the relationship between thought and feeling throughout the book.) How these parts of the limbic system function is very relevant to your understanding of how your brain makes you feel anxious even when you don't want to.

Thalamus. Think of the thalamus as the relay, taking information from the outer world via sensory input and immediately relaying it to the other parts of the limbic system as well as sending it upward to the cortex. It might be considered the quarterback for sensory information from the external environment. That is, it receives information and relays it onward so that another part of the brain can take action on it. The "ball" of sensory information, hiked to your thalamus, is passed on to the amygdala, the hypothalamus, and the hippocampus. Each of those structures has a part to play in responding to the input. The thalamus has several other tasks, but for anxiety, the speedy uptake of incoming sensory information is critical in starting a response.

Hypothalamus. The hypothalamus is both a monitor and an initiator. It constantly scans the inner environment for hormone levels, hunger and thirst, oxygen levels, and other important internal data and initiates adjustments to those levels. When the thalamus relays information needing a response or the hypothalamus notes an internal demand, the hypothalamus instantaneously initiates responses to incoming stresses. Connected to the thalamus as well as the amygdala and hippocampus, both of which also send signals in response to the thalamus's relay, the hypothalamus immediately responds to information that you are being threatened or are under a need to respond. All of the structures of the limbic system are closely connected, and the interchange of information and response is immediate—and amazingly rapid. Faster than you can begin to think, the hypothalamus sends stress hormone (CRF) to the pituitary and activates the autonomic nervous system as it calls for norepinephrine. Thus, when there is a need for energy, your heart rate accelerates faster than you can recognize the stress.

Your hypothalamus may have too many of the neurons that respond to stress, so it may send out a flood of demands for a stress response. This is one way that small things feel very big to anxious people and may be a cause of overreacting emotionally and physically to normal, not-so-big stresses. Because it is your way of feeling things, you would probably need some convincing that the small things really are small. But once you are convinced, you can take charge of calming down your stress response by talking to the hypothalamus and providing it with physical calming messages, like breathing.

Hippocampus. The hippocampus is the part of the limbic system that registers details for you. It plays a role in recognizing the incoming information without emotion, functioning like the Joe Friday of your brain—"Just the facts, ma'am." It records details—data and facts—and sends them up to your cortex, which thinks about them. But it also works with the other structures of the limbic system to retrieve information and to form a context for the arousal that's going on. Registering the details while the amygdala is responding to threat allows for correctly identifying threat. If you need short-term or long-term memory to be made from the details the hippocampus is recording, then other parts of the brain get involved to make those memories happen.

Amygdala. Your amygdala is a key player in developing anxiety. It can be like the Little Red Hen; whenever something negative shakes it up, it cries out, "The sky is falling!" This is not detailed information. It is purely emotional. Your amygdala is an early warning system; if a threat is present, it instantaneously notifies other structure in your brain to prepare for problems. The amygdala immediately communicates to the hypothalamus to get the stress response going and to get norepinephrine (the "energizer" neurotransmitter) pumping to prepare for fight or flight. All that excitement occurs long before the cortex of the brain can form context so that you can think about how serious the situation might actually be.

The amygdala registers *all* emotions, not just negative ones, but it *prefers* to notice the threatening, scary ones. The action of the amygdala is something like a smoke detector for your body and brain. A smoke detector doesn't respond to the pleasant aroma of baking bread, but if that bread starts to burn, it causes quite an alarm. You don't have to be alert to incoming joy in order to survive in this world. But if you want to survive, you'd better do a good job of noticing incoming trouble, such as someone looking angry or intending to hurt you. But the amygdala is also not the place to appraise that threat. While ready to respond to incoming information that sets off the alarm, it doesn't think about it. Once your amygdala learns what is dangerous, it tries ever after to protect you from whatever scared you. This is how cues and triggers develop to cause anxiety or panic: the amygdala and the hippocampus work together to learn what is dangerous and then remember so that you continue to respond quickly to the cues relayed from the thalamus and the hypothalamus.

The Basal Ganglia

Between the limbic system and the cortex lie the basal ganglia. A ganglion is a concentrated group of neurons. Each ganglion in the basal ganglia (BG) has a role in this system, which has many functions. These several interconnected ganglia work together to induce motivation, create energy to meet goals, and even coordinate physical movement with emotion. The BG are located under the cortex (covering) of the brain, where you do your thinking, and over the limbic area. One part of the BG, called the nucleus accumbens, is specialized to interpret pleasure when it receives the messenger dopamine. When you do something that stimulates dopamine and it flows to this part, you feel good. This makes you want to repeat whatever you were doing that made you feel good. For this reason, the BG strongly affect motivation and energy.

The basal ganglia are also involved in the level of general arousal and energy you typically feel. If you have a good supply of dopamine and norepinephrine in the BG, you will feel full of energy and have high drive, but if GABA isn't working effectively, then your energy can get *too* high and result in tension. When people are highly energetic, they may face a risk for generalized anxiety, as situations that raise norepinephrine—involving tension, conflict, or the need for caution—may raise the level to the point of anxiety. Additionally, even for no real reason but just out of the blue because GABA isn't working as it should, overexcited activity in the neurons of the BG can trigger panic attacks. In the case of BG energy, some is good, a lot can give you drive but make you tense, and too much can flip you over into panic.

A third role of the BG is formation of habits: chunks of physical activity that we do at first on purpose and then without thinking. Tying your shoes, brushing your teeth, and driving a car are good examples of things you can do without paying attention once they're habits. And certain responses to feelings of anxiety can be habitual. In working with anxiety, we want to identify habits that keep anxiety in place—things like avoidance, substance use, and stress eating.

The Cortex

The structures of the limbic system work together to send messages to the thinking parts of the brain—the cortex. *Cortex* means "bark" or "covering," and in human beings, that covering on the lower brain is very thick. Such a thick cortex is necessary to deal with social information. Our ability to think about our own thinking and about our emotions, as well as our ability to think about what others are thinking and feeling, is possible because of the cortex. To understand anxiety, it will be useful to look at activity in these parts of the cortex:

- The *anterior cingulate cortex* (ACC), the filter and amplifier of information
- The *insula*, where physical sensations are formed into a context so they can be interpreted by the prefrontal cortex
- The *orbitofrontal cortex* (OFC), the place where working memory is held
- The *prefrontal cortex* (PFC), the "CEO" where all information is ultimately received, analyzed, and responded to

A lot of information from your senses and from the organs of your body needs review by the prefrontal cortex. The information must be organized so that the responses from the cortex back to the emotional brain can return swiftly and appropriately. All the structures of the cortex combine to make that organization of information and interpretation happen efficiently. Problems in these parts of the brain result in misinterpreting, making cognitive mistakes, or taking impulsive action.

Anterior cingulate cortex. The anterior cingulate cortex (ACC) is located at the part of the cortex closest to the limbic system. It is sometimes referred to as paralimbic (*para* means "next to") because of this position. It works like a gear shift, switching between emotion and thought. If you think about the action of a car, when you need to increase speed, the car shifts to a new position, moving along smoothly. If you suffer from anxiety, the analogy of a car with a manual transmission may make sense. When you need to shift to a different speed, you do it deliberately, putting in the clutch to separate the gears and moving the gears to a new position so the car can function smoothly at a lower or higher speed. When the ACC doesn't have a good balance of neurotransmitters, it can get stuck on negative feelings and be unable to shift them forward, thereby making it less efficient at sending analysis back on to the amygdala. The ACC may also have insufficient structural connections to the cortex and limbic structures, making it hard to modulate emotion or control impulses. If your ACC gets stuck, you may experience worry or rumination on negative thoughts, oppositional behavior, ineffective problem-solving, and resistance to trying new options or responses to situations. Therapy can teach you how to put in the clutch and deliberately shift gears, improving your ability to manage worry and become more flexible.

Insula. The insula gathers data on the way your body is feeling, noting all the sensations and forming an interpretation of this somatic (bodily) experience. It takes in the information from your somatic nervous system as well as all the data about your visceral sensations from the enteric as well as the sympathetic and parasympathetic nervous systems. The insula registers the arousal of your body and helps label it (e.g., "Is this anger or excitement or sexual arousal?"). When the insula combines these sensations with the limbic system data, it creates the whole context of a situation for your thinking brain to work with. Therapies that work with somatic experience focus on the contribution of the insula to the memories you have and the responses you make without conscious intention.

Orbitofrontal cortex. The orbitofrontocortex (OFC) helps to organize information from all the other parts of the brain and pass it along to the frontal cortex for analysis and decision-making. It's like the vice president in charge of forming context and preparing reports for the CEO of the brain—the prefrontal cortex—and sending the CEO's recommendations back out. It takes the details sent in from the hippocampus and the emotional tone from the amygdala, along with the somatic experience of the situation, and puts them together for analysis. All of this must occur smoothly to allow for effective brainstorming. The OFC commands the process called working memory, which holds pieces of information just long enough for you to use them to complete tasks of everyday mental functioning. Also, working memory—or short-term storage—allows your OFC to compare information with other memories of similar situations. This work is necessary to generate several possible, reasonable responses to problems, and then the data is sent forward to the prefrontal cortex for analysis and decision-making.

When this part of the cortex is functioning correctly, you have good impulse control; that is, you don't act on "half-baked" ideas. Rather, you make decisions based on information. For this to occur, the "wiring" of the OFC up to the prefrontal cortex and down to the limbic system has to be sufficient for efficient and controlled responses. When neurotransmitters are in balance in the OFC, your mood is optimistic and it seems that things can be explained or solved and aren't hopeless. If you're low on serotonin, you may be prone to poor problem-solving or tend to frame your situation in a negative context. The OFC is quite important in managing anxiety because it helps to control fear through its optimistic, problem-solving activity.

Prefrontal cortex. The prefrontal cortex (PFC) is the CEO of the brain. This is where all the information from your entire body and all the other parts of your brain is ultimately received and where decisions are made about how to respond to it. The buck stops here. When the PFC gets good data from the rest of the brain, it has what it needs to analyze whether a situation is actually threatening or not. It decides whether the data should be put into long-term memory storage or dismissed as unnecessary. It creates new solutions to problems and plans how to carry those out. The PFC needs clarity and energy to do this. When it is short on neurotransmitters like serotonin or dopamine, or they are out of balance or excessive, your thinking is impaired.

The Peripheral Nervous System (PNS)

The peripheral nervous system comprises the somatic nervous system and the autonomic nervous system. The latter has three branches: the sympathetic and parasympathetic systems and the enteric system. When talking about anxiety and how to control it, it is important to understand that the actions of the autonomic nervous system are *automatic* and operate without your control, but you can take it over on purpose.

The Sympathetic Nervous System (SNS)

The SNS is the system that tells organs in your body to get busy and respond to a demand for action. If you walk up a steep flight of stairs, the SNS will demand a little extra heart activity and respiration so that your muscles can get more oxygen while they work harder. If you think you're about to be mugged, your SNS will immediately get your heart rate and respiration ready for a fight or a fast run out of danger. The sudden and intense arousal of this system is called "fight or flight," and many people experience this as a panic attack. When the hypothalamus gets a threat cue from the inner environment or when other limbic structures relay signals of threat from the outer environment, it activates the SNS by ordering up norepinephrine to be released to arouse the body.

The Parasympathetic Nervous System (PSNS)

The PSNS restores homeostasis after fight or flight. It kicks in to calm down action in the body and takes over when you need to rest and relax. The signal travels via the vagus nerve from the brain to the body to reduce your heart rate, slow your respiration, lower your blood pressure, and signal your enteric system to restore blood flow and peristalsis (the normal movements of the digestive track). The PSNS restores homeostasis without your deliberate action; it occurs automatically when the threat is over. When you have an anxiety disorder, however, you overperceive threat or react too strongly. When that happens, you can stimulate the vagus nerve intentionally to initiate PSNS calming by performing diaphragmatic breathing, meditation, deliberate humming, or even splashing cold water over your face. Anxiety management techniques encourage PSNS calming by focusing on self-soothing through breathing, relaxation, and thought management.

The Stress Response System

The stress response system is called the *hypothalamus-pituitary-adrenal (HPA) axis*. The pituitary gland, located within the brain, is considered the "master gland," directing activity throughout the endocrine system. For your body to have the energy it needs when the sympathetic nervous system (SNS) cranks up the organs of your body, you need some chemical assistance from hormones. When your hypothalamus activates the SNS via norepinephrine, it simultaneously starts HPA activity—an endocrine response to provide energy for arousal. The hypothalamus sends a message via the pituitary to your adrenal glands to release adrenaline and cortisol. These hormones travel through your bloodstream and mobilize your body to release stores of fuel (glucose and fat) to be used in the energy burning that muscles perform when they work hard. This is the stress response: a system to get you energy when you need it. It can work for any length of time, from brief and inconsequential little releases of energy to short, powerful bursts of energy to sustained and extended stress responses, such as when you're under the burden of difficult emotions or expectations. Whether you're sitting by a sick child in the hospital emergency room or on your third day of 16-hour workdays to meet a project deadline, your stress response is working to make energy available.

As you might imagine, a stress response can't go on forever without relief. You can become very anxious as the result of unremitting stress. Damage to the brain-body occurs when stress is unremitting. You may experience fatigue, weight gain, and difficulty sleeping. When the persistent stress goes on for long periods, you may have even more problematic outcomes. You might find yourself getting sick too often. You might feel depressed as well as anxious. Stress creates inflammation, and your brain-body reacts to that by slowing down mental and physical energy. Cortisol itself, when released for too long, can damage the hippocampus, showing up in problems with memory and cognition in general.

This system has built-in ways to protect your brain-body from the possible damage of chronic stress. First of all, cortisol has a role in completing the feedback loop by going up to the brain and braking the stress response. That means that stress responses will naturally come to an end. Cortisol can be depleted by chronic stress, which can lead to trouble turning off the stress response, circularly increasing stress damage. The neurochemicals neuropeptide Y and galanin are also released during the simultaneous activation of the SNS and the HPA. They protect the brain, buffering the impact of stress and promoting replenishment of neurons. Under chronic stress, however, they can be depleted, creating problems with becoming calm and replenishing neurons.

HOW ANXIETY IS MADE

Now let's look at how neurotransmitter activity and brain function produce symptoms of anxiety.

The Role of Neurotransmitters

The quantity of neurotransmitters in different parts of the brain affects what kinds of anxiety symptoms you experience. Having described the neurotransmitters and the parts of the brain relevant to understanding anxiety, I want to review briefly how it may be that you don't have a good supply of neurotransmitters. Then I will chart how symptoms of anxiety might be generated by the activity of neurotransmitters in different parts of the brain.

A person may not have enough neurotransmitters for any number of reasons. For example, you might just not have been born with a plentiful supply. You may not have enough to feel good. This is likely true when people feel they have been depressed or anxious most of their lives. Life circumstances can make that problem worse. Trauma or illness can deplete the supply of some neurotransmitters, like serotonin, or intensify levels of norepinephrine and therefore heighten the impact of the trauma or illness, which, if left untreated, can continue for years. Chronic stress uses up your extra supplies of neurotransmitters and creates a deficit while preventing the opportunity to rebuild your supply. Poor sleep and nutrition also diminish neurotransmitter supplies. So, depending on your circumstances, there could be one or many reasons your neurotransmitters have gotten out of balance.

Take a look at the neurotransmitters, one at a time, to see how they interact with the parts of the brain to cause anxiety symptoms (Table 1.2). The neurotransmitter with the most wide-ranging impact in creating anxiety symptoms is serotonin (SE). When serotonin is low, it wreaks havoc

Table 1.2 How Brain Structures Are Affected When Serotonin Levels Are Low

Brain Structure		Anxious Symptom
limbic system (amygdala)	$\longrightarrow$	negativity, worry, sensitivity to threat
prefrontal cortex (PFC)	$\longrightarrow$	poor planning, unable to push negativity away or find a positive frame, loss of emotional control or affect regulation
orbitofrontal cortex (OFC)	$\longrightarrow$	poor impulse control, irrational responses to problems
anterior cingulate gyrus (ACG)	$\longrightarrow$	ruminating worry, inflexible attitude

in most of the brain systems. Serotonin's main function is to regulate, and losing regulation has predictable results for the calm, orderly assessment of a threat and your response to it.

The next neurotransmitter with powerful influence in creating anxiety is norepinephrine (NE). NE causes trouble primarily when it's too high. The level of NE sets a tone of tension throughout the brain and body. Like the energizer it is, NE causes small stresses to trigger big responses. Because the level of tension in an anxious person is already so high, it doesn't take much of a bump from NE to push their tension level over the top into panic or acute anxiety. Table 1.3 shows some of the major ways high NE can result in anxiety.

Dopamine (DA) is an interesting neurotransmitter because it has implications for anxiety when it's too low *and* when it's too high, again depending on where its message is being received. In the basal ganglia (BG), it affects

Table 1.3 How Brain Structures Are Affected When Norepinephrine Levels Are High

Brain Structure		Anxious Symptom
throughout the brain	$\longrightarrow$	general overarousal, inner jitteriness, physical and mental tension
prefrontal cortex (PFC)	$\longrightarrow$	hypervigilance, scattered thoughts
basal ganglia (BG)	$\longrightarrow$	restlessness, "wired" sensation
sympathetic nervous system	$\longrightarrow$	panic attacks or acute anxiety, sense of doom

Table 1.4 How Brain Structures Are Differentially Affected by Dopamine (DA) Levels

Brain Structure		Anxious Symptom
basal ganglia		
high DA	$\longrightarrow$	high drive, high motivation, perfectionism
low DA	$\longrightarrow$	loss of interest or pleasure, low motivation
prefrontal cortex (PFC)		
temporarily high DA	$\longrightarrow$	over-focus on detail may trigger subsequent panic or acute anxiety
chronically high DA	$\longrightarrow$	psychosis or delusional states

pleasure and energy, which translates into motivation. When levels are low, there is an absence of good feelings. People with social anxiety and low interest in social interactions may well have impaired ability to receive DA, thus decreasing their motivation for facing their anxiety. In the prefrontal cortex, DA is necessary for paying attention, so when it's low you might be inattentive, but when it's sufficient you can pay attention and focus on tasks. Dopamine can be temporarily high during a time of trauma, differentially released by stress, and during that time it contributes to the creation of powerful cues for anxiety. These very high but temporary levels of dopamine during crisis affect the brain differently than chronically high levels of DA. Table 1.4 summarizes the impact of high and low DA levels in different areas of the brain.

The final neurotransmitter that is very important in creating anxiety is GABA. GABA neurons are found throughout the brain in vast numbers because GABA is the brain's "stop" signal, needed to slow down the firing of

Table 1.5 How Brain Structures Are Affected When GABA Is Ineffective

Brain Structure		Anxious Symptom
entire brain	$\longrightarrow$	agitation from glutamate imbalance exacerbates other problems caused by neurotransmitter imbalances
basal ganglia (BG)	$\longrightarrow$	heightened energy tone, panic attacks

neurons in your brain. It balances the effects of glutamate, the neurotransmitter that acts as the "go" signal. When GABA is insufficient or is not being easily received by neurons waiting for its signal to stop firing, the result is overactivity in whichever part of the brain GABA is not working. Table 1.5 shows the most significant disruptions from ineffective GABA.

Left Brain, Right Brain

You may have heard about differences between right-brain and left-brain activity and wonder if this is important for anxiety as well. The short answer is that every structure of the brain described above (in the section on the central nervous system) has two sides, right and left. Your brain is efficient—it doesn't double up on activity—so the right and the left sides, called "hemispheres," have, in effect, subspecialties within their individual functions. For example, the right side of the amygdala (which, you will recall, is responsible for noticing what's important, especially if it's threatening) swiftly recognizes cues of danger and immediately alerts the hypothalamus to start responding. The left side of the amygdala compares the current cue of danger to those encountered previously to see if the situation is as dangerous as it seems. If the situation turns out to be different from a former situation, the left amygdala adjusts the reaction so that the next time the cue comes in, the amygdala will be able to use the new information. For example, if a person with social anxiety is in front of a group of people and feels alarm because the group chuckled at something he said but then realizes they were laughing in humor, not humiliation, his left amygdala will note that this group is safe. In future experience with the group, his right amygdala won't react as intensely.

The two hemispheres of the cortex also share the load of analyzing, although the left prefrontal cortex is the final decision-maker. In general, the right hemisphere of your cortex handles nonverbal information. It hears the tone of voice and sees the facial expressions that communicate what the words you hear really mean. It contributes to understanding spatial information. The left brain provides the vocabulary of words and math symbols and the analytic work of the meaning of experiences. A big bundle of connecting neurons called the *corpus callosum* rapidly fires information back and forth across the hemispheres so they can function in unison to understand communications, correctly interpret information, and form good responses. Effective intercommunication makes for good modulation of limbic emotion as well.

Anxiety management techniques aim to control your anxious symptoms primarily through the left brain, using words, analysis, and decision-making to direct the rest of your brain and your body. Psychotherapy methods that activate other parts of the brain are certainly available, and necessarily so, because difficult problems such as resolving long-standing trauma, changing the impact of childhood experiences, and altering dark moods such as despair require different work than just anxiety management techniques. If your anxiety stems from a history of trauma, then you will likely need psychotherapy to release the impact of that trauma. Your anxiety may be hard to diminish or may repeatedly return if deeper therapeutic work is not done. However, the 10 best-ever techniques presented in this book will put your left prefrontal cortex to work to manage symptoms while you do other therapy work.

Repetition Changes—and Strengthens—Pathways

A principle of how the brain forms memory and how it is susceptible to worry and panic involves how repetition of a thought or an action increases the likelihood of thinking the thought or having the panic. When you think a thought, a network of activity occurs. The pathway of that network lights up with the excitement of glutamate and calms back down again with the action of GABA. But more happens if the thought gets repeated. The brain recognizes repetition as an indicator of significance, and it begins almost immediately to change the very structure of the brain to help repetition become easier. As a thought is repeated often (the way worry works!), the brain starts to provide vascularization and glial cell support for it—that is, more blood supply and white matter. Now those neurons in the cognitive pathway can fire faster and more efficiently, making a worry pathway into a worry highway, and it becomes easier and easier to get onto that highway. Repetition strengthens! And, in the typical way of the brain to have a feedback loop, as soon as the repetition is eliminated, the brain erases the traces of that neurobiological superhighway and takes it back to a worry path that is fading. Therapy for worry is often focused on eliminating repetitive negative thoughts and actions that are common in generalized anxiety and social anxiety.

A similar process called sensitization occurs when it gets easier for the brain to fire neurons. When cells in the basal ganglia are triggered to set off a panic attack, they become easier to fire. The more often you panic, the more often you will panic. Subsequent arousal occurs more easily. Thus, reducing the intensity, duration, and eventually the frequency of panic events reverses sensitization and makes panic events slower to get going.

COULD IT BE SOMETHING ELSE?

A look at other conditions that look like anxiety is warranted, because in those situations, brain structure and function are working differently than when the condition is anxiety alone. (My book *Tough-to-Treat Anxiety* takes an in-depth look at how anxiety appears when other mental health conditions are primary and how treatment for anxiety might need to be altered in those situations.) These conditions are attention-deficit hyperactivity disorder (ADHD), which is important to rule out with both generalized anxiety disorder (GAD) and social anxiety disorder (SAD); alcohol and marijuana use contributing to panic; and autism spectrum disorder (ASD), which is most important to screen for in people with social anxiety.

ADHD

Without going into lengthy descriptions of symptoms, let's look briefly at the impact of ADHD on anxiety. When people suffer from GAD, worry is a dominant symptom that interferes with attention and feels physically distracting as well. At times, those with ADHD have similar experiences that have to be treated in the context of how ADHD affects learning and memory. (That discussion is beyond the scope of this chapter, but see *Tough-*

Table 1.6 Generalized Anxiety Disorder Without ADHD vs. Generalized Anxiety Disorder With ADHD

GAD Without ADD	GAD With ADHD
Feeling of anxiety precedes cognitive worry	Feeling of anxiety precedes cognitive worry
Worry interferes with concentration	Worry interferes with concentration
Concentration is fine when worry is not present	Concentration is poor even when worry is not present; poor concentration causes mistakes, and the fear of making mistakes causes worry
When mistakes are made, worry causes mental freezing and inaction	When mistakes are made, worry causes mental freezing and inaction
Excessive worry about how to correct a mistake or face a problem causes difficulties with problem-solving, which can lead to further inaction	Difficulties with problem-solving give rise to worry about making a mistake or facing a problem, which can lead to further inaction
Both pleasurable distraction and work-related activity can temporarily relieve anxiety	Pleasurable distraction can temporarily relieve anxiety, but work-related activity is often associated with anxiety about deadlines or failure

to-Treat Anxiety for a thorough look at it.) Table 1.6 provides a glimpse of GAD with and without ADHD.

ADHD has a role in social anxiety (SAD) as well. Suffering from social anxiety leads people to avoid settings where they fear they may fail—school is one prominent example. But when a person has ADHD, school failures can lead to school avoidance, and that plus some other coping strategies can look like SAD. Table 1.7 compares these symptom profiles.

Panic and Alcohol or Marijuana Use

When panic strikes, I always want to investigate underlying brain-based causes. Those will be highlighted in Chapter 3 for Technique #1—"Change Your Intake." One common phenomenon that needs to be ruled out is the

Table 1.7 Comparison of Behavioral and Emotional Symptoms Between Social Anxiety and ADHD

Social Anxiety	ADHD
Low interest in social clubs and extracurricular activities	Apparent low interest in clubs and extracurricular activities related to fear of failing
Excess time spent computer gaming with others online as a way to avoid in-person interactive social experiences while feeling somewhat connected	Excess time spent computer gaming with others online as a manifestation of ADHD problems with impulse control and delayed gratification
Anxiety preceding avoidance or withdrawal from engagement with others	Anxiety that leads to withdrawal from engagement with others
Feelings of anxiety when expected to meet social demands; worry about being successful	Feelings of anxiety when expected to meet social demands; worry about being successful
Parents may do the work of daily life; the passivity of the person with SAD allows it	Parents may do the work of daily life; the inability of the person with ADHD to get organized allows it
Forgetfulness may be avoidance; calendar reminders will be ignored	Forgetfulness is unavoidable; using calendar reminders can help
Environmental stimuli disrupt concentration	Environmental stimuli disrupt concentration

impact of alcohol and marijuana on experiencing panic attacks. Table 1.8 demonstrates how panic can in fact be triggered by use of those substances.

SAD and ASD

At times the distinctions between severe social anxiety and autism spectrum disorders are blurry. The emotions and actions can be quite similar. However, a look at these disorders' respective symptom presentations will make it clear how they differ. ASD is not responsive to standard anxiety interventions, so exploring treatment for someone with ASD won't be part of this discussion. Table 1.9 highlights distinctions between ASD and SAD.

Table 1.8 The Relationship of Alcohol and Marijuana Use to Panic Disorder

Panic & Alcohol	Panic & Marijuana
Due to the high correlation of panic and alcohol, evaluation for abuse is necessary	Due to the high correlation of panic and marijuana, evaluation for abuse is necessary
Bingeing on alcohol can create a risk of panic during detoxification	First use can result in a panic event
Panic predicts using alcohol to calm it down	40% of weekly users have panic attacks
Vicious cycle occurs in which alcohol is used to decrease anxiety but results in increased anxiety, which causes increased use of the drug	Vicious cycle occurs in which marijuana is used to decrease anxiety but results in increased anxiety, which causes increased use of the drug
Panic is suspected to prompt relapse in alcohol abusers (insufficient data)	Panic is suspected to prompt relapse in marijuana users (insufficient data)
Nearly 90% of adults in the U.S. have drunk alcohol, 50% to 60% with some regularity; they often drink to diminish anxiety	Harder to obtain statistics, but more than 40% adults have tried marijuana and 2% of the population are daily users; many report using to be more relaxed

Table 1.9 Autism Spectrum Disorder vs. Social Anxiety Disorder

Autism Spectrum	Social Anxiety
Underreactivity to others' emotions	Overreactivity to others' emotions
Inability to label emotions	Ability to label emotions
Social difficulties are due to social learning disabilities; person must be taught specific behaviors for each situation, and generalization to other social environments is poor	Social difficulties are due to inexperience caused by avoidance; person can learn appropriate behavior when exposed to the situation and generalize it to similar situations without special instruction
Engages in parallel play; that is, person will do an activity side by side with someone but has a harder time when interactions are contingent on another's actions	Engages in interactive play; that is, in activities with others, the person can engage in back-and-forth, contingent actions that demand some flexibility of response
Special interests are soothing (regardless of whether they are socially acceptable)	Interests and talents are underdeveloped due to fear of scrutiny and avoidance of possible embarrassment when performing in public

Any childhood gregariousness or desire for interpersonal interaction is gradually replaced by social withdrawal due to social errors and inability to generalize to similar situations	Almost without exception, shyness is present from childhood, although once familiar with a situation, the person can interact appropriately and generalize to similar situations
Difficulty understanding social nuances and a tendency to assume one's actions are correct despite disapproval from peers or authorities	Understanding of social nuances but an overestimation of negative responses; may be overly concerned about peer and authority approval
Scrutiny from others feels alarming because the nervous system is easily triggered	Scrutiny is uncomfortable because of the cognitive belief that others will find one wanting
Calming includes removal from overly stimulating environments but may require intensifying the stimulation of the nervous system through stimming (repetitive movements like hand-flapping that release high energy)	Calming is achieved through breathing and muscle relaxation that slows the nervous system (sometimes in addition to removal from the overly stimulating environment); raising nervous system stimulation will not help

CONCLUSION

Knowing how your brain can make you anxious doesn't teach you what to do when you feel anxiety—that's what the 10 techniques are for! But knowing that you have considerable ability to change that anxiety and ultimately change your brain *can* encourage you to take charge. Anxiety symptoms will lessen as you employ the methods given to you in this book, and as I describe each method, I will reference what the brain change goal is so you know how significant the techniques are. When you feel anxious and are thinking over what to do to handle a situation, you might remember what part of your brain is contributing to that feeling or you might not. All you really need to remember is which techniques to apply to manage the symptom. The more you apply the techniques, the better chance you will have of calming down your brain and decreasing the likelihood that the symptoms will continue to bother you. So read on—the 10 best-ever anxiety management techniques are in the chapters ahead!

TWO

Managing Your Brain With Medication

Typically, people get medication for anxiety symptoms before they receive psychotherapy to control their anxiety. When people have panic attacks, they go to the emergency room or consult their physician and get a prescription for medication instead of a referral to a psychotherapist. When people see an MD for a medical complaint, such as heart palpitations, shortness of breath, frequent nausea, a lump in the throat, or temporomandibular joint pain (TMJ), they *expect* to get a medical test or a prescription. They interpret these common anxiety symptoms as problems with their heart, lungs, stomach, and so on, so consulting a medical doctor is logical.

It may take some time and some negative test results before a physician feels comfortable identifying the cause of the symptoms as anxiety, but once anxiety is determined to be the culprit, she or he may prescribe one of several drugs for relieving the anxiety. A primary care physician is medically trained and may not know the efficacy of psychotherapy. Competent psychotherapy can help you eliminate symptoms without medication; however, there are times when medication is an important aid to feeling better and calming your brain so that these techniques can work faster and more effectively at the start. Medication can make you start feeling better a little faster than psychotherapy, but it is psychotherapy that will change your thoughts and behaviors and give you strategies that you can use anywhere for the rest of your life without the side effects of or need for medication (Farchione et al., 2012; Harvey, 2015; Keefe, Webb & DeRubeis, 2015; Kroenke, 2007; Otto, Misra, Prasad, & McRae, 2014; Teding van Berkhout & Malouff, 2016).

How do you know if you should be using medication? Talk with your doctor, of course. In my years of working with anxious people and reading research results, I've noticed certain clues that indicate whether or not medication will contribute to the effectiveness of psychotherapy. If you can answer yes to any of the following questions, you may be helped by medication.

- Are you having panic attacks a few times a week or more? My experience with people who have panic disorder leads me to think that if people are having attacks that frequently, they might benefit from medication. Their brains may be so agitated that it will take some time to calm the panic. It may be too discouraging for them to have to get their thoughts and behavior in control without the help of medication.

- Are you able to push aside ruminating worry when you have something important to concentrate on but find yourself worrying again the minute you have nothing to focus on? You may do okay without medication, but if it's a huge effort or you can't draw your attention away from worry even for short times, medications are in order.

- Do you feel sick to your stomach with dread much of the time and find that it interferes with your eating and sleeping? If so, you will probably respond better to anxiety management techniques with the help of medication, because this level of distress should be interrupted as quickly as possible. Having an agitated brain without relief isn't good for your emotional or physical self.

- Do you immediately flush and have shaky legs, a quivering voice, and a palpitating heart even at the thought that someone might watch you leave a theater, watch you speak up at a business meeting, or observe you ordering food or eating in a restaurant? You might benefit from using medication on an as-needed basis while trying techniques to get over those signs of social anxiety.

- Do you feel so terrified of attending a party or being in a busy public place like a shopping mall, airport, or school that you refuse to go? You will probably benefit most from a combination of medication and treatment methods, because this is about the most difficult situation in which to calm yourself. Medication will allow you to focus on using new anxiety-controlling skills and social skills that will help you in your interactions with others.

IF YOU'RE ALREADY ON MEDICATION BEFORE STARTING THERAPY

Often people are given prescriptions for medications before they decide to try techniques to manage anxiety. Whether you're trying techniques on your own or working with a therapist, it's *not a good idea* to stop taking medication abruptly. Always discuss with your prescribing physician any decision to reduce or discontinue your medication. Many medications have withdrawal effects. And, if you are benefiting from your medication, it just means that you'll have a head start on feeling better. The major downside to using medication while practicing anxiety control techniques is that it's harder to know what it's like to feel and control anxiety without the effects of the medication in your system. But you can prepare for that. Be aware that you will feel different when you stop taking the medication, so plan to review these techniques or go back for a few "booster sessions" of psychotherapy.

WHAT DO MEDICATIONS DO FOR YOUR BRAIN?

Medications are used to change specific brain or neurotransmitter functions. There are several mechanisms by which they work to control anxiety. I suggest you take a look at the book *Successful Psychopharmacology* by Steven Sobel if you want an in-depth but very readable look at how medications are used in mental health treatment. The kinds of medications most commonly prescribed for anxiety disorders are selective serotonin reuptake inhibitors (SSRIs), benzodiazepines, bupropion, and buspirone.

Selective Serotonin Reuptake Inhibitors

When serotonin (SE) levels are insufficient, people can be negative, worry excessively, lack concentration and attention, and have trouble suppressing worry and panic. They may have difficulty paying attention, feel preoccupied, be overly tense, and have a hard time seeing good solutions to their problems. Their limbic system becomes overactive in producing negative, worrying thoughts, and their cortex lacks energy to suppress the negativity. The anterior cingulate cortex gets stuck on worry thoughts and doesn't efficiently transfer information between the limbic system and the cortex for modulating worry and negativity. The orbitofrontal cortex can be inefficient in its work to compare and evaluate new situations with old ones, which contributes to negative appraisals of new situations and difficulty in coming up with new, creative solutions to problems.

Improving serotonin levels or action in the brain promotes regulation of thoughts and mood, making the brain work more effectively so that techniques can be learned faster. Selective serotonin reuptake inhibitors (SSRIs) are intended to make serotonin more available in your brain. They are not mood-altering; you won't immediately feel relief when taking them. Therefore, they are not addictive. These medications help your brain increase its production of SE by enhancing the growth of new SE neurons and blocking the return of SE molecules into the cells that released them. When a cell that releases the serotonin doesn't pick any back up from the synapse (gap) between cells, it gets a message that there isn't enough serotonin, so the brain goes to work to make more serotonin neurotransmitters in the cells. Figure 2.1 shows a neuron releasing serotonin (drawn as little diamonds) into a synapse, with its receptor sites blocked (indicated by short black lines).

The most commonly prescribed SSRIs are:

- Prozac (fluoxetine)
- Zoloft (sertraline)
- Paxil (paroxetine)
- Luvox (fluvoxamine)

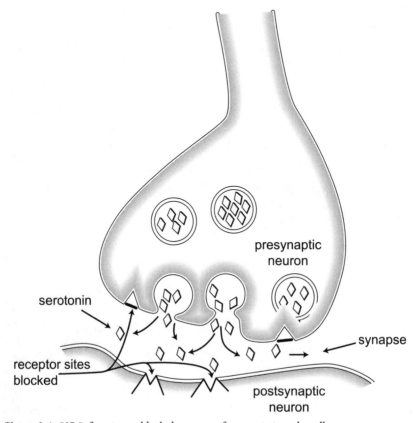

Figure 2.1 SSRIs function to block the return of serotonin into the cell.

- Celexa (citalopram)
- Lexapro (escitalopram)

Two newer medications combine SSRI action with other ways to increase serotonin availability in the brain:

- Viibryd (vilazodone)
- Trintellix (vortioxetine)

The following three medications are also commonly prescribed but are SNRIs (serotonin *and* norepinephrine reuptake inhibitors):

- Effexor (venlafaxine)
- Cymbalta (duloxetine)
- Pristiq (desvenlafaxine)

Although SSRIs and SNRIs have a small impact on serotonin availability right away, it usually takes weeks for the brain to start producing enough additional serotonin neurotransmitters to change anxiety. It takes *months* for the brain to maintain that level of production without the medication, and it requires nutrients and sleep during that time to produce the serotonin. Vai and others (2016) found that while brain changes of increased positive perception occur fairly quickly after beginning medication, it takes some time for habits of observation and thought to change. This speaks to the role therapy may play in helping people to notice their thoughts and deliberately change them, essentially working with the medication to prompt faster changes in symptoms.

People taking SSRIs or SNRIs should expect to be on these medications for some time, typically for a year or more. These medications should be discontinued only under the supervision of a physician.

Choosing SSRI Medication

In the past, choosing a medication for anxiety meant taking the chance that a medication used by a family member might be best for you, or the physician might base the decision on other factors, but it was common for people to try two or more medications before finding the one that gave a good result without difficult side effects. Several kinds of tests are available to measure serotonin levels and may or may not be used for choosing medication, but physicians are increasingly utilizing pharmacogenomic (genetic analysis) testing to find out which medication might work best for individual patients. A small blood or saliva sample can help determine:

- Whether a specific medication may be effective
- What dose of the medication may be most effective
- Whether a person might have serious side effects from medications

With increasing sophistication of methods for analysis, people may find better and faster responses to medication.

If a physician prescribed one of these medications before you started learning anxiety management techniques, it is usually best to continue using it until it has had enough time to work—usually several months. When the drug is discontinued too soon, the symptoms may come right back. In fact, reemerging symptoms indicate that it was doing a good job. A person can keep on learning techniques while getting help from the medication. If the physician agrees it is time to try handling anxiety without medication, he or she will suggest a medication withdrawal plan to prevent you from feeling sick from discontinuing it too quickly. This is a good time to work with a therapist, who can help you use the techniques without medication to make sure the transition is smooth.

Benzodiazepines

Benzodiazepines have been in use for decades, and they are very effective for relieving sensations of anxiety; however, they come with risks, and many physicians prefer to avoid utilizing this drug class for anxiety except with a specific, targeted approach and careful monitoring.

The most commonly prescribed benzodiazepines include:

- Xanax (alprazolam)
- Ativan (lorazepam)
- Klonopin (clonazepam)

The benzodiazepines work on GABA, the neurotransmitter that slows down the firing between brain cells. The activity in the basal ganglia that leads to symptoms of panic, tension, and social anxiety is slowed down to reduce those symptoms. The calming effects of benzodiazepines work within 20 to 30 minutes and last for several hours, depending on the person's response to the specific medication. That is why they are considered mood-altering. They help GABA to do its job, but only while they are active in your system.

Risks in using this class of medication occur:

- In children who have not reached puberty, who have a higher risk of responding with increased agitation rather than calming
- In elderly patients, who have an increased risk of memory problems and an increased fall risk
- In people recovering from addiction, who should avoid mood-altering drugs
- In people using this medication daily over long periods of time, who may then develop dependence and ultimately may suffer memory impairment or other risks

Dependence

Benzodiazepines are potentially addictive, and this poses a risk in people who have been addicted to alcohol. Benzodiazepines greatly increase the effects of alcohol, so they should never be used *with* alcohol. Also, people who *have been* addicted to alcohol, even if they no longer drink, may develop an addiction to these drugs quickly. Therefore, more caution in using benzodiazepines is needed in this population. Physical and psychological dependence are both possible if the medication is prescribed for daily use over periods of months or years. Most physicians have become aware of these risks and prescribe benzodiazepines with caution.

Many people who use these medications to decrease anxiety try hard not to use them too often, and that is not always a good idea. Following the prescriber's plan is best. Benzodiazepines work best to decrease the high degree of physical arousal that is experienced in generalized anxiety. If that is needed, typically they will be prescribed in tandem with an SSRI to be used while the SSRI achieves therapeutic results (for the first few weeks on that medication). Even after three to four weeks of use, benzodiazepines should not be discontinued abruptly but rather weaned off to avoid potentially unpleasant or serious effects of discontinuation, depending on the length of time they have been used.

The best recommendation for taking a benzodiazepine when a person suffers persistent, acute generalized anxiety is to take it daily for several weeks, and typically in combination with an SSRI. There is great benefit in calming the brain on a consistent basis over a period of a few weeks. Often people decide on their own to take the medication only when they think they need it, but this inconsistency won't yield the desired calming effect and is likely to trigger more tension, panic, and anxiety. If you don't take the drug the prescribed number of times per day, you lose the benefit of soothing the brain. Typically, your physician will prescribe this drug for a brief period—weeks, not months.

Sometimes this class of medication will be used for the unpleasant physical arousal that goes with panic attacks. Those who are prescribed one of these medications for "as-needed" use (when they panic) should be aware that panic will stop without medication. The medication can relieve some of the disturbing aftermath of a panic attack. Occasional use does not create the risk of physical dependence but might lead to psychological dependence if the person believes she or he needs medication to get through panic.

Benzodiazepines are typically prescribed for use on an as-needed basis to people who have visited an MD or emergency room for panic symptoms. If you are taking these medications on an as-needed basis, it would be helpful to talk with a psychotherapist to decide how to coordinate medication use with learning techniques. There are some cases when as-needed medications are helpful for mastering anxiety in social settings. Planning to use medication to promote mastery over anxiety is the best idea when using these mood-altering drugs. They can be extremely helpful for gaining control over your anxious body—eventually without medications.

Buspirone (BuSpar)

Buspirone is an atypical anti-anxiety drug in the class of medications called azapirones. These medications work on the serotonin system differently than the SSRIs. Buspirone has some impact on the dopamine system and is more likely to "take the edge off" anxiety than to eliminate it. It doesn't work immediately but rather takes a few weeks. People with generalized anxiety may benefit from using this medication for a period of months.

Other Medications

Some medications are used "off label" to control the symptoms of social anxiety. ("Off label" means that the drug isn't marketed for the use the physician is prescribing it for. Many drugs have been found to help treat problems other than those they were developed and marketed to treat.) Heart medications called beta blockers may occasionally be prescribed on as-needed basis for limiting the heart palpitations and skin flushing that goes with the physical discomfort of social anxiety. When people are practicing techniques to be more comfortable in front of others, benzodiazepines or beta-blockers may be used prior to a practice session to make the practice more effective. This, however, should be very carefully planned with the therapist and medical doctor.

Bupropion (Wellbutrin) is more often used to raise levels of interest and energy, as it works on the dopamine levels in the reward pathway. Like the SSRIs, it is called an antidepressant, but it is not often used for anxiety. It can serve a helpful role for socially anxious people who display passivity and low motivation but is otherwise not considered for use with anxiety. Additionally, the class of medications called anticonvulsants may be used for people with social anxiety to diminish the physical symptoms they experience.

NATURAL REMEDIES

Many natural remedies and supplements are recommended for anxiety, and the boom in herbal remedies has not often coincided with good research support. In part, that has to do with financial realities—research is expensive and herbs won't necessarily return the costs involved. However, practitioners of integrative medicine and naturopathic physicians may offer excellent help for anxiety management via herbs, supplements, and essential oils. They may test saliva, blood, or urine for levels of serotonin, norepinephrine, and dopamine to make recommendations for nonmedication pathways to increase the levels or adjust the balance of these neurochemicals. The Resources section at the back of this book has recommendations for exploring these options.

COMPLICATED SITUATIONS

Medication choices may become more complicated when other psychiatric problems overlap with anxiety. People who have obsessive-compulsive disorder may experience severe rumination; other people may have depression or other kinds of mental health problems. People on the autism spectrum may suffer from anxiety of different causes, such as difficulty turning off their response to environmental stimulation or the emotional stress caused by autism. People with bipolar II disorder may feel very anxious, especially when in the manic phase. In those cases, drugs that can improve thought clarity and mood stability may be used to augment other medications. For example, quetiapine (Seroquel), an atypical antipsychotic, has been getting some attention for this purpose with generalized anxiety.

These are complex individual situations, and I will suggest to you what I suggest to my clients with complicated situations: "See a psychiatrist." Psychiatrists, more than other medical doctors, know how these medications affect people at different ages or with different symptom expressions, as well as what medications work best for people who have more than one anxiety problem or who have other mental health conditions. They are also more aware of trends and new ideas regarding augmenting medication for mental illness. It is well worth a visit to get your medication right.

Medication is a first-line treatment according to insurance companies and medical protocols for all kinds of anxiety disorders. But medication will not teach you techniques that will help you use your brain to change your brain. Medication can, however, calm your brain enough to allow you to learn and effectively use anxiety management techniques. The best use of medication occurs when a psychotherapist and an MD work together to plan how to effectively integrate medication and anxiety management techniques that will diminish or eliminate anxiety symptoms altogether.

PART II

MANAGING YOUR ANXIOUS BODY

People with panic fear the physical feeling of being afraid. The intensity of the experience of having a panic attack is so unpleasant and scary that they *never* want to have the feeling again. Your heart races, your breathing becomes rapid and shallow, your chest may hurt, and you may feel dizzy, dry-mouthed, shaky, or unpleasantly tingly. When people become afraid of having another panic attack and begin to curtail their activities because of it, panic disorder sets in. It is completely understandable that you would never want to have a panic attack. The attacks are physically painful and terrifying. However, as I will discuss later, they are not lethal. You can control many factors that will reduce the frequency and duration of panic attacks.

If you have panic disorder, you may feel:

- A rapid heart rate
- Shallow respiration or hyperventilation
- Nausea
- Tingling
- Ringing ears
- A lump in your throat
- Dizziness

Other types of anxiety have unpleasant physical symptoms as well. People with generalized anxiety (the worrywarts among us) suffer significantly from tension-related problems. Temporomandibular joint (TMJ) or jaw joint pain, neck pain and headache, and stomach and gastrointestinal pain are just a few examples. In addition, the sensation of acute anxiety—the physical sensation that something is very wrong—is decidedly painful as well. Managing the body is very relevant to helping those with generalized anxiety suffer less physical discomfort and to reducing the feeling of being anxious as well. If you have generalized anxiety, you will see some of the following symptoms:

- A sense of doom or dread
- Achiness
- Muscle tension
- Agitation or restlessness

Sufferers of social anxiety squirm at the very idea that others could perceive them as looking frightened. Kross and colleagues (2011) demonstrated that emotional pain is felt physically (see also Chen, Kipling, Williams, Fitness, & Newton, 2008), and this is especially is true for social anxiety pain. Rejection hurts (Kross & Berman, 2011). Flushing, sweating, heart palpitations, and quivering muscles or quavering voices are transient symptoms—uncomfortable but not long-lasting if you can escape the feared scrutiny of others. But there is also evidence that the discomfort of knowing that others may observe these symptoms hurts, and that ongoing fear may keep the discomfort prominently in your thoughts. Our mental representations of emotional pain make us feel pain. People who have social anxiety tend to be overly sensitive to their own feelings as well as to events outside themselves (Aron, 1996; Lonigan & Philips, 2001; McNally, 2002). This creates more physical pain than they would have simply from the outward signs of their anxiety. Social anxiety sufferers may experience:

- Flushing or blushing
- Sweating
- Quivering muscles
- A quivering voice
- Heart palpitations

A person may have any or all of these symptoms, and the intensity may vary dramatically from one person to the next. For many with anxiety, there is a vicious circle wherein the body triggers anxiety and anxiety triggers physical arousal. Interrupting this cycle helps to slow down the arousal and diminish the frequency and intensity of anxious symptoms.

BEFORE YOU START PSYCHOTHERAPY, GET A MEDICAL CHECKUP

Too many possible physical causes of anxiety exist to list them all here, and it would just make you more anxious if I did. Even if you have always been prone to worry, nervousness, or shyness, it is important to get a medical check for heart, hormonal, and blood sugar issues, especially if your symptoms have worsened recently. For example, changes in thyroid function can mimic anxiety, and mitral valve prolapse can trigger panic. Changes in estrogen and progesterone can affect the way your brain receives neurotransmitters, and when neurotransmitters change, so do physical sensations, mood, thought, and behavior. If you have a medical problem causing anxiety, you may have limited success with the techniques in this book because that underlying medical problem will not be addressed.

More typically, when people consult their family physician or go to the emergency room with a panic attack, they are given a battery of tests that come back negative (i.e., show no physical problems). They are told there is no evident medical cause for their symptoms. In frustration, they turn to therapy. These people may be hard-pressed to believe that definite physical symptoms can be managed with psychological techniques. They believe that if no medical treatment is required, they must not have really experienced the physical issues at all. But anxiety *really* is felt in the body, since the brain creates physical symptoms, and when you are clear that no disease or medical condition is causing the symptoms, the techniques I provide will make a world of difference.

This section reviews methods that calm the physiology (physical symptoms) of anxiety. Research shows that calming the body calms the brain, which is, after all, part of the physical body (Amen, 2015; Benson & Proctor, 2011; Childre, 2008; Gallo, 2000; Hanson, 2016; Schwartz, J., 2011). The brain responds to all the stressors from outside and inside the body; the phone ringing can be as disturbing as eating the wrong foods. Whatever disturbs your brain is going to show up in your physiology, your thoughts, and your behavior. Implementing physical changes can make a big difference in the way you think and feel and thus in your anxiety.

There are many methods for managing the anxious body, including energy therapies, eye movement desensitization and reprocessing (EMDR), neurofeedback, HeartMath, and biofeedback. (Further information on some of these methods can be found in the Resources section at the end of the book.) But these techniques require specialists. Fortunately, several tried-and-true techniques exist that you can practice completely on your own. This section identifies four:

- Technique #1: Change Your Intake
- Technique #2: Breathe
- Technique #3: Practice Mindfulness
- Technique #4: Rest and Relax

These four techniques will calm your brain activity and, consequently, arousal in your body. The calmer your brain is, the less you will feel the unpleasant physical sensations that are the hallmark of all types of anxiety.

THREE

Technique #1

Change Your Intake

Your body has to process whatever you take in. Whether you are taking in chemicals or high stimulation from the environment, your body (including your brain as an organ) responds to restore balance in all of your systems. Physical symptoms of anxiety are one cost of being out of balance. Calming your anxious body starts with changing your intake, including your intake of foods or drugs that trigger anxiety as well as intake of stimulation and the demands that stress your brain and body. Technique #1 is one you can start practicing today.

LIMIT C.A.T.S.

C.A.T.S. stands for caffeine, alcohol, tobacco, and sugar and sweetener. Research demonstrates that these substances play a role in causing physical anxiety, and when you change your intake of these substances, your body immediately becomes less anxious. Knowing *how* limiting intake of C.A.T.S. can modify the physical symptoms of anxiety will help you decide if limiting your intake of one or all of these substances is a good first step.

Caffeine

Avoiding caffeine may seem like a no-brainer if you notice that you don't like the jittery, overstimulated feelings you get when you drink coffee, tea, or caffeinated soft drinks. But you may not realize how these caffeinated substances are affecting you. Research has demonstrated that out-of-the blue panic that is caused by a person's genetic makeup tends to be triggered by caffeine consumption (Alsene, Deckert, Sand, & de Wit, 2003; Nardi et al., 2007). Even fairly small amounts of caffeine can trigger panic. One young man, who saw me because he was having panic sensations daily and occasional major panic attacks that drove him to the emergency room, stated that he couldn't believe that caffeine was a cause of his panic because he consumed so little of it. He drank only one cup of regular coffee in the morning and occasionally a soda in the afternoon. He made some improvements in the frequency and severity of his panicky feelings by using other techniques, but after another terrible panic attack he finally decided to eliminate caffeine altogether. To his amazement, he could immediately tell the difference— his panicky feelings decreased considerably, and he didn't have another big panic attack. However, caffeine does more than just trigger panic. People who are worriers, who may have generalized anxiety, are typically physically tense, and their tension levels will increase with the intake of caffeine due to its effect on the nervous system (Fisone, Borgkvist, & Usiello, 2004; Fredholm, Bättig, Holmén, Nehlig, & Zvartau, 1999). Caffeine also has an impact on people with the social anxiety symptoms of flushing, sweating, and shakiness. By heightening the arousal of their nervous system with caffeine, they become more likely to experience the signs of distress that they don't want the world to see.

In general, caffeine is a contributor to all kinds of anxiety. Notice the amounts of caffeine in the everyday products you may use, such as soda, coffee, tea, chocolate, and energy drinks or tablets. It's easy to find the milligrams of caffeine in these products on the Internet. People vary widely in their tolerance to caffeine, and some can't consume even small amounts, but if you keep track of your changes in mood, tension, and anxiety after consuming it, you will quickly be able to find your limit and alter your intake accordingly.

Alcohol

Many people regularly use alcohol as a way to reduce stress, handle fear, and avoid unpleasant emotional states. A moderate amount of alcohol can quickly and temporarily induce a relaxed state of mind or body. However, the impact of alcohol on the anxious body is more complicated than it initially seems.

People under stress tend to consume alcohol in larger quantities or with more frequency than they might when not stressed. At times of unremitting stress—such as during a divorce, a particularly difficult project that requires long hours of work, or caring for a family member who is ill—people may use more alcohol. All of these situations can interfere with relaxing or getting to sleep, and alcohol may help induce sleep.

Alcohol can also ameliorate social fears. It can make a person feel less anxious about facing a social demand, like attending an office party. Trying to get rid of unwanted feelings or to create states of relaxation they desire, people use alcohol and unwittingly create a bigger anxiety problem.

Although alcohol may temporarily help you relax, it is actually a profound anxiety-*causing* agent. When it leaves the body, detoxified by your liver, alcohol actually leaves nerves in an agitated state. People who have a couple of drinks at night may find it easier to get drowsy and fall asleep, but they often awaken halfway through the night and can't get back to sleep. The best solution to middle-of-the-night awakening, if you are not going to eliminate alcohol altogether, is to restrict alcohol consumption to earlier in the evening so this phase of detoxification is complete before heading to bed.

A better solution is to use herbal teas with calming properties (such as kava, chamomile, catnip, lemon balm, hops, or valerian) at bedtime to achieve drowsiness without the rebound. The herbs in these teas help calm the brain and promote sleep with no "hangover" effects in the morning. Whenever using herbal substances, make sure you have checked how they might interact with each other and with other medications you're taking. Even though the FDA doesn't control these substances, they still work with or against other herbs or drugs you are taking.

A more obvious problem with alcohol as it pertains to anxiety is the effect it has on the day after drinking too much. Young people commonly drink excessive amounts of alcohol. Binge drinking is dangerously popular, often starting in late adolescence. This is not "social drinking" and has consequences that should be assessed as a risk factor for addiction as well as for anxiety, both of which may develop from frequent alcohol use. (Alcohol addiction, when present, requires separate treatment from anxiety management—addiction won't disappear just because a person can control their anxiety.) The reaction of anxiety occurs many hours after the binge ends, so people don't always recognize anxiety as connected to alcohol. They may no longer feel drunk or hungover, but the anxiety can set in intensely. The liver can detoxify the body at the rate of an ounce of alcohol per hour. If a binge has an excess of 12 ounces of alcohol (not unusual), the anxiety reaction will hit about 12 hours after the consumption ends and the person may feel acute anxiety that can even become panic. You might think of it this way: alcohol that first sedates, later irritates.

The agitated brain trying to recover from the consumption of alcohol is primed to experience more anxiety and panic. One way of identifying the impact of alcohol on your body is to keep an anxiety or panic diary. Keep track of how much alcohol you drink the night before, and record your overall level of anxiety or occurrence of panic the next day. Regularly maintaining this diary over the course of a few months will tell you a lot about how alcohol affects your system.

Tobacco

Tobacco use has so many downsides that it's difficult to even say why any of us might logically use it. However, when we're in the throes of anxiety, sometimes it's hard to be guided by logic, as I myself experienced at a younger, anxious age! Those who smoke find tobacco to be relaxing, and the actions associated with using it contribute to that relaxation. The rituals of tobacco use—lighting up the cigarette, pipe, or cigar, or the act of chewing—are often strongly associated with creating a space of calm and separation from stress in which the smoker has time to step out, relax, think, and soothe himself or herself. There is no faster way to make an anxious person more anxious than to announce that she or he has to quit smoking.

A better strategy is to track the relationship between the sensations of anxiety and the use of the tobacco. Many anxiety-provoking effects of smoking exist, among which are sensations of dizziness, tingling, shortness of breath, or just the nagging belief that you shouldn't be smoking because of the health concerns associated with it. You can't truly recognize exactly how smoking affects you until you track your reactions. Try keeping a simple record of sensations before, during, and after smoking, which you can do on paper on in notes on your mobile device.

You will quickly be able to see if your tobacco use has a relationship with the intensity of your anxiety. One client recently reported that the constant edge of anxiety that made him fear he was about to have a panic attack disappeared immediately when he quit smoking. He thinks it was because he felt guilty about every cigarette but didn't want to openly acknowledge it. Several of my clients have noted that smoking decreases their anxiety while they're doing it but increases it afterward. When you are working on managing the physical sensations of anxiety, a positive way to change your intake of tobacco is to do some diaphragmatic breathing or one of the quick breathing relaxers (see Chapter 4) before you light that cigarette. These exercises may help to relieve your underlying anxiety so you feel less compelled to pick up the cigarette in the first place.

Sugar and Sweeteners

Intake of sugar and nonnutritive sweeteners poses a variety of anxiety-stimulating problems. First of all, sugar can create anxiety-mimicking effects for people who might be hypoglycemic. Hypoglycemia is low blood sugar, and the symptoms of low blood sugar (e.g., sweating, flushing, nausea, shakiness) are quite similar to most of the physical sensations that accompany all kinds of anxiety. Like most health problems that become a fad and go through a phase in which they are overdiagnosed, hypoglycemia was at one time blamed for a lot of physical and mental problems. Andrew Weil (2004) wrote that unstable blood sugar is unusual because your brain depends on a stable supply of blood sugar and the body has many different ways to ensure that levels stay within an appropriate range. But some people do have hypoglycemia, and some people are more sensitive to the effects of changes in their blood sugar levels. Many people with anxiety feel physical symptoms more intensely and pay more attention to them than others might. When someone with hypoglycemia ingests foods that turn to sugar quickly (e.g., simple carbohydrates like a doughnut or plate of pasta), the level of blood sugar rises quickly. Shortly thereafter, the blood sugar level drops quickly, causing symptoms that feel very much like anxiety. Eating complex carbohydrates rather than simple ones, balancing your meals with protein, and minimizing caffeine are good ways to counteract this problem.

The issue of nonnutritive sweeteners, aspartame in particular, is complicated because the research on its negative effects is controversial. Many studies report no consistent negative reactions to these substances, but other studies demonstrate a connection between increased anxiety and intake of aspartame. There is convincing research that aspartame affects nerves directly by changing the myelin sheath (the protective covering on the nerves) (Blaylock, 2004; Muller, Peterson, Sonnewald, & Unsgard, 1995; Walton, 1988). Additionally, a large number of anecdotal reports citing the negative responses to aspartame, including many from my own clients, suggests it may be beneficial to eliminate aspartame to control any role it plays in triggering anxiety or panic symptoms.

On the subject of nonnutritive sweeteners in general, judicious use of sugar may be the wisest choice; however, if you need to avoid sugar altogether because you are sugar-sensitive, nonchemical, nonnutritive sweeteners made from plants are widely available in natural foods stores. Chemicals in our foods challenge our physical ability to process them, and many people with anxious bodies react not only to aspartame but to other chemicals as well. For health in general, reducing intake of all chemicals is sensible, and eliminating aspartame is an obvious way to do that. Again, keep track of your anxiety levels after using aspartame or sugar, and if you notice an increase in symptoms, it makes sense to use less or eliminate it.

CREATE DEMAND DELAYS

Our current culture has created a special category of stress—the demand for an instantaneous response to communication. Many of us have become accustomed to the idea that we should immediately answer the phone, respond to an email, or send back a text rather than a "snail mail" letter. You might be among the people who have high drive—lots of energy to keep on going and doing, no matter what activity you undertake—so you may not be aware of the toll this communication demand takes.

Every time the computer or phone "dings" to tell us there is a waiting message, our brains register an alert. The amygdala hears a ding as a demand for attention. That alert is not calmed until we respond to it, and if we don't respond right away, it takes mental energy to push away the urge to respond. Even hearing someone else's phone ringing creates mental (and therefore, physical) tension. All of our communication-related technology has created an artificial "on-call" status that we live with daily—a constant level of alertness and readiness to respond promptly. It's easy to feel the demand of email, voicemail, text messages, instant messages, and so on. Workplace expectations increase that feeling. "Oh?" the boss says with arched eyebrow. "You didn't get the message? I sent you an email at nine o'clock last night to tell you the meeting this morning was to start an hour early." The implication is that you should be checking in with work at all hours of the day. Many companies directly instruct employees to check email on weekends, and healthcare professionals, especially mental health professionals, are often expected to be on call without a break, sometimes for days on end. The stress of remaining alert is subtle but constant, and it plays a definite role in creating physical tension.

It may be a good idea to reduce "response demand" stress to see how it is affecting you. Mike, a client of mine who used to joke that his Bluetooth earpiece had been surgically implanted, forgot his phone one day on a business trip. He realized that it felt great being unable to answer the phone, respond to texts, or answer email while he spent the day with his customer. He was attentive to the customer, focused on his work, and felt that he did a better job than he could have if he had been responding to the constant rings and dings coming in on the phone. He felt some anxiety without the phone, but because he had no choice, he was able to set the anxiety aside, and he felt calmer on the job than he had in a long time. Even traveling home, he felt better, being able to listen to music rather than returning calls during the commute. Because changing your pattern of responding to communication demands may briefly increase anxiety before it provides relief, create a fair test period in which to observe this. Turning off contact makes you anxious about what you're missing. You will have to get used to the sensation of being out of touch. And then you might like it.

Adolescents in particular will have intense anxiety if separated from their cell phones. They are at the developmental stage in which social engagement is a primary motivator, and they will find many of their friends and acquaintances sending texts and tweets, messaging via Instagram and Snapchat and WhatsApp, and using whatever the next terrific messenger app is as soon as it's out. They often need parental control to learn limits—the temptation to check the phone all night is common. Many adolescents sleep with their phone in hand or next to their pillow. This is far from ideal, and as we become more sophisticated with technology, measuring the impact of constant connection, for good or ill, is an important challenge.

To reduce the impact of this stress, make a deliberate choice to limit your availability for answering these many means of messaging and see how your anxiety level changes. This is called creating *demand delays*. Try one of the following ideas for at least a full week, choosing the one that fits best with your work life. The ultimate goal is to be in control of *when* you will respond to all of your technology demands, but start with one thing at a time. Rate your anxiety level each day on a scale of 0 to 10 (with 10 being high) before, during, and after the technology-free time you create.

- Wait to check your email for at least an hour into your workday. Try getting some work done first.
- Try checking voicemail at specific times in the workday when it suits your schedule to take messages and return calls. (You may want to let callers know about these times—when they can expect a return call—on your outgoing message.)

- Turn off things that ring and ding while you are focusing on work.
- Turn off everything at home that rings, including cell phones, while you eat your meal. Make mealtimes a "no-calls zone."
- Leave your cell phone in the car when you go into a restaurant, or at least turn the ringer to silent (not on vibrate) so that your attention is completely on your meal and your companions. (Do the same thing in theaters, meetings, churches, lectures, and so on.) One group of friends I know all put their cell phones face down on a restaurant table when they dine out. The first person to pick his or hers up pays the tab! (If none do it, they split the tab.) What an incentive to enjoy the company of friends and stay in the moment with them.
- Don't leave your cell phone number as an alternative to your work number unless you are required to do so. People will automatically use it, knowing you are likely to have it with you. If you use a cell phone for work and you want a work break, either have a work cell phone separate from your personal phone that you can turn off when not at work or, at a minimum, turn it off soon after finishing work for the day and let your outgoing message indicate you will return calls at a later time.
- To a reasonable degree, don't mix personal and work-related numbers so that you can elect to not answer the work phone without missing family or friends' calls. Additionally, don't answer work calls on personal time.
- If you are required to take a computer home or to work from home, make a specific agreement with your supervisor about exactly which hours you are expected to work. Don't respond to messages from work except during those hours. The temptation to be at work nonstop will not be discouraged by your boss; you have to set the boundaries.
- Track the impact of communication demands and how they affect your anxiety level. This may be perceived as tension or alertness rather than nervousness. It is also helpful to track how

DEMAND: Don't answer email until an hour into workday	Day 1	Day 2	Day 3	Day 4	Day 5	Day 6	Day 7
Before delay	8	7	9	5	3		
During delay	10	10	7	3	0		
15 min. after delay	3	2	7	1	1		

Figure 3.1 Demand Delays. Rate your anxiety level each day 0–10 (with 10 being high) before, during, and after the technology-free time you create.

anxious it makes you to step away from communication availability. Both versions of anxiety can keep your brain revved up and ready to be anxious over seemingly unrelated things. One method of rating anxiety and how its levels change when you try to create some communication boundaries is to create demand delays and track the results. You can use an ordinary index card to do this or use the sample to create a similar tracker into your method of keeping notes in your phone. Figure 3.1 shows an example of a partially filled out card.

LOWER YOUR STIMULATION INTAKE

Getting a break from high-stimulation environments at work can be extremely helpful to lowering stress (Jabr, 2016; Schaubroeck & Ganster, 1993). Although people don't always report feeling stressed from the noise of working in an open workplace, their bodies reveal the impact of constantly having to block out the noise, showing stress hormones at higher levels than those of people working in less noisy offices (Evans & Johnson, 2000). For people who are very sensitive to high degrees of stimulation, these kinds of breaks from being on demand can be lifesavers for lowering stress and tension levels (Aron, 1997; Aron and Jaeger, 2003).

If you're not conscious of the impact of stimulation in your environment, you might need to take breaks even without feeling the pressure to do so. The more sensitive you are, the higher the toll the environment takes on you, so time out from stimulation can really pay off in calmer physiology. Try some of these breaks at least every 90 minutes at work:

- Take a moment to look outside and let your mind wander.
- *Actually go outside*, even for a few minutes.
- Have a picture of your favorite people or place handy, and when you look at it, take a moment to feel deep appreciation and love.
- If you go to Facebook or other social media for a relaxer, think carefully about whether you will instead view or read things there that stress you out: news, competitive posts, nasty comments.
- Walk up and down a hallway, take a drink of water, or take a trip to the bathroom, even if you don't need it, just to move and be away from your workstation.
- Try a two-minute mental vacation. This is great for any age. Close your eyes and imagine a place you love. Then run through what you experience there in each of your five senses. By the time you have set the scene, it will be about two minutes, and you can come back to the present with the feeling that you have had a small break.

People feel stress in environments other than work as well. Students may feel crabby or act overexcited as the result of too much stimulation in the classroom, cafeteria, or hallways of school. After spending a day with children in the house, most parents want to send them outside to play, but those who are sensitive to stimulation really need to do this if they want to avoid anxiety-provoking tension. Shopping (especially in malls), commuting on busy streets by car or public transportation, attending conferences with lots of people and new information, or being exposed to noise, fluorescent lighting, or other kinds of environmental irritants may all create the need for a stimulation break. If you have the option to limit the amount of time you spend in situations that will be too stimulating, that can be a big help. Plan breaks in a day of shopping, like taking time to sit down for lunch or have a cup of tea. If there are too many people around the house, disappear into a quiet room for a break. If you notice yourself becoming more irritable, tired, angry, or anxious, take time to calm down your body after situations that stimulate you. Rest, read, listen to music, nap in a quiet space, breathe, or distract yourself with an activity that draws you in but doesn't require intensity.

INCREASE YOUR INTAKE OF NUTRITIOUS FOODS

Your brain makes neurotransmitters from the nutrients in the food you eat, and most of the production of brain cells and neurotransmitters occurs while you're sleeping. Your brain needs protein from animal or plant sources (Delgado et al., 1994; Goldberg, 1997) while you're sleeping, and the digestive process requires 12 to 15 hours for the proteins to become available in the brain (DesMaisons, 2011). This is yet another reason why a good breakfast is a good idea! To make protein available throughout the night, eat protein three times a day, but you only need 3 or 4 ounces per serving—a portion about the size of a deck of cards.

You also need vitamins to make sure your brain is operating as it should and producing necessary neurotransmitters (Amen, 2003; DesMasions, 2011; Weil, 2007, 2017). The best route to getting nutrients is from food itself, but vitamin supplements can be a good idea if you're lacking in some areas. The surge in the use of acid reflux medications has created an unexpected problem for those with anxiety. We need vitamin B12 for healthy, nonanxious brains. Those medications interfere with absorption of B12 and folic acid, so it might be a good idea to supplement those vitamins if you take a proton pump inhibitor.

Remember that calories and nutrients are not the same thing. *What* you eat is much more important than how *much* you eat when it comes to brain health. Folic acid from dark green vegetables like spinach is essential to producing serotonin (Delgado et al., 1994; Wolfersdorf, Maier, Froscher, Laage, & Straub, 1994) and, if you are on SSRI medication, for making the medication work at its optimal level. Make sure you get other vitamins by selecting colorful orange, red, and yellow vegetables and fresh fruits. Healthy fats from olive oil and fish, like the omega 3 oils, have a good reputation for helping your brain do its work. See *Change Your Brain, Change Your Life* by Daniel Amen, *How to Use Herbs, Nutrients and Yoga in Mental Health Treatment* by Richard Brown, Patricia Gerbarg and Philip Muskin, *Good and Cheap: How to Eat Well on $4/Day* by Leann Brown, *Potatoes not Prozac* by Kathleen DesMaisons, and *8 Weeks to Optimum Health* by Andrew Weil for more information on building a healthy brain through nutrients.

Then, get some sleep! Your brain builds neurotransmitters while you sleep from the nutrients you provide during the day. Over history and in different cultures, people have had different sleep patterns, but most adults in Western industrial societies are sleeping straight through the night and need seven to eight hours a night, not just to manage stress but to repair and grow new cells. Children need more sleep than adults, and in 2016, the American Academy of Pediatrics supported the American Academy of Sleep Medicine's (AASM) 2014 recommendation that adolescents start school later so they can get their needed eight and a half to nine hours of sleep per night. (See the article on the AASM website *Recharge with Sleep* at www.aamnet. org/articles.aspx?id=6326. Many children show learning and behavior problems as an outcome of insufficient sleep.)

Research demonstrates that the brain restores itself overnight. During sleep, the neurons shrink and cerebrospinal fluid increases to carry away toxicity from the brain. Without sleep, numerous mental health problems can occur or worsen. During sleep, we put information into long-term storage; that is, we learn, and we also forget—we let go of unnecessary memories of experiences. See the website for the American Academy of Sleep Medicine (www.aasmnet.org) to obtain information about sleep disturbances and what kinds of treatment can work. There are also apps and technological devices that you can use to promote good sleep; see the Resources section for an example. Chapter 6 explores ideas to promote better sleep.

So, to help increase your intake of nutritious foods:

- Add protein, which builds brain neurotransmitters.
- Add dark green, leafy vegetables, which help the brain build new brain cells.

- Take a multivitamin to make sure you have all the trace elements you need.
- Eat regular meals so nutrients are available to you consistently.
- Pay attention to consuming healthy fats and avoiding hydrogenated oils.
- Get enough sleep so your body can use the nutrients for building and repairing cells.

CONCLUSION

Taking charge of the things that make your body anxious is not always easy, but it is always productive. Soothing physical agitation occurs with mental effort but also by making changes in your physical environment—both the inside environment of your body and the outside environment of the world around you. In the next three chapters, I'll present other significant techniques for calming your overaroused brain and anxious body.

FOUR

Technique

#2 Breathe

––––––––––

To manage the anxious body, there is no single technique as effective as breathing. It's almost miraculous what controlling your breath can do to calm your physiology. The beauty of breathing is that it works even if you don't believe it's going to. You already know how to breathe, so you aren't starting from scratch when you learn to apply breathing to feelings of anxiety. No matter what physical arousal symptoms you experience, breathing will make you more comfortable immediately if you learn how to apply it and remember to use it. Different aspects of breathing have applications for all kinds of anxiety. Some breathing methods include:

- Diaphragmatic breathing to interrupt panic *before* it starts
- Breathing to diminish and then stop panic when it has already started
- Associating deep breathing with progressive muscle relaxation such that taking a breath can relieve tension by cueing muscle relaxation
- Using breathing to keep your body calm as a way to keep stress from building

PRACTICING DIAPHRAGMATIC BREATHING

Try this before you read any further: take a nice deep breath and slowly release it. If you tried it, you just demonstrated how diaphragmatic breathing works its magic. You made an executive decision in the prefrontal cortex (PFC) of your brain to breathe, and the cortex sent instructions to the parts of your brain that would make sure the breathing was carried out by all the muscles and organs necessary to execute a breath. In your medulla, a primitive part of your brain, respiration and heart rate are constantly directed and monitored without any conscious effort on your part. But you can, by making a conscious decision, change the rate of that respiration. This starts parasympathetic activity, which stops sympathetic arousal by stimulating the vagus nerve that initiates activity in that part of the autonomic nervous system. If you keep up the breathing, your panic symptoms will subside.

The optimal rate of diaphragmatic breathing depends on your individual lung capacity. Most people normally take around five breaths per minute, but being faster or slower doesn't affect how effective this method is. The difference between the inbreath and the outbreath is the key. The optimal ratio is 1:2. That means that when you breathe slowly in, you should exhale twice as long. When you use apps, as I suggest later, the best ones demonstrate this ratio.

Diaphragmatic breathing is the most reliable way to stop a panic attack once it has begun. It's the only thing you can do as an act of will, even without believing it can work. Breathing changes your physiology immediately. When the body is tense, breathing is affected even before panic starts. But in panic, breathing gets shallow and rapid instantly and often without warning, and can change into gulps or gasps. This rapid breathing can become hyperventilation, which causes dizziness. Diaphragmatic breathing is the counter to hyperventilation.

Getting ready to start, carefully observe your breathing. Write down these observations so they don't get lost. Answer these questions: Is your breathing pace regular on inhaling and exhaling? Do you pause in your breathing? When? Do you feel short of breath or rushed? Can you tell if you're filling your lungs or breathing into your chest only? What do you notice?

The next time you're under pressure, set aside a part of your attention to observe how your breathing changes when you're tense. If you have to speak at a meeting and that makes you nervous, notice your breathing. If you're having a disagreement, note how you breathe. Even if you are feeling time pressure, take a moment to feel your breathing. It may surprise you to find that you haven't been filling your lungs or that you've been holding your breath when you inhale.

Make a chart, such as the one shown in Figure 4.1, to observe your breathing. Put a check mark next to all of the items that apply and add a note if you find any other observations about your breathing.

Breathing can be done anywhere, anytime. Whether you are tense at work or at home, whether in public or in private, you can breathe without being obvious. If you practice this breathing rigorously, you will be able to use it for panic attacks right away. You will immediately notice a reduction in the length of a panic attack. Over a period of a few weeks, if you are successfully diminishing the impact of any panic attacks that arise, you will see a decrease in the frequency of the panic. Stopping panic in its tracks calms the basal ganglia and causes them to trigger panic less often.

Practice the first time by lying down or standing—after that, you can breathe anywhere without anyone noticing. Be aware that the goal is not to change the way you breathe as you go about your daily activities, but rather to consciously change the way you breathe when you begin to feel panic coming on.

1. Lie down flat on your back or stand in a relaxed manner, feet slightly apart, knees loose. This is so you can sense the movement in your abdomen, which should move out when you inhale and pull in when you exhale.
2. Rest your hand on your abdomen. This will help you notice whether you're breathing deeply enough and whether your chest is tight.

	Short or impeded intake *Notes*:		Even, but fast *Notes*:
	Gasping *Notes*:		Relaxed *Notes*:
	Long in, short out *Notes*:		Holding breath *Notes*:
	Shallow *Notes*:		Panting *Notes*:
	Gulping *Notes*:		Hyperventilating *Notes*:

Figure 4.1 Breathing Observations Checklist

3. Next, exhale the air in your lungs so you are completely empty to start the practice.

4. Breathe in through your nose. Inhaling must be done evenly, as if you could fill your lungs from bottom to top in equal, even amounts. One way to imagine this is to think about a balloon filling up with water when you attach it to a faucet. The bottom fills and widens first and then the water expands the upper portion. Form an image of your breath filling a balloon in your abdomen, becoming heavy and warm as you inhale. It will help you to breathe evenly if you find a pace that allows you to measure your breathing in and out. Count until you feel exactly full (e.g., a slow one, two, three, four) to help you get a measured, even breath. Chances are you will take between three and six counts to fill your lungs with smooth inhalations. If you don't like the idea of counting, breathe while thinking a sentence with an even rhythm, such as, "I am steadily filling my lungs with air. I am emptying my lungs slowly and evenly." Fill up evenly, no gulps or gasps, so that you reach the top of your imagined balloon just in time to release the breath at the same even, measured pace.

5. Exhale evenly, taking twice as long as you did to inhale, until your lungs feel empty. The pace of exhaling should be slow and steady. Imagine you're blowing at the flame of a candle enough to move it but not blow it out. Your body needs time to exchange the oxygen and carbon dioxide or you can get dizzy—a sign that you are trying to eliminate, not encourage!

6. If you are uncomfortable or feel pressured to push air out while you are exhaling, stop the exhale at a comfortable point and simply pause for two counts before you start to inhale again. (Just try to make the exhale longer than the inhale before you pause.)

7. Practice! Diaphragmatic breathing is for you to use to calm down a panic attack. Most people who panic immediately forget their panic control measures unless they've practiced them. It's essential to use diaphragmatic breathing the moment you sense a panic

attack beginning, so you must practice frequently, whether or not you are sensing panic at the moment.

Create "Breathing Minutes"

For 30 days, try this "breathing minutes" exercise 10 or more times per day. For a minute at a time, practice diaphragmatic breathing whenever you're waiting for something. Remember, you don't need to be standing or lying down. You can do this whenever:

- You're stopped at a stoplight
- You're on hold on the phone
- You're waiting in line at the store
- You're waiting for the microwave to heat your food
- You're waiting for a friend at work or school
- You're waiting in the car to pick someone up
- You're waiting for the computer to boot
- You're waiting for the teacher to hand out the test papers
- You're waiting for someone to return a text
- You're waiting for a meeting to start

After practicing for seven days, pick one time of day when you can predict that you will be uninterrupted for a few minutes. For most people, it works best to pick early morning, late evening, or your lunch break. During this one uninterrupted period per day, you are going to *add one minute of breathing*. For the next seven days, you will continue the one- to two-minute practices seven to nine times a day, but you will add one minute each day to the time you picked when you can be uninterrupted. By the end of the week, you may be practicing for seven to eight minutes once per day. Once you can breathe for this long, you have set the stage to breathe for other important purposes, such as for profound relaxation, for meditation, and for cueing the stress response to turn itself off.

As you become better at automatically using diaphragmatic breathing when you feel panic symptoms set in, you can eventually stop practicing.

However, if you suffer from the tension and tightness that goes with being "uptight" or "wired," you can continue to use daily breathing for a different reason—to trigger muscle relaxation. By consciously noticing how your muscles relax as you breathe, you create a cue for relaxing. Later, when you deliberately breathe in that slow, deep way, your muscles will automatically let go of the tension they have acquired. Chapter 6 discusses the technique for cued muscle relaxation.

Obstacles to Diaphragmatic Breathing

Without exception, people will encounter obstacles before they can make diaphragmatic breathing work for them. But practice is necessary to make it a habit. Common obstacles include the following.

"I'm a Mouth Breather!"

Some people with significant allergies or physical obstructions such as deviated septa may find it hard to breathe through their nose. You may then feel anxious about breathing because you won't feel like you're getting enough oxygen. You may, of course, do diaphragmatic breathing through your mouth. The only problem is that you may get a tickle in your throat from the longer breathing practice drying you out. Just pause and swallow in between some breaths, and you may find it works well.

Forgetting to Practice or Forgetting to Breathe When Anxiety Strikes

I suggest linking breathing to several times, places, and activities throughout the day so that you don't forget to do it. It may be easier to remember if you:

- Visualize yourself practicing breathing—for example, at the sink, in the car, watching a show or working on your laptop, or using your cell phone. This will remind you to practice in those places.
- Keep track. Some people remember better if they write things down. You can keep a note the old-fashioned way on paper or in your phone. Noticing when you practice will also set it more

clearly in your mind and help you remember the next practice more readily.

- Remind yourself to breathe with a note or a task reminder. Forgetting to breathe when anxiety strikes is common, so a reminder from your calendar keeps you in the habit, and a tangible reminder on a note card in your pocket or purse can trigger you to breathe when anxious. The apps you can load on your phone become handy reminders as you see the icon on the screen even before you open the app to direct your calming breath.

When Breathing Creates Anxiety

Some people get anxious when they start to breathe deeply. Some are afraid to try this because they fear they will panic while doing something new. Being conscious of the act of breathing reminds others of their panic or can be alarming to people with anxiety. It may help you to realize that you breathe automatically in exactly the amount you need to breathe, controlled by the same kind of process that keeps your heart beating without conscious effort. But when we are stressed by thoughts or situations, our breathing can change, and we can make a conscious effort to regulate it.

Most often, when the conscious effort to regulate breath increases anxiety rather than soothes it, this is caused by incorrect technique or by giving in to anxious thoughts, so you may need one of two kinds of help. Work with someone who can watch you breathe and correct your technique. If that doesn't eliminate your discomfort with breathing techniques, try to articulate your thoughts about it and possibly talk about those with a therapist. You will benefit from talking with a counselor if you need to explore whether trauma or another, deeper cause of fear makes it too hard for you to do breathing exercises without anxiety.

When Breathing Doesn't Seem to Help

It is very rare for diaphragmatic breathing to have no positive impact on panic reduction whatsoever. Observe how you're practicing. You may be filling your chest while keeping your abdomen tight or holding your breath during part of the breathing. I once debated two graduate students in my class who insisted they had to suck in their stomachs while breathing in. They were doing the *exact opposite* of what their bodies would have done naturally, but they had breathed in this wrong way for so long that they kept reversing the action. They were amazed to see how different it felt when they learned to let their abdomen expand while inhaling. It may be helpful to have someone watch you while you breathe, as it can be hard to recognize what you're doing on your own.

When You Have Difficulty Concentrating

When practicing breathing, everyone has distracting thoughts that flit through their mind. This is especially likely when you're adding a minute a day to one of your breathing practices. The best way to handle distractions is to:

- Notice that you've been distracted and mentally say to yourself, "Oh. A thought." Just notice, with no judgment against yourself for getting distracted. Don't feel upset with yourself or impatient with the breathing. Consider thoughts as clouds in the sky, just drifting by. You have no need to stop them, examine them, or be irritated that they're there.
- Redirect your attention to your breath.
- Focus on the physical sensation of breathing, noticing the feeling of your lungs expanding, the sensation of your waistband against your abdomen, or how your back shifts against a chair. Feel your breath move through your nostrils or out of your mouth.
- Count to measure your pace and help keep your focus on the breath.

When Inhaling Feels Restrictive

You may feel as if you are tight or have an obstruction, as if there is a block in your airflow, or you may feel unable to fill your lungs completely. This is typical when you're feeling anxious. First, make sure you are upright and loosen any restrictive clothing, such as tight jeans or neckties. If the problem isn't as obvious as this, the source may be emotional, and it would be best to practice breathing in a therapy session to examine your emotional responses to the breath. Ask yourself:

- Where is the restriction or obstruction located?
- How does it feel? Is there a word or phrase that describes it?
- What does it look like? What is its shape or color or size?

Then:

- Visualize the block clearly.
- Send your breath to the center of that block.
- Watch what happens as you breathe and pay attention. Obstructions or restrictions that have an emotional basis will often disappear when you become aware of them, as long as you don't fight to push them away.
- Ask yourself what it would take to make the block smaller or disappear and imagine doing that.

When You Have Physical Limitations

Some people have difficulty breathing due to asthma or other lung diseases. If this is the case, you may need to work with your pulmonary specialist to find a faster breathing pace, a shorter duration, and a less intense breath to make it work. Decreasing intensity and duration of breath are usually the keys to making diaphragmatic breathing useful for those with chronic lung disease or pulmonary problems.

A LAST WORD ABOUT DIAPHRAG- MATIC BREATHING

You will notice more about your breathing as you practice. This technique is simple to do but not easy to master. For breathing to effectively reduce tension, you first have to remember to use it! Until it becomes a habit, you may forget to breathe under anxiety or tension. It takes some time for this process to become smooth and easy. Breathing effectively requires practice and attention until it comes naturally. As the ads used to say about driving a VW Beetle stick shift, "After a while, it's automatic!"

Breathing for Minimal Arousal

When people are in situations that make them uncomfortable, they tense up and try not to show it. They tend to hold still, making their breathing shallow and tightening their bodies. In other words, they create incredible muscle tension and set a hair trigger on their anxiety, getting ready to produce flushing, sweating, shaking, and quivering as soon as they think anyone is looking their way. They may even have a panic attack as soon as they start to think they're not going to be able to control the situation. When you have that degree of tension, it's important to take preventive action by breathing to keep your brain calm and help yourself stay relaxed as you prepare to do what you fear. If you focus on your breath, you are less likely to focus on your fears, and if you are breathing, your parasympathetic nervous system can help you avoid unnecessary physical arousal. The less tense you are, the less likely you are to experience symptoms of anxiety.

For example, you may be in a business meeting where you're expected to give a report on your activities and you don't like the feeling you have when everyone is looking at you. While you wait to speak, you can breathe to avoid getting too tense. Perhaps you're getting ready to try something you haven't done before—try out for a sports team or give a speech or speak up to your manager at work about a problem you're having. In such situations, you can do diaphragmatic breathing preventively. You will stay calm physically even if you are in situations that are trying.

A particularly good one-minute breathing exercise that is helpful when you have only a short amount of time and have to be subtle is the "in two, out two-four-six-eight-ten" method of relaxation breathing. It goes like this:

1. Inhale to the count of two.
2. Exhale to the count of two.
3. Inhale to the count of two.
4. Exhale to the count of four.

5. Inhale to the count of two.
6. Exhale to the count of six.
7. Inhale to the count of two.
8. Exhale to the count of eight.
9. Inhale to the count of two.
10. Exhale to the count of ten.

Nasal Breathing

Another version of this breathing is nasal breathing, which is especially calming and centering. This way of breathing is one of the best stimulators of the release of nitric oxide (NO). This is the neurochemical that helps your brain cells connect more readily, so you may find yourself more able to unlock "brain freeze" of the anxious mind (see Chapter 10 on TMA, or "too much activity"). When NO is released in the linings of your blood vessels, encouraged by nasal breathing, it functions as a vasodilator and relaxes your muscles. It's easy to understand how this works. Breathing in and out through your nose, you take 10 (minimum) very slow breaths, all the while just noticing your breath.

You may also find yourself in hectic or emotionally trying situations from which you need a break but can only get a short time away. A breathing method called the "five-count energizing breath" works well, but it's hard to do subtly. It's a good option if you can take a moment to leave the room or go to the restroom. In fact, if you're washing your hands, you can use this breathing method while shaking water off your hands with five short shakes on the exhale.

1. Inhale smoothly to a quick count of five.
2. Exhale by huffing your breath out in short bursts to the count of five: huh-huh-huh-huh-huh.

After taking a few minutes out of the high-stimulation environment and breathing off the tense energy you've accumulated, you can reenter with less tension but also with the energy to cope. You will be less likely to get too anxious to handle the situation, and your mind will be clearer to respond to whatever is happening.

CONCLUSION

Breathing is easy to learn but not always so easy to remember when you're panicking, tense, or frightened about what will happen next. Practice breathing until it comes naturally, because anxiety has a way of making you forget what you're supposed to do. Even when you become a master of anxiety control, breathing techniques remain useful, as they form a basis for meditation, relaxation, and otherwise dealing with the normal tensions of life in a very positive way.

FIVE

Technique #3

Practice Mindfulness

Mindfulness—a way of being fully present in the moment you are living and observing without judging or making meaning—has come into prominence during the last 20 years as a powerful way to improve physical and mental health. Mindfulness is a practice that becomes a way of living in which you disengage from strong attachment to your own beliefs, thoughts, and emotions (Kabat-Zinn, 2013). When people become able to live in the moment, they have a greater sense of emotional balance and well-being. Engaging in mindfulness directly relieves anxiety. it prevents the self-criticism that plagues those with social anxiety and relieves a person from the rumination about the past or worry about the future that is part and parcel of generalized anxiety.

Mindfulness is finally getting the attention it deserves from psychotherapists in research and practice. Several ways of working with anxiety have sprung from studying mindfulness and include the modalities of acceptance and commitment therapy (ACT) (Hayes, Strosahl, & Wilson, 2016) and Mindfulness-Based Stress Reduction (MBSR) (Kabat-Zinn, 2013; Stahl & Goldstein, 2010). These are by no means the only programs based in mindfulness, but they include structured training in mindfulness meditation as the core of the modality. The MBSR program intends to teach people how to take better care of themselves and live healthier and more adaptive lives, and research supports the success of that. Mindful awareness has benefits far beyond its use as a technique to manage anxiety—it improves physical health and dramatically reduces utilization of health care providers for both physical and mental health concerns.

Living mindfully involves staying in the moment as much as possible and staying open to what may come without judging it to be good or bad but just observing. While this may not sound related to managing the anxious body, it is a powerful way to accept the presence of disturbing physical sensations without deciding they are harmful. It can allow you to stop reacting so immediately to the world around and to more intentionally respond both to stressors and to your own fear. A delay in making meaning out of sensations allows you to observe an increased heart rate or sensation of fluttering in the gut and say to yourself, "I observe my heart is beating quickly," instead of, "Oh no! I am about to panic!" Without ascribing cause or meaning, it is possible to observe sensations coming (and going!) without fear. Mindfulness practice allows you to stop before getting to the imagination of fear.

Such presence in the moment is the antithesis of anxiety. Anxiety by its very nature is worrying about what was or what will be. The three types of anxiety discussed in this book demonstrate this. Simply put, panic disorder is fear of fear, social anxiety disorder is fear of humiliation, and generalized anxiety is worry about any kind of negative outcome (in hopes of preventing such a possibility). It is rarely focused on the moment. If something bad is happening *right now*, you are probably not anxious about it. You are more likely occupied with handling it. Of course, something happening right now could scare you, but even so, you are still dealing with a threat occurring in the moment, not actually worrying about it happening later.

People who have researched the impact of mindfulness on the brain and body can demonstrate that practicing mindfulness has a calming effect on the brain. Mindfulness diminishes the physical impact of stress by allowing people to be more focused, more able to see solutions to problems, and more able to remain peaceful in the face of the normal wear and tear of life (Benson, 2015; Hanson, R. 2016; Kabat-Zinn, 2013; Newberg & Waldman, 2010) Schwartz, Gulliford, Stier, & Thienemann, 2005; Siegel, 2010; Williams, Teasdale, Segal, & Kabat-Zinn, 2007).

MINDFULNESS MEDITATION

Mindful *meditation* allows you to use meditation to increase your ability to stay in the moment in daily life. Meditation in general brings so much benefit to developing a calm body-mind. The psychological, spiritual, and physical benefits of meditation were first highlighted by Herbert Benson and his co-author Miriam Klipper in *The Relaxation Response* (2000), and he went on to look at beliefs as they affect health (Benson & Proctor, 2004). Mindfulness meditation is one way to do that, and deriving the full benefits of it requires you to be disciplined. Most meditation practice requires 20 minutes at minimum, and MBSR recommends 45 minutes, typically on a daily basis, although research has shown that as little as 10 minutes of meditation, done daily, has lasting benefits for stress reduction, memory, and calmness (Chiesa, Calati, & Serretti, 2011). Other styles of meditating produce very positive outcomes in health, memory, attention, and empathy and reduced anxiety and depression (Newberg & Waldman, 2010).

The discussion of mindfulness in this chapter is not intended to teach meditation. There are various techniques for mastering that very rewarding practice, and you can learn about meditation from other sources. Websites I have found helpful are listed in the Resources section.

It is not possible here to teach all the ways to introduce the practice of mindfulness to your life, but there are some concepts from this practice that you can employ to start along the path to living free from judgment and to open your ability to see others as less threatening and yourself as more competent.

Learn to Observe

One way to begin being more mindful is to practice observing. A simple way to do this is to think of yourself as a detective who is observing details. The goal is to observe before deciding meaning, just as a detective gathers clues before deciding what theory they may fit.

You can do this in any setting:

- Walk outside and observe through your five senses. What do you hear, see, taste, smell, and touch?
- Observe without speaking at the next meeting you attend. How do people speak, act, relate to each other? How do they speak to you? Look at you? Remember, no judging about what they are thinking or feeling. Just observe what you see and hear.
- Watch family members at a family gathering. Watch who says what and observe what others do when a person speaks. Observe the give-and-take, both verbal and nonverbal, without deciding what the meaning of it is.
- You might even be able to observe your thoughts as they occur. Just notice the thoughts. Later, you may choose to act or not act on them. You may decide the thought is useful or may even decide your thought is not true or correct.

Even without devoting yourself to a life change in this direction, there is a mindfulness exercise that can bring immediate benefit to those who are excessively focused on worrying about what is happening in their bodies. This exercise will assist you over time in telling the difference between what is real and what is imagined, and it will help you to ignore fleeting and inconsequential physical sensations.

Body Scan Meditation

A starting place for most mindfulness practice is the body scan meditation. This meditation is done lying down and involves developing awareness of each part of your body in a systematic scan from toe to head. The goal of meditation via the body scan is to create a sense of awareness that unifies the perceiver and the sensation. Kabat-Zinn (2013) wrote that in the body scan, we open to the give-and-take that occurs between the sensations themselves and our awareness of them.

The body scan meditation may become a start to your development of a meditation practice. But even if it doesn't, at a different level you may have great benefit from it for anxiety relief. At first, in doing a body scan, you sense that your body is you but that *you* are also in some way distinct. When people suffer panic, social fears, or even worry, they often have the sense that they have no control over their physical sensations and begin to believe that their behavior must be ruled by those sensations. However, the body-scan meditation creates awareness that sensations can be experienced without losing control and that sensations will pass.

The scan takes about 20 minutes (or longer) and involves the following steps:

1. Lie down comfortably.
2. Allow your breath to slow and deepen.
3. Turn your attention in an interested, open, and loving way to your body, slowly moving through it in the following pattern:
   • Starting with the left foot, attentively scan the toes, the foot, the ankle, the shin and calf, the knee and kneecap, the thigh, the hip.
   • Repeat that awareness with the right leg.
   • Continue from the right hip to awareness of the buttocks and genitals.
   • Move your attention to the abdomen and the lower back.
   • Gradually move your attention up through the torso, the middle back, the stomach.
   • Note the chest, the heart, the lungs, and then the upper back.
   • Bring your attention to the shoulders.
   • Slowly, allow your attention to focus on the arms, starting with the left fingers first, then the hand, wrist, forearm, elbow, and upper arm and then the right. Then return to the shoulders.
   • Then scan upward through the neck, the throat, the jaw, the face, and the scalp.
   • Breathe.

This body scan may result in surprising awareness of sensations that you had not attended to. It may result in brief intensifying of sensations, and those often pass as you recognize them. I learned early in my career that if you notice sensations, they pass—what an important message for people with anxiety! Your mind-body awareness helps you know how you are being affected by stress, by interaction with others, and even by your own thoughts. If you want to have guidance in doing your body scan, do a quick search on the Internet to find guided meditations. I would suggest finding one based on the MBSR model.

MINDFULNESS WITH SHIFTING AWARENESS

Sara, a client of mine who had developed debilitating panic attacks in adulthood, began to master the techniques of breathing, which helped diminish her fear of dying while having a panic attack. However, she developed another problem as well. She began to fear that she would always be afraid. "After all," she said, "this panic took total control over me, and I was always so strong." Sara paid too much attention to every small physical sensation, believing each tingle heralded a panic attack. She was essentially creating panic out of small, normal changes in her physical state. A slight chill or a momentary flutter in her stomach was all she needed to start hyperventilating in fear that panic was on its way, which of course it would be with her attention riveted to the sensation.

Sara needed to learn to turn her attention away from her physical state to the other aspects of her life as it was in the moment. It was important for her to learn to notice the outer world rather than her inner world. Remember that our brains are registering data from all of our senses at the same time that our hypothalamus is monitoring information from our organs and bloodstream. Paying attention to the outer world can complete our mindfulness, and learning to direct focus and attention are important aspects of being mindful.

By focusing your attention on what is happening around you, you gain some sense of control over how you are experiencing life. You are *choosing* what to attend to. You also enhance your ability to observe yourself. Observation of your own thinking and feeling requires prefrontal cortex activity.

Our uniquely human capacity to use the brain to control the brain is at the heart of anxiety management, and it is most obvious in selecting what to pay attention to. When physical sensations are troubling and there is no real purpose served by focusing on them, focusing away from those physical sensations to observations of the outer world is a good way of calming yourself. This is called "self-soothing," and it is an important life skill.

People who suffer from panic attacks tend to be particularly aware of physical sensations and changes. People with flushing, sweating, or shaking associated with the fear that other people are watching and judging them are also highly aware of how they feel. Anytime you focus on these kinds of sensations, you are dooming yourself to having the physical reaction you most fear. This technique, on the other hand, will help you immediately stop focusing attention on perturbing body sensations so that you won't develop the symptoms you fear. You will learn to shift from awareness of your inner sensations to awareness of the world around you.

Practicing Mindfulness With Shifting Awareness

It is helpful to do this technique for the first time with a partner who can lead you through the exercise while you devote attention to your own awareness. Have your partner read aloud the following steps:

1. With your eyes closed, follow your breath into your body as you inhale through your nose. Notice each sensation of inhaling.
   - Notice the coolness of the air.
   - Notice the pressure of the airflow.
   - Notice how the movement feels through your nose, throat, trachea, and into your lungs.
   - Notice the feel of your body shifting against your clothing and the chair you are sitting on.
   - Follow the breath out of your body, exhaling through your nose or mouth.
   - Notice the warmth of the air.

- Notice the pressure of the airflow reversed past your throat, sinuses, and nose or mouth.
- Notice how the movement of air feels through your lungs, trachea, throat, and nose or mouth.
- Notice the change in the feel of your body shifting against your clothing and the chair you are sitting on.

2. Exhale your awareness to the world around you without opening your eyes.
   - Direct your awareness to every sound in the environment, paying special attention to location and intensity.
   - Shift your awareness to the smells in the environment.
   - Shift your awareness to the sense of movement in the environment if you are in a place with other people nearby.

3. Now, shift your awareness back to your body, and inhale again.
   - Notice the coolness of the air.
   - Notice the pressure of the airflow.
   - Notice how the movement feels through your nose, throat, trachea, and into your lungs.
   - Notice the feel of your body shifting against your clothing and the chair you are sitting on.
   - *Add this awareness:* Feel your heart beating.
   - As you exhale, notice the warmth of the air.
   - Notice the pressure of the airflow reversed past your throat, sinuses, and nose or mouth.
   - Notice how the movement of air feels through your lungs, trachea, throat, and nose or mouth.
   - Notice the change in the feel of your body shifting against your clothing and the chair you are sitting on.

4. Now, with your eyes remaining shut, exhale your awareness into the room.
   - Direct your awareness to every sound in the environment, paying special attention to location and intensity.
   - Shift your awareness to the smells in the environment.

- Shift your awareness to the sense of movement in the environment if you are in a place with other people nearby.

5. Now, shift your awareness back to your body as you inhale.
   - Notice the coolness of the air.
   - Notice the pressure of the airflow.
   - Notice how the movement feels through your nose, throat, trachea, and lungs.
   - Notice the feel of your body shifting against your clothing and the chair you are sitting on.
   - Feel your heart beating.
   - *Add this awareness:* Feel the movement of blood or energy through your body or limbs.
   - Notice the warmth of the air.
   - Notice the pressure of the airflow reversed past your throat, sinuses, and nose or mouth.
   - Notice how the movement of air feels through your lungs, trachea, throat, and nose or mouth.
   - Notice the change in the feel of your body shifting against your clothing and the chair you are sitting on.

6. One more time, shift your awareness to the external world as you exhale.
   - Direct your awareness to every sound in the environment, paying special attention to location and intensity.
   - Shift your awareness to the smells in the environment.
   - Shift your awareness to the sense of movement in the environment if you are in a place with other people nearby.

7. Prepare to open your eyes by becoming aware of light coming through your eyelids, and then gradually allow your eyes to open, taking in the color of the light and then the things you can observe with your vision as you become fully present and aware of the situation you are in.

- Notice the pressure of the airflow reversed past your throat, sinuses, and nose or mouth.
- Notice how the movement of air feels through your lungs, trachea, throat, and nose or mouth.
- Notice the change in the feel of your body shifting against your clothing and the chair you are sitting on.

2. Exhale your awareness to the world around you without opening your eyes.

- Direct your awareness to every sound in the environment, paying special attention to location and intensity.
- Shift your awareness to the smells in the environment.
- Shift your awareness to the sense of movement in the environment if you are in a place with other people nearby.

3. Now, shift your awareness back to your body, and inhale again.

- Notice the coolness of the air.
- Notice the pressure of the airflow.
- Notice how the movement feels through your nose, throat, trachea, and into your lungs.
- Notice the feel of your body shifting against your clothing and the chair you are sitting on.
- *Add this awareness:* Feel your heart beating.
- As you exhale, notice the warmth of the air.
- Notice the pressure of the airflow reversed past your throat, sinuses, and nose or mouth.
- Notice how the movement of air feels through your lungs, trachea, throat, and nose or mouth.
- Notice the change in the feel of your body shifting against your clothing and the chair you are sitting on.

4. Now, with your eyes remaining shut, exhale your awareness into the room.

- Direct your awareness to every sound in the environment, paying special attention to location and intensity.
- Shift your awareness to the smells in the environment.

- Shift your awareness to the sense of movement in the environment if you are in a place with other people nearby.

5. Now, shift your awareness back to your body as you inhale.
   - Notice the coolness of the air.
   - Notice the pressure of the airflow.
   - Notice how the movement feels through your nose, throat, trachea, and lungs.
   - Notice the feel of your body shifting against your clothing and the chair you are sitting on.
   - Feel your heart beating.
   - *Add this awareness:* Feel the movement of blood or energy through your body or limbs.
   - Notice the warmth of the air.
   - Notice the pressure of the airflow reversed past your throat, sinuses, and nose or mouth.
   - Notice how the movement of air feels through your lungs, trachea, throat, and nose or mouth.
   - Notice the change in the feel of your body shifting against your clothing and the chair you are sitting on.

6. One more time, shift your awareness to the external world as you exhale.
   - Direct your awareness to every sound in the environment, paying special attention to location and intensity.
   - Shift your awareness to the smells in the environment.
   - Shift your awareness to the sense of movement in the environment if you are in a place with other people nearby.

7. Prepare to open your eyes by becoming aware of light coming through your eyelids, and then gradually allow your eyes to open, taking in the color of the light and then the things you can observe with your vision as you become fully present and aware of the situation you are in.

MINDFULNESS AND PANIC ATTACKS

Mastering the mindfulness technique above will help you to stop fearing physical sensations that trigger worry about whether an anxiety attack is headed your way. People tend to control panic by avoiding situations in which they previously panicked. When they are trying to reenter those situations, they commonly state that they are on the lookout for panic to recur. Sometimes these people are afraid of the consequences of ignoring panicky sensations. They may ask, "How can I do this? What if I panic and I don't notice it coming?" I always ask right back, "Have you ever had a panic attack that you failed to notice?"

If a panic attack is coming on and you are not yet practiced enough with breathing or mindfulness to ward it off, the attack may in fact develop. The next section—Part III—will discuss techniques to control the thoughts that go with this. However, it is a good idea to develop the attitude that you don't need to be afraid of panic happening. All you need to do is make a plan for what to do if the panic attack develops. Write this plan down and carry it with you in case you need a reminder. Clearly, identifying options for situations such as driving, being in a public place, and so on is necessary. You can review the written options before entering the situation the next few times. The confidence you get from having a plan can reduce the likelihood of feeling anxiety. Often, the best option is just to stay where you are and breathe until the panic is gone. Driving is a little different in that you want to be sure that you don't endanger anyone, so the plan might be to pull over and breathe until the anxiety passes.

A client of mine responded very well to this wonderfully simple technique. Diverting her attention to the external world was particularly helpful when she started to drive on the highway again. As she started to feel sensations that might be the harbinger of a panic attack, she did some diaphragmatic breathing and diverted her attention back to the road and the actions of controlling the car. Even though her plan allowed her to stop if the symptoms increased, shifting her focus of attention to the road was sufficient to avoid a full-blown panic attack. It only took a couple of trips on the road without panicking for her to regain confidence that she could resume her driving without fear.

MINDFULNESS AND FLUSHING, SWEATING, AND EMBARRASSMENT ANXIETY

As stated earlier, warding off the anxiety that others will notice—small signs of flushing, sweating, or shaking—is a critical part of having fewer attacks of nervousness. These symptoms are triggered by the peripheral nervous system, and once under way, they are harder to interrupt than panic itself, in part because others *do notice* these symptoms. Ultimately, if you stop caring whether you flush, you diminish the tendency to do so, but the best way to keep these symptoms at bay is to learn how to discreetly stay calm in situations that could provoke anxiety. Mindfulness with shifting awareness can take you either inward or outward, depending on which is the most helpful direction at the moment. If you're shy, staying focused on your inner breathing rather than on the surrounding hubbub can help you avoid the overstimulation that can trigger blushing, sweating, or flushing when you feel flustered.

CONCLUSION

Because you can practice mindfulness with shifting awareness in any setting without being obvious—as long as you simply keep your eyes downcast and not closed—it is a terrific tool for pulling your mind away from worry or panic and simply directing your attention to the present moment. As I said earlier, the antithesis of worry is to be in the moment and not in the future or past. Whether you're feeling worried, anxious, or panicky, the technique itself doesn't vary—you can use it in any of these situations—but the timing of it may. Because worry and panic can occur anywhere for any reason, this "do it anywhere" technique is terrific for those of us who fret.

SIX

Technique #4

Rest and Relax

The anxious brain uses up a lot of energy—energy to push back against negative thinking, energy to recover from bouts of strong sensations of anxiety, and energy to manage stress. When people are under stress, the stress hormone initiates a cascade of responses in the brain-body, and one outcome is muscle tension. Stress signals muscles to contract in the same way you might deliberately tighten to spring into action at the starting line of a race. This tightness shows up as physical tension.

Under stress, people can develop illness and pain that intensifies any anxiety they might have. This is a circular problem. For example, increased tension can cause irritable bowel syndrome (IBS) to become much worse, and the IBS then compounds the tension by making people afraid of the pain of the stomach cramps and the disruption of their activities as they suffer alternately from diarrhea and constipation. Learning to relax and get rid of stress will reduce the impact or frequency of these kinds of illnesses.

THE IMPACT OF STRESS AND THE IMPORTANCE OF REST AND RELAXATION

Stress comes in two primary categories that I call *quantity stress* and *quality stress*. Quantity stress occurs often because people in today's nonstop culture, which strongly values productivity, get themselves into a position in which they are capable of doing every task on their list but don't have enough time to get it done. Their sense of stress (and their body's response to stress) escalates when they feel the pressure of undone tasks. If a person doesn't feel some measure of control, their stress response is even more intense.

Quality stress is what happens when people must do tasks they are not able to do. They need skills or education or training, and without it they believe they will fail. In this situation, a sense of control also matters. If people know they will be trained and/or believe they can learn the task in time to complete it, then they won't produce as much stress hormone and their body will not get as tense.

Recovering from and even preventing the damage from stress involves four arenas of stress management. Robert Epstein (2011) listed those four arenas as follows:

1. Eliminate the stressor
2. Manage time and environment
3. Manage attitude
4. Learn to relax

I discuss time management in Chapter 8, "Stop Anxious Thoughts," and I look at eliminating stressors and managing both environment and attitude in Chapter 10, "Control TMA." This chapter is about Epstein's stress management skill #4: learning to relax. Rest, including taking breaks from stress and sleeping, is essential to overall good health, not just for managing the anxiety born of stress. It will increase mental and physical calmness. Relaxation has many applications for managing the anxious body: staying calm in anxiety-provoking situations, shifting gears at the end of a trying day, clarifying thinking, diminishing the physical and emotional impact of stress, and so on. This chapter offers several approaches to preventing stress damage from the different kinds of tension and anxiety people feel.

RELAXING THE TENSE BODY AND MIND

The description "uptight" is very apt for people who are stressed out. Most people react to stress by literally tightening up physically. And they don't notice the tension until they have knots in their backs or headaches. Physical relaxation doesn't come naturally to people suffering from anxiety, and they, like everyone else, won't notice how they have tightened up in the neck or shoulders, lower back, buttocks, or legs until they have pain somewhere. Tension headaches are born of tense muscles in the head and neck that restrict blood flow or affect nerves.

Tension in the body often stems from mental tension. For example:

- People who are prone to panic tend to anticipate trouble, which causes tightness.
- People with social anxiety fear they are going to be humiliated, causing them to feel tension prior to being in a public situation.
- People with generalized anxiety are in mental overdrive. This also produces tightness.

Physical tension is the result of too much norepinephrine (NE) that causes cognitive vigilance and enhances the physical "wired" feeling generated in the basal ganglia. While anyone can enjoy the release provided by an exercise for muscle relaxation, people with generalized anxiety are most likely to need to practice relaxation as a lifelong habit. Their mental and physical stress is the mental equivalent of standing at the starting line of a race. Their muscles contract in anticipation of the need to move, but often their lives don't allow for a lot of muscle activity that would release that tension. In addition to experiencing the stress-related tension of vigilance and high drive, they also cope with the mental tension of the ruminating anterior cingulate cortex (ACC; see Table 1.3, How Brain Structures Are Affected When Norepinephrine Levels Are High, in Chapter 1) that makes muscles gradually tighter and tighter. Worriers can learn to cue relaxation on a frequent basis to defeat the tension that accumulates during the day.

The ability to relax is not just necessary for people with worry as their main version of anxiety. People who suffer panic can fare better if they know how to let go of mental and physical tension prior to a situation in which they fear they could panic. It is harder to flare into panic if you start from a calm place mentally and physically. People with social anxiety have the same benefit if they can relax their bodies and stay calm in their mind before they enter a public situation they fear.

Tense-and-Release Progressive Muscle Relaxation

Progressive muscle relaxation for tension release is a "first-line" treatment for the physical tension of the anxious body. It directly counteracts the symptoms and ailments that go with continual tightness in the neck, back, jaw, and so on. The intentional relaxation of muscles with slow, deep breathing helps the parasympathetic nervous system to slow the heart rate and respiration and to lower blood pressure. This not only eliminates tension-related stiffness and aches but also lowers arousal levels so that it's harder to trigger anxious physical symptoms. Methods such as yoga or meditation, or even some of the martial arts, are good ways to learn deep relaxation, but they require specific training from a practitioner of those arts. The form of progressive muscle relaxation offered here is a method everyone can learn and is the best option for people with generalized anxiety.

The basic goal of this technique is to relax all muscle groups in a systematic manner. It will take 10 to 15 minutes. The following script provides directions for this particular method (I present others later in the chapter). Feel free to expand the instructions to include reminders to feel warmth as the muscles release. People who are very logical and pragmatic do better without imagery, but if you want to enhance this technique, you can add imagery to steps 3 and 5 (adding imagery works especially well with children). However, if you are leading someone else in this relaxation technique, check before starting that the relaxation imagery you use is soothing to the other person.

1. Make sure you are in a relaxed position, lying flat or sitting with your neck upright.
2. Close your eyes. Focus entirely on the sensations of each muscle group.

3. Add an image to the process. For example, imagine you are lying outside and the sun is gradually shining on you, touching your toes first and then moving along your body as you go through this exercise. (Other images such as ice cream melting or Jell-O or butter softening in a patch of sun work, too.)

4. If you are sitting up, begin at your head and move down. If you are lying down, begin at your feet and move up, working one group of muscles at a time.
    • Tense, hold, and then relax the muscle group. For example, tense your toes—curl them tight, tight, tight. Now release.
    • Feel the warmth flood into them. Feel the energy and warmth suffuse those muscles. With each exhalation of breath, feel the warmth flow into your toes.
    • Repeat the tense, hold, and release three times. (It is amazing how much tension remains after just one or two tightenings.)

5. With each muscle group, notice the warmth and then energy that suffuses the muscles as you release the tension. If you are using a specific image, such as the sun beginning to touch each part of you, think of that image as you go through each group.

6. The order of muscle groups named may be:
    • Scalp—raise your eyebrows to tighten the scalp.
    • Forehead—wrinkle your brow.
    • Face—squint your eyes, wrinkle your nose, and purse your mouth to tighten the face.
    • Neck—don't do neck circles, as they are hard on the spine. Try this instead:
        − Let your head drop forward with the weight pulling your chin toward your chest. You will feel the stretch down your back, even as far as your lower back if you are very tight.
        − Return your head to a full upright position before leaning it back in the opposite direction.
        − Tilt your head to one side, with the ear moving directly toward the shoulder, and you will feel the stretch as far

down as your shoulder blade. When your head returns
upright, feel the warmth flow in where the stretching was.

- Shoulders—raise your shoulders up, hunch-
ing them, and then release the tension.
- Arms—tighten your forearm, wrist, and
hand by clenching your fist.
- Back and abdomen—tighten this area by imagining a string pulling your belly button (navel)
toward the spine and then release slowly.
- Buttocks—tighten by squeezing together.
- Thighs—tighten by tensing and releasing your quad muscles.
- Calves and shins—tighten by pointing your toes
and feel the stretch down the shin and the contraction in the calf. Then reverse, by pulling the
toe up and pushing the heel down. Feel the stretch
down your calf and the contraction in the shin.
- Feet and toes—tighten by either curling the
toes or pushing the foot into the earth.

7. If you did the exercise from the top down, end with an awareness
of the soles of your feet feeling connected to the earth through
the floor. If you did it from the bottom up, end with an awareness of feeling completely relaxed, from head to toe.

8. Notice how totally relaxed, warm, and peaceful you are. Give
yourself permission to remain relaxed as long as desired, or, if
you are going on to another activity, give yourself permission to
remain physically relaxed, yet refreshed, alert and fully present,
while doing it.

Muscle Relaxation With Children and Elderly Adults

Because this technique can be done seated or lying down, there is no reason
that older adults can't do it. As with all exercises, an important reminder is
to never do anything that hurts. Sometimes stretching out tense muscles can

feel a bit achy, but it's more like "good soreness" than outright pain. Be sure you, or those you're instructing, understand this distinction.

If you are using this technique with children, you can improve their attention by making the stretching and relaxing of muscle groups into a game. Children don't usually have sore muscles from tension, but learning to relax is a good way to develop healthy habits. With younger children, use images of animals they can relate to, such as a cat stretching out in the sun or a lion opening its mouth to yawn. Using the language of "stretch and release" instead of "tense and release" works very well with these images. In a classroom setting, stretching as a group exercise can help children and adolescents relax before doing stressful things like taking a test.

Sphere-of-Light Imagery for Relaxation

As I indicated above, imagery for muscle relaxation works very well for many people. It has the same benefits of slowing down respiration and heart rate, opening capillaries, and inducing parasympathetic calming. There are many different imageries for relaxation, but the "sphere of light" works particularly well.

1. Imagine that there is a sphere of light and energy above your head.
2. The light is the color you most associate with peace, calm, healing, or energy. It is in abundant supply and cannot be depleted, so you can draw as much as you want into yourself.
3. As you inhale, breathe this beautiful, warm, vibrant, colorful energy through the top of your head.
4. As you exhale, feel the flow of energy streaming through your scalp.
5. Repeat this with each of your body parts (face, head, neck, shoulders, arms, hands, fingers, torso, hips, buttocks, thighs, knees, shins, calves, ankles, feet, and toes), breathing energy and light to each of the muscle groups as you inhale and feeling the energy flow through those muscles as your exhale.

6. Become aware of each body part, feeling the flow of the beautiful, warm, vibrant, colorful energy.

7. Imagine the energy flowing through your spine and out, as if you were sending roots into the earth.

8. Imagine energy flowing through the soles of your feet and into the earth, which can absorb any amount of energy and turn it all into the energy of life.

9. Experience the energy exuding from your pores to surround your body.

10. Find a word that you associate with the sensation of total relaxation, such as *calm* or *peace*, or even a sound, such as *ah* or *mmm*.

11. This energy provides a barrier to negativity for the day, preventing all criticism, disapproval, harsh words, or ill treatment from penetrating your heart. The barrier is permeable to all positive energy, such that words of praise, approval, and affection can immediately be received into the heart.

12. As the envelope of energy fades through the day, you can renew it with a deep breath, imagining the energy and light and saying or hearing the relaxing sound or word you chose.

One-Breath ("Cued") Muscle Relaxation

While practicing muscle relaxation techniques, diaphragmatic breathing occurs almost automatically. It is natural to breathe evenly while relaxing the tension in each group of muscles. Start noticing, as you practice any form of muscle relaxation, how your body feels when it is relaxed. You are likely to notice as you finish a relaxation that your breath is even and deep, as relaxed as your muscles.

Muscle relaxation is a lifelong method of handling physical tension. Because physical tension may result from activity in the basal ganglia or excess norepinephrine, it is not going to disappear with one session of relaxation. It is going to reappear constantly and not necessarily as the result of overt stress. The tension level resulting from activity in the basal ganglia can only be interrupted with muscle relaxation, which has to be learned and then integrated into an ongoing symptom-control plan. Relaxing the muscles reduces the high tension level and resulting pain in people with anxious bodies.

"One-breath" or "cued" relaxation also helps people with social anxiety or panic. People who need to stay calm in situations in which they have previously panicked or in social settings that set off embarrassed flushing and sweating can use cued relaxation as a tool to keep their bodies calm prior to entering a difficult situation.

Once you have learned diaphragmatic breathing and progressive muscle relaxation, you can pair them to produce cued relaxation. The pairing of breathing and muscle relaxation has many effects:

- Breathing encourages parasympathetic calming of the organs and the neuroendocrine system, which is activated in stress. In people who have excess activity of norepinephrine, sympathetic nervous system arousal is easily set off and contributes to higher degrees of physical and emotional tension. The decision to breathe is the best example of harnessing the brain (the prefrontal cortex decision-making function) to control the body.
- For people who have overactivity of the stress response system, such as those with social anxiety or those who have been traumatized, breathing with muscle relaxation can help interrupt or diminish the stress response.
- Pairing breathing and deep muscle relaxation forms an association between one or two full diaphragmatic breaths and total relaxation. Once you make that association, it will allow you, at any time or in any place, to cue relaxation by taking a controlled deep breath.

Once you have learned diaphragmatic breathing and muscle relaxation, it is fairly simple to expand that experience into a cued relaxation:

1. Several times a day, encourage physical release by taking a deep, diaphragmatic breath, recalling the way you feel when deeply relaxed.

2. Use an image that represents letting tension go—such as plugging your feet into the earth—and as you exhale, send negative energy out of your body and let relaxation flow in behind it throughout your whole body. Another good image is to send roots from your feet into the earth to draw calm in and send tension off into the atmosphere.

3. Accompany a slow, deep breath in with a calming statement, such as, "Now I am breathing in all that is of peace. Now I am breathing out all that is not of peace." Whether using an image or a phrase, draw peaceful relaxation inward as you inhale, and exhale the negative energy.

4. When you exhale, send the energy off or out in the way you have imagined it. Note how the muscles from your scalp to your toes are letting go of tension. Repeat this many times a day to discharge the muscle tension that accumulates from the normal stresses of life as well as from the extra tension of the anxious body.

As you get comfortable with this pairing, you will be able to take one breath and feel all of your muscles release. In this way, you can cue muscle relaxation on demand, anywhere or anytime, without anyone noticing the change from tight to relaxed.

EXERCISE TO RELAX

Physical pain, muscle soreness, headaches, digestive upset, and so on are particularly evident signs of an anxious body in people with high levels of stress. People who are worriers suffer the physical outcome of tightness throughout their bodies. If you are a "worrywart," you are likely to take stressful circumstances more seriously than others. Worriers not only suffer more from everyday stress but also bring on extra amounts of it.

Ongoing stress for any person can result in physical tension, higher blood pressure, or problems in almost any system in the body (Laber-Warren, 2015; Myers et al., 2015; Schmidt, Beck, Rivkin, & Diestel, 2016), and these problems will be worse in those who have the tendency to worry excessively. Exercise can be a great way to get rid of the impact of stress and worry.

A stunning amount of research demonstrates the many ways exercise is good for your mind and body. Exercise also has a positive impact on your ability to relax. For the high-energy person with a tense, anxious body, physical activities are better sources of physical relaxation than sitting still. Aerobic exercise is the best. At times of high stress, vigorous activity uses up the adrenaline of the stress response and helps to rid the body of toxic cortisol. It also helps the body to avoid the weight gain caused by constant stress (Bidonde & Busch, et al., 2017 Talbott, 2007). Finally, vigorous exercise promotes relaxation because muscles that are used are stretched and relaxed afterward. There is really no downside to exercise.

Exercise also promotes many aspects of mental health (Bartholomew, 2005; Dunn, et al., 2005) and is as important for children as it is for older adults (Larson, 2006; Nelson et al., 2007; Ratey & Hagerman, 2013; Zahl, Steinsbekk, & Wichstrøm, 2017). It fosters a sense of self-efficacy that promotes a willingness to take charge of one's life in other ways (Craft, 2005). In fact, physical fitness is a buffer against damage from stress (Schmidt et al., 2016) and helps you bounce back from stress effectively. Physical exercise is critical for overall health, and the significance of exercise is so broad that it should be considered a major intervention to reduce the impact of stress on both the brain and body.

Exercise increases blood flow to the brain, which is associated with many aspects of brain health, and it can benefit your neurotransmitter levels as well as the overall functioning of parts of the brain. Therapists are beginning to understand that exercise is as important to recovering from mental illness as many other interventions. (Bartholomew, 2005; Cynkar, 2007; Penedo & Dahn, 2005; Ratey, 2013). It may affect serotonin levels more positively in people who have problems with serotonin to begin with, as seen in research with depressed persons (Kiive, Maaroos, Shlik, Toru, & Harro, 2004), but other factors also boost depression and reduce anxiety (Busch, Ciccolo, Pus-pitasari, & Stults-Kohlemainen, 2015; Weil, 2017). Considering that about 50% of people with anxiety suffer from depression as well, it may be reasonably extrapolated that what will help with depression is also going to be important to treating anxiety.

The Mayo Clinic (www.mayoclinic.org/diseases-conditions/depression/in-depth/depression-and-exercise/art-20046495) currently tells us:

> Exercise helps prevent and improve a number of health problems, including high blood pressure, diabetes and arthritis. Research on anxiety, depression and exercise shows that the psychological and physical benefits of exercise can also help reduce anxiety and improve mood.

Similar recommendations as those for general physical health have been shown to have a positive impact on anxiety.

> To promote and maintain health, the ACSM/AHA [American College of Sports Medicine; American Heart Association] writing group recommends that "all healthy adults aged 18 to 65 years need moderate-intensity aerobic physical activity for a minimum of 30 minutes on five days each week or vigorous-intensity aerobic activity for a minimum of 20 minutes on three days each week." (O'Riordan, 2007)

And the Office of Disease Prevention and Health Promotion (ODPHP) website on https://health.gov/paguidelines/guidelines recommends:

For substantial health benefits, do one of the following:

- 150 minutes (2 hours and 30 minutes) each week of moderate-intensity aerobic physical activity (such as brisk walking or tennis)
- 75 minutes (1 hour and 15 minutes) each week of vigorous-intensity aerobic physical activity (such as jogging or swimming laps)

- An equivalent combination of moderate- and vigorous-intensity aerobic physical activity

Do aerobic physical activity in episodes of at least 10 minutes and, if possible, spread it out through the week.

For even greater health benefits, do one of the following:

- Increase moderate-intensity aerobic physical activity to 300 minutes (5 hours) each week
- Increase vigorous-intensity aerobic physical activity for 150 minutes (2 hours and 30 minutes) each week

Doing more will lead to even greater health benefits, and the guidelines include the option to do various levels of exertion or types of exercise:

> Combining exercises is also acceptable, with people allowed to meet the recommendations by walking briskly or performing an activity that noticeably accelerates the heart rate for 30 minutes twice during the week and then jogging for 20 minutes, or performing any activity that causes rapid breathing and a substantial increase in heart rate on two other days. (O'Riordan, 2007)

Another ACSM and AHA report states that less than 50% of adults in the U.S. meet standards for minimum physical activity for heart health (Haskell et al., 2007). There is no real agreement on the perfect amount of exercise. What your goal is can be a determining factor in how you decide. Is your goal heart health? Is your goal physical strength? Is your goal resilience? Is your goal better memory? Is your goal feeling less depressed? It seems that for anxiety relief, you could try the following amount of exercise: five to seven days a week for 25 to 45 minutes at 70% of your maximum heart rate, a pace that will make conversation hard but not leave you breathless (Amen, 2015; Sobel & Ornstein, 1996).

Getting Started With Exercise

For people who are not already regular exercisers, the biggest problem is getting started. Start by getting educated about how important exercise is. Remember that the anterior cingulate cortex (ACC) and the orbitofrontal cortex (OFC) in your brain (see Table 1.1. How Brain Structures Are Affected When Serotonin Levels Are Low in Chapter 1), both of which are involved in creating new options to problems, sometimes fail in those tasks. The ACC can get stuck on "I can't," and the OFC can fail to generate solutions. The brain can fail in its role to connect motivation to the process of exercise. This is when creating an intention (the work of the executive decision-maker, the prefrontal cortex) even in the absence of motivation, is a necessary part of getting the ball rolling for exercise. Take time to develop both the understanding and motivation to try this method.

You may recall in the discussion about stress and neurochemicals that some neurochemicals get depleted when stress is ongoing. The ability to turn off the stress response depends on sufficient levels of cortisol, and the brain needs to buffer the impact of norepinephrine and stress hormone with neuropeptide Y and galanin. What has been depleted must be restored. You might feel a little more inclined to exercise when you know that this is one of the best ways to promote the growth of the neurotransmitter-producing neurons. Exercise causes the brain to release brain-derived neurotrophic factor (BDNF), which promotes neuron growth. Exercise also stimulates galanin—necessary to protect the limbic system from stress as well as to stimulate neuron growth.

So, if you are developing the motivation to exercise but have not been doing it, you could consider starting small. A big step for someone who is not exercising might be to walk the dog for one extra block or five extra minutes, or it might be getting off the bus one stop early. Start by figuring out what activity will work and then make a commitment to try it. The following questions and guidelines will help you establish an exercise plan.

- *What physical things do you like to do?* (If the answer is "nothing," ask yourself, "What do I *remember* liking to do?") Don't exclude anything at first. Remember playing sports? Playing in the yard as a kid? Remember riding bikes for fun? Did you play tennis or racket sports or swim?

- *What opportunities do you have to do this activity?* Look for something that is similar to what you enjoy, even if you can't do exactly that. Maybe you played basketball when you were in school. Can you shoot baskets in the park? In your yard? Join a community team for adults? Get creative about what could work. Talking this over in therapy, or talking it over with a friend or family member, can provide ideas that otherwise may elude you if you're distracted or anxious.

- *Who might do this activity with you?* An exercise partner can increase both motivation and accountability. This can be problematic if you're starting from scratch. You might feel some embarrassment, especially if you have some social anxiety, at the thought that you are not as good as someone else. If you can afford it, working with a trainer can be a great place to start, because that person will know how far you can go physically. But even agreeing to meet a friend at the gym to start and finish at the same time or meet at the local track and not necessarily go at the same pace will encourage you to get started and keep at it. Even if you can only make a commitment to your dog to take longer walks, having someone—a pet or person!—depend on you will make you more likely to get out and do it.

- *Decide! What is the biggest possible step you can take in the direction of exercise?* Answer this question each week until you have achieved the goal of 25 to 45 minutes of aerobic exercise at 70% of your maximum heart rate. The weekly goal should produce increases in duration or pace of exertion, even though they may be slight, which will also promote motivation, as success encourages people to do more.

- *Make a commitment to an action plan.* It is best to make your plan with another person who will ask whether or not your commitment has been kept and what you plan to commit to next week.

	Day 1	Day 2	Day 3	Day 4	Day 5
EXERCISE GOAL (type and duration):					

Figure 6.1 Exercise Record

- *How will you be accountable?* One simple way to be accountable is to use a simple record-keeping method, such as that in Figure 6.1.
- *Evaluate your success and set the next week's goal in writing.* Aerobic exercise is best for short-term stress reduction and relaxation of tight muscles. It is also great for short-term boosts in neurochemicals. Over time, it promotes the healthy production of brain chemicals and may help with improved neurological function through increased blood flow to the brain.

Alternatives to Traditional Exercise

Some people find it very challenging to begin an exercise routine. All is not lost. There are other ways to diminish the impact of stress and relax tension. For example, the benefits of yoga for not just physical but also mental health are well-documented (Brown, Gerbarg, & Muskin, 2012; Weintraub, 2012). Practicing yoga is a way to promote peacefulness, as it specifically assists in centering awareness in the body, stretching out tension, breathing, and mindfulness (Weintraub, 2012). Another great aspect of yoga discipline is the contact it involves with others and the leadership that is typically available in a group. The support of an instructor and the sense of camaraderie in a group are very calming to people with anxiety. That is a side benefit, especially for people who have some social anxiety, and it is one of the subtle assists that any group experience can give to slow down anxiety.

STRETCH TO RELAX

Staying loose physically also helps with all kinds of anxiety:

- For panic, staying physically calm helps the brain cool down. This makes it harder for panic to occur.
- If you have social anxiety, the more relaxed you feel, the less likely your peripheral nervous system will be to set off the palpitating heart and flushing face you fear. The state of physical calm translates into brain calm.
- For the worrier, loosening tensed muscles is especially helpful.
- In general, stretching increases blood flow and readjusts tensed-up posture, which results in greater muscle relaxation.

Follow this simple, general rule about stretching for release of tension: *Never do anything that hurts! If it hurts, stop immediately.* The stretches can be done anywhere. Several of the stretches below can be practiced while at work or sitting in school or sitting in any confined place, such as a car or airplane seat. Plus, they take relatively little time to do. You can do a stretch while thinking about the next question on a test, holding on the phone, or waiting for your computer to perform a function. One 15-second stretch is sufficient, but some stretching experts recommend several 2-second stretches to loosen up. Do what feels best to you. Following is a list of stretches that can be done anywhere.

- *Arm stretch.* Simply yawn, stretch your arms upward, and release. Repeat.
- *Back stretch.* For gentle back stretching, try torso relaxation. With your feet comfortably spread apart for support, let your torso fall forward with your head gently leading the way down, bending at the waist, and then come back into an upright position

by reversing the motion. Imagine that you are a puppet being released and then drawn upright by a string.

- *Overhead stretch.* Try continuing the back stretch into an overhead stretch once you are upright. Lift up your arms, reaching high overhead, and gently tilt your head by lifting your chin until you gaze directly up. Make this and all releases gentle.

- *Leg lunges.* If you get up to walk somewhere after sitting for a while, pause for a moment and try some gentle leg lunges.

- *Calf stretch.* If you have the opportunity to go up or down a few stairs, pause and, with your toes balanced on the edge of the stair, let your heel drop, thereby stretching the back of the leg. Do this for 2 seconds and then release. Repeat it a few times. You can do this one leg at a time with the other foot firmly planted on the stair so you don't have to worry about balance.

- *Seated-at-your-desk head tilt.* You can do a simple head-tilt stretch while on the phone, looking at the computer, or reading and not even lose time from work. *Do not rotate your neck in a circle.* Let your ear fall toward your shoulder as far as it can without hurting. Then raise your head upright. Now let your chin drop slowly to your chest, feel the stretch down your back, and raise your head upright again. Then drop your other ear toward the other shoulder and, again, raise your head before letting your head feel heavy and drop slowly backward. Return your head to an upright position before repeating this.

- *Seated-at-your-desk arm stretch.* Raise one arm straight overhead and then bend it at the elbow, reaching with that hand down and toward the other side of your body as if you were going to scratch your other shoulder blade. Then relax. Take the same arm and reach across your chest and wrap your hand around the opposite shoulder. Using the unoccupied hand, grasp the elbow of the reaching arm and gently exert pressure to increase the stretch in the shoulder and upper arm.

- *Seated posture change.* One other way to prevent inadvertently tightening up is the seated posture change. This preventive measure can be practiced constantly if your job requires you to sit all day. It involves regularly rotating through changed positions. Have a stool (or just a box) by your feet on which to rest them. For 15 minutes in each position, sit with one foot raised, then the other, then both, then neither. Put a back pillow or rolled towel behind your lower back, then your middle back, and then do without it.

Practicing these stretches will help keep you loose when work or life intervenes to make you uptight.

SLOW DOWN TO RELAX

Rest is far more important than you might imagine. If you want to learn new information, understand yourself and others better, grasp the implications of new information, or spark new ideas, you need mental rest (Immordino-Yang, Christodolou, & Singh, 2012). Your brain has a network for doing exactly that, called the default mode network, or DMN. This is the network that engages when you are not focused on external goals or on deliberate cognitive activity. The DMN may initiate for a second at a time or for long periods when you're daydreaming. But without it, you will learn less, know yourself less well, and may not be as good at reading others (Schlichting & Preston, 2015). Without going into a lengthy treatise on this network, suffice it to say that you need time to rest mentally—not just sleep, but rest your mind from high activity.

One challenge to accomplishing mental rest is the tendency to let mind-wandering turn negative. That is a special challenge when people have generalized anxiety. Worry may be too interruptive of default mode activity. A way to access the powerful action of the DMN is to do mindfulness meditation, which changes the brain and allows it to move into less negativity (Garrison, Zeffiro, Scheionost, Constable & Brewer, 2015). People with high-activity anxiety (see Chapter 10) are likely to resist downtime and so should learn how important it is. How do you otherwise encourage the DMN to engage?

- Get out in nature and wander around
- Sit and gaze—at water, at art, at the night sky
- Set aside time to contemplate

Those among us who are not inclined to sit and who value productivity may find it hard to believe that practicing contemplation will, after a period of weeks, demonstrate its value. In an article for *Scientific American Mind*, Ferris Jabr (2013) writes:

> Downtime is in fact essential to mental processes that affirm our identities, develop our understanding of human behavior and instill an internal code of ethics—processes that depend on the DMN. Downtime is an opportunity for the brain to make sense of what it has recently learned, to surface fundamental unresolved tensions in our lives and to swivel its powers of reflection away from the external world toward itself.

Mental fatigue can make it harder to regulate your emotions (Grillon, Quispe-Escudero, Mathur, & Erns, 2015), and when it comes to anxiety, that can make you much more vulnerable to the impact of worry and fear.

Downtime might also include just taking things slowly, taking some time off being goal-oriented. I hear this described often as "being, not doing," and its benefits for reducing stress, increasing mental flexibility, and detaching from worry are profound. It's a good idea to remember that you can be slow and leisurely without feeling anxious about what you *ought to be doing* with that time. You may need to consciously decide that the (in)activity is worth the time so that you don't yell at yourself for not being productive. When you believe your anxiety will decrease if you take care of yourself, it may be easier to commit. Some activities that involve leisurely use of time will ultimately calm the anxious body. The person with anxiety often needs a good reason to do something that seems lazy or unproductive, so here are some good reasons behind a few obviously relaxing activities:

- *Get a massage.* The therapeutic value of massage has been recorded in several studies. It has been shown to reduce stress and anxiety; relax muscles; aid in circulation, digestion, and excretion; and reduce pain perception. Being touched stimulates oxytocin, a hormone involved in feelings of being soothed and calmed (Field, 2002; Kosfeld, Heinrichs, Zak, Fischbacher, & Fehr, 2005). It is also a good way to stimulate the release of nitric oxide (NO) to relax your muscles and mind. (Northrup, 2016). There are many different types of massage—effleurage, deep-tissue, and relaxation massage. Even the simplest massage from a family member may convey a feeling of being cared for and literally reduce the impact of stress. A study by Field (2002) in postpartum mothers showed how massage corrected the effects of stress. The massage group had statistically significant changes in saliva cortisol levels after their sessions—the better to turn off stress—and was the only group to show decreases in anxiety scores.
- *Take a warm bath and use aromatherapy.* A warm bath also stimulates oxytocin, and warmth relaxes muscles. Aromatherapy is the practice of using essential oils to reap the therapeutic benefits of the plants from which they are derived. Essential oils are commonly used to enhance relaxation or to target symptoms of tension and anxiety. The oils are highly concentrated substances distilled from plants known to have therapeutic benefit. The mechanism of action of topically applied essential oils is not clear, although the oils may work by absorption through the skin or by inhalation of airborne, physiologically active compounds. The oils most consistently used for depression and anxiety are lavender, jasmine, ylang-ylang, sandalwood, bergamot, and rose. Several of these oils have been shown to have muscle-relaxant and sedative properties.

- *Stroll in the sun.* The skin should be protected from the UV rays of the sun, but our brains need the stimulation of light to develop good circadian rhythms (promoting sleep) and to prevent depressed and anxious states. Thirty minutes of walking outside provides enough light stimulation to help prevent loss of serotonin in gray weather seasons. Being in the warmth of the sun is also a good muscle relaxer.
- *Be in the green of nature* through walking or hiking. The greenness itself is connected to increasing cognitive flexibility by stimulating creative thinking. The air and the sights allow for relief of mental and physical tension. (See the National Geographic YouTube presentations from 2014 and 2015 called "This Is Your Brain on Nature!")
- *Spend time near lapping or running water*—a lake, a river, an ocean—and breathe. The sounds are soothing, and the ionization of the air near bodies of water allows for greater relaxation.

SLEEP!

This is really slowing it down! Good sleep underlies good health, including good mental health. Recent studies demonstrate that, without sufficient sleep, the structures of the brain that cause anxiety (the amygdala and anterior cingulate cortex in particular) become overactive, mimicking anxiety. And people prone to anxiety suffer more of this outcome of insufficient sleep (Cirelli & Tononi, 2015)

Why Sleep?

Many children show learning and behavior problems as an outcome of insufficient sleep. Children need more sleep than adults, and in 2016, the American Academy of Pediatrics adopted the recommended hours of sleep for children prescribed by the American Academy of Sleep Medicine (Paruthi et al., 2016)

The recommendations are provided (as follows) on the website of the

American Academy of Sleep Medicine at www.aasmnet.org/jcsm/ viewAb-stract.aspx?pid=30652):

- Children 1 to 2 years old should sleep 11 to 14 hours per every 24 hours (including naps)
- Children 3 to 5 years old should sleep 10 to 13 hours per every 24 hours (including naps)
- Children 6 to 12 years old should sleep 9 to 12 hours per every 24 hours
- Teenagers 13 to 18 years old should sleep 8 to 10 hours per every 24 hours (the Academy also included a recommendation for adolescents to start school later so they could get their needed hours of sleep per night)

Most adults need seven and a half to eight hours of sleep per night.

> Sleeping the number of recommended hours on a regular basis is associated with better health outcomes including: improved attention, behavior, learning, memory, emotional regulation, quality of life, and mental and physical health. Regularly sleeping fewer than the number of recommended hours is associated with attention, behavior, and learning problems. Insufficient sleep also increases the risk of accidents, injuries, hypertension, obesity, diabetes, and depression. Insufficient sleep in teenagers is associated with increased risk of self-harm, suicidal thoughts, and suicide attempts. (Paruthi et al., 2016)

Research demonstrates that the brain restores itself overnight. During sleep, the neurons shrink and cerebrospinal fluid increases to carry away toxicity from the brain (Xie et al., 2013). Without sleep, numerous mental health problems can occur or worsen. Sleep deprivation immediately impairs your ability for emotional discrimination ("Am I safe with you/ not safe with you?") as the viscerosensory networking between heart and amygdala is degraded (Goldstein-Piekarski, Greer, Saletin, & Walker, 2015). During sleep, we put information into long-term storage; that is, we learn (Whitehurst, Cellini, McDevitt, Duggan & Mednick, 2015), and to do this we also have to forget—to let go of unnecessary memories of experiences (Poe, 2017). We build healthy brains by building new neurons and replenishing neurotransmitters during sleep (Des Maisons, 1998).

Why Aren't You Sleeping?

When a person experiences anxiety, sleep suffers for several reasons, depending on the cause of the anxiety. A number of brain components are involved in this. When serotonin levels are low, the production of melatonin by the pineal gland can also be disrupted. Melatonin governs getting drowsy and reawakening and is linked to daylight and nightfall. When anxiety interferes with sleep, the natural rhythm of melatonin production goes off track. When norepinephrine levels are too high, the arousal makes it hard to get to sleep and, moreover, makes it hard to get deeply asleep. The role of dopamine in the basal ganglia is also becoming more clear; sufficient dopamine is necessary to get to sleep and sleep deeply.

Restless sleep or short nights due to the stress of overwork and trying to keep up with activities can make everything else about having anxiety harder. Suffering from stress can affect everyone, but people who have anxiety disorders have stress from anxiety itself. When they are also under stress from other sources, they have a "double whammy" to deal with when it comes to their sleep. (Learning stress-coping skills will help sleep. Also, see the ideas in Chapter 9 on containing worry for calming the brain before sleep.)

Get Ready to Sleep

Managing anxiety means managing your night's sleep. The profound mental relaxation promoted by good rest is not obtainable in any other way.

Even meditation, which can give many positive results for mental and physical health, is not a substitute for sleep. Following are some simple ways to improve the quality of your sleep:

- Doing things that reduce physical arousal will help you to achieve a deeper sleep. When the basal ganglia contribute to high drive, settling down at night might be very hard. Long before your actual bedtime, focus on how you handle evening activities so that basal ganglia overdrive can be settled with activities that promote calming at the physical and mental levels.
- Making time between activities is also important for giving your nervous system a chance to regroup and rejuvenate itself. Create transitions between stimulating activities such as school and any after-school social events. Take a little walk, rest, read, or close your eyes and listen to some music.
- Make sure you take time to rest and get organized after a big event—like a vacation—before returning to work. To that end, make sure that rest and quiet are part of your après-fun plans, and you will find that the fun is much more pleasing.
- Create time to refocus between activities. Highly energetic people with a basal ganglia–generated drive to get things done may not need as much time as the person who is more affected by stimulation, but they still need some transition time to keep their drive level focused and thus their activities less stressful. Especially if you are a person who prefers order, the disorganized feeling of moving on to something different before you're ready can stress you out and make it hard to settle your mind. Always finish one activity before beginning the next.

Settle Your Mind with Small Breaks

In a busy day, big stretches of time for relaxation may just not be possible. Small breaks can really help to settle your mind and reduce the impact of high activity. There are many different ways to take a break. For example:

- Sit in a quiet space and do something quiet like reading, meditating, or just breathing
- Get away from the stimulation, even for just 15 minutes.
- Take regular breaks at work. Don't skip times just because you're not feeling stressed at the moment.
- Take 10-minute naps. One recent study indicated that a 10-minute nap has amazing benefits; it is powerfully restorative of focus and mental clarity (Brooks & Lack, 2006). But if you want 30 minutes, that's a good idea, too!
- Limit time in overstimulating venues, such as shopping malls or sporting events. Take time off or time alone after big events.
- Take a 20-minute warm bath—great for the muscles and mind, as it stimulates oxytocin.
- Concentrate on something that requires focus but is not intense, like playing an instrument or doing needlework.
- Run cool water over your hands while exhaling slow breaths.
- Listen to music that soothes you.
- Spend a few minutes playing a computer game that requires all your concentration.
- Switch from the indoors to outside—get a look at trees or gardens if possible.
- If you can't get out of the indoor environment, try breathing (see Chapter 4) or focusing on the most important part of the activity you must do. Keep refocusing to screen out the extraneous stimulation.

Regularly getting downtime should occur throughout the workday, not just during breaks like days off, vacations, or the time you make at the end of every workday. The report about the significance of downtime (Jabr, 2016) reiterated what every study on taking breaks has shown: people are *more productive, better at problem-solving, less irritable, and healthier* if they take regular breaks. We also know they are calmer in mind and body and will find it easier to fall asleep.

Set a Pattern of Sufficient Sleep

People find it easier to fall asleep, stay asleep, and wake up rested when they are regular about the times they sleep. Sleep is part of the rhythm of the body, governed by the pineal gland, melatonin secretion, and circadian rhythm, much of which is mediated in the basal ganglia. When the anxious body is forced out of its rhythm by anxiety conditions or by caffeine ingestion, overwork, or staying up too late, those rhythms are disrupted and are hard to reestablish. To get back on track, go to sleep and get out of bed at the same time every day. This will take a while to work, so don't get discouraged and quit trying too soon. Even on weekends or days off from work, you should not vary your sleep schedule by more than an hour.

Another aspect of getting sufficient sleep is making time for it. People in the United States seem to think that sleeping is a sign of weakness. Anxious individuals who typically sleep very short hours may have trouble accepting the value of sleep or staying asleep even if they try it. But there is a real payoff to sleeping more for the highly active person, both mentally and emotionally. Research indicates that the well-rested person gets as much work done as the person who is awake longer because that person is more energetic and efficient during the day.

To start getting enough sleep, you have to go to bed early enough to stay in bed for a full eight hours, even if you wake sooner than that for a while. Until you can sleep for eight hours, you should plan to stay in bed and rest while practicing the sleep hygiene methods (listed on the following pages) that will eventually help you stay asleep. Once you are sleeping on a regular schedule, and fairly well, you will find that you naturally awaken when you are rested, and you will discover exactly how much sleep your body needs to feel rested.

With adolescents, it is useful to remember that they are in a special category regarding their circadian rhythms. Biologically, they may not be ready for sleep until midnight (unless exhausted) and not ready to awaken until 9. School is at exactly the wrong time for the adolescent body! A bigger problem is establishing time limits on using the computer, phone, or video games in the evening so that homework and school activities can be finished in time to sleep.

Elderly people may sleep more restlessly for a range of reasons, including needing to use the bathroom frequently or no longer producing sufficient melatonin to maintain sleep cycles. Many older adults live in extended-care environments that may be too noisy or too light. Changing components of their environment and lifestyle to make them more conducive to sleep can help. If their health will permit, try herbal teas such as spearmint or chamomile, or a brief trial of supplements such as L-tryptophan or melatonin, to calm the brain or produce melatonin before using meds (Weil, 2017). New formulas of herbal sleep remedies have emerged, and they may be very helpful, as may other supplements. To see if those might be a good idea, check with reliable sources such as the books *Change Your Brain, Change Your Life* by Daniel Amen and *How to Use Herbs, Nutrients, and Yoga in Mental Health Treatment* by Brown, Gerberg and Muskin, or with a local naturopath. Herbs and supplements interact with many health conditions and medications, so careful attention to those are necessary if you want to use supplements.

Make the Environment Conducive to Sleep

Sleep in a room that is as cool and dark as possible. These are the best conditions for establishing a good circadian rhythm that will promote sleep on a regular cycle. The amygdala functions in sleep as in waking, staying alert to warning signals that danger might be near. It responds to variances in sound, smell, and so on, so the brain wakes up when it notices a change. Screening out environmental noises (like people talking in another room or noise from the street) is very important to eliminating the amygdala response.

Although a quiet room without television or lights is generally better, many people say they *need* light or noise (like television or radio) to block out other sounds. But there are better things than television for this purpose. A television changes in pitch, tone, and volume, causing too much alertness in the amygdala. If you *must* use television to fall asleep, remember that most televisions have sleep timers. Set the timer and then have a white-noise background to block environmental noises.

Make the Anxious Brain Ready for Sleep

Below are several ways to get your anxious brain ready for sleep.

- Eliminate violent or exciting television for several hours before sleep—that means skipping late-night news programs! Television comes complete with amygdala-jarring music, unexpected and often gruesome visuals, and overexcited voices. Its *sole purpose* is to keep people watching for *fear* of missing something important.
- Take a warm bath for 20 minutes before sleep, as was mentioned above for relaxation purposes. It relaxes tight muscles and stimulates oxytocin, a hormone that soothes.
- For your brain to build itself during sleep, it needs nutrition too. You can help your brain build cells by eating well during the day and then having a small high-carbohydrate snack before sleep. This gives the brain the insulin and blood sugar levels necessary to use the proteins and nutrients that build neurotransmitters during sleep.
- Avoid caffeine and energy drinks or energy supplements. These stimulants can disrupt falling asleep. If you suffer from restless sleep, examine all your beverage intake—you may not realize the places that caffeine hides or the small amounts that can disturb you. People who suffer from panic disorder have a higher likelihood of caffeine sensitivity than others.

Plan for Worry Dreams and Wakeful Times

Anxiety can cause restless sleep for several reasons, but not sinking into deep dream sleep, called rapid eye movement sleep, or REM, is particularly troublesome. People who are worriers or are very tense do dream, but differently. They tend to have what I call "worry dreams"—restless sleep with dreams about daily problems that seem insoluble during the night. It is generally recommended that restless sleepers should stay in bed and try to go back to sleep if they awaken, but when it comes to worry dreams, staying in bed and trying to go back to sleep usually results in the dream continuing in its ruminative, never-ending way. Try handling worry dreams this way:

- Awaken fully for a few minutes
- Shake the dream off by consciously finishing the topic
- Ask yourself if anything should be done in the middle of the night (if so, do it!)
- Dispel its importance—remind yourself it will look better in the morning
- Focus on something pleasant while falling back to sleep.

Restless sleepers can also benefit from planning for awake times. Each night before sleep, pick a topic to think about in case you awaken. You may awaken with a sense of foreboding that is caused by your brain chemistry rather than anything actually being wrong. (See Chapter 9 for a discussion of the chemistry of foreboding feelings.) It is best to refuse the urge to think about what might be wrong and rather immediately direct your thoughts to the topic you selected for the night and try to fall back to sleep with the pleasing thought.

USING TECHNOLOGY

There has been an explosion of technologies that assist in calming the mind-body, and I expect that will continue as the availability of technology to every person at every age continues to burgeon. These range from virtual reality therapy for overcoming phobias or changing activity in brainwaves, like *Deep*, to HeartMath heart rate variability technology (Childre & Martin, 2000) and neurofeedback (Demos, 2005), which have been around for some time and continue to benefit people learning to calm their mind-body. While many technologies require the instruction of a skilled practitioner, certain devices, such as Alpha-Stim for reduced anxiety and improved sleep or the Fisher Wallace Stimulator for depression and anxiety, can be used at home to bring about deep relaxation and stress relief while setting the stage for a better understanding of one's emotions.

Apps for relaxation and improved sleep abound. There are so many that it is impossible to list them all. They range from white-noise or nature sound generators to cover background noise and help you fall asleep to relaxation meditations, sleep music, and guidance for muscle relaxation and breathing. Explore these and use what works best for you. I fully expect that by the time this book gets into print, there will be even more new ones!

CONCLUSION

Rest and relaxation can be achieved in many different ways, and learning what works best may take time. Working to understand the way anxiety is personally affecting you, and learning the types of distraction and tips for calming and relaxing that work best, will help you to manage it. This may be some of the most productive time and effort you will ever put into managing anxiety for a lifetime.

PART III

MANAGING YOUR ANXIOUS MIND

Techniques for managing the anxious body do not actually require people to believe that the techniques will work; they work if you do them. But managing the anxious mind goes into the territory of *willingness* and *belief*. The anxious mind persistently generates worry and fear. If you want to master the techniques, you must have willingness to make a consistent effort. The methods you will find in this section come from cognitive behavioral therapy (CBT) in addition to other sources. CBT is remarkably helpful to those who have anxious minds (Beck & Dozois, 2011; McMullin, 2001; Wilson, 2016). CBT methods like cognitive reappraisal (such as the worry management methods in Chapter 8) directly reduce the stress response (Davidson & McEwen, 2012). Research consistently demonstrates CBT's effectiveness for anxiety (Farchione et al., 2012; Otto, Misra, Pasad, & McRae, 2014), and it works for people of different ages and life circumstances (Beck & Dozois, 2011). CBT can even work better than medication for some anxiety conditions. I would like to point out again that while medication might make you feel less anxious pretty quickly, it doesn't teach you anything. If you want to feel better for life, learn the skills that make your brain generate less anxiety and learn to manage anxiety that comes with stress and adverse life experiences.

Believing that the techniques can work is also necessary to staying motivated, and learning how these techniques can change the brain promotes the belief that relief is possible. The research is clear on this as well; psychotherapy can often be important for successfully managing the anxious mind, and changes can be seen in the function or structures of the parts of the brain most connected to worry and fear (Bruhl, et. al., 2014; Opialla, et.al. 2015).

Knowing how practicing these techniques can change your brain will enhance your willingness to do the work of CBT. This knowledge may be hard to gain without guidance, but a therapist can provide the necessary information about the brain. Plus, therapy is the best place to get direction on how to use the techniques, many of which are simple to understand but not easy to put into effect. Knowledge of how this works will also promote willingness. A therapist is a consistent source of encouragement, help, and support in applying the techniques, which promotes success and can carry you forward when your progress seems to slow. Without knowledgeable support, it is harder to apply the techniques and to keep up the effort when anxiety is strong.

DO YOU HAVE AN ANXIOUS MIND?

The anxious mind shows itself in a variety of ways. This section is going to address how panic, worry, and social anxiety show up in typical ways. For people who panic, the symptoms of the anxious mind include:

- Catastrophizing the outcome of panic
- Catastrophizing the outcome of any physical sensation
- Fearing feeling panic in the future

The worrier with generalized anxiety suffers much more from the persistence of negative thoughts but also suffers from catastrophizing. Additionally, worriers suffer from:

- The tendency to catastrophize feeling angry
- Guilt
- Perfectionism
- Procrastination
- Inability to plan

- Reassurance seeking
- Dread, even without a good reason

Social anxiety sufferers have a different relationship to worry. They tend to worry about whether they will experience their symptoms in settings where they previously felt and looked anxious. Their thought process specifically promotes behaviors that avoid rather than confront anxiety. They suffer from:

- Catastrophizing that everyone will reject them
- Catastrophizing that their problems are unavoidable
- Self-talk about incompetence and lack of confidence, which leads to avoidance behavior

This section covers techniques that address the typical problems of the anxious mind:

- Technique #5: Stop Catastrophizing
- Technique #6: Stop Anxious Thoughts
- Technique #7: Contain Your Worry

SEVEN

Technique #5

Stop Catastrophizing

This technique is intended to stop anxiety-producing thought processes. When a thought begins with "Oh, no!"—what is known as "catastrophizing"—your mind will perceive the situation as awful or terrible or assume that the worst is about to happen. When you believe the worst is going to happen, you act as if the worst will happen. Both thought and behavior are changed by that assumption. You will want to find ways to stop the behavior and alter the catastrophic thinking that started it.

Catastrophizing is definitely engendered by brain activity. If someone with panic disorder notices a change in her physical sensations and immediately worries that a panic attack is coming on ("Oh, no!"), she is likely to actually panic, thus "proving" her belief that panic was starting. Aaron Beck (Beck & Beck, 2011) described that cognitive model of panic as circular. The more you focus on sensations, the more you notice the sensations, thus "proving" that the risk of panic is real. This speedy process can flip a person into panic very fast. And once a person panics, it undergirds the false belief that those sensations reliably herald a panic attack, encouraging subsequent panic whenever those sensations occur. The brain remembers strong emotion, and panic is about as strong as it gets. Overwhelming physical arousal, with a racing heart, shallow, rapid breathing, dizziness, nausea, tingling, and the emotion of terror, is a state that will be instantly memorized and easily remembered the next time there may be any cue—including a physical sensation—that reminds one of a terrifying incident, including a state of panic.

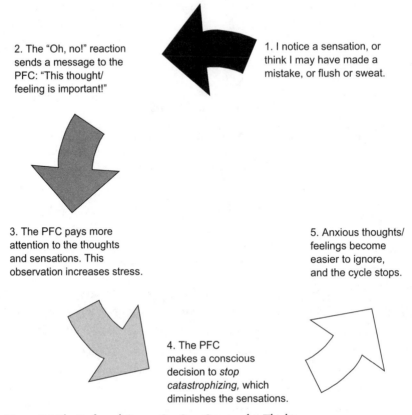

2. The "Oh, no!" reaction sends a message to the PFC: "This thought/feeling is important!"

1. I notice a sensation, or think I may have made a mistake, or flush or sweat.

3. The PFC pays more attention to the thoughts and sensations. This observation increases stress.

5. Anxious thoughts/feelings become easier to ignore, and the cycle stops.

4. The PFC makes a conscious decision to *stop catastrophizing,* which diminishes the sensations.

Figure 7.1 The Prefrontal Cortex Can Stop Catastrophic Thinking

But it isn't just about panic that people catastrophize. When some situation—for example, that a mistake might have occurred—triggers a worry, the sensitive, overactive limbic system goes into "Oh, no!" mode. A stab of adrenaline strikes almost immediately in response to the "Oh, no!" thought and causes the sensation of stomach-sinking fear. So, if someone with primary worry symptoms is concerned over whether he made a mistake, his "Oh, no!" can quickly skyrocket to acute anxiety, making the mistake seem like an insoluble *catastrophe* rather than just a mistake.

And social anxiety comes into this as well. When people suffer the hallmark blushing, sweating, and trembling symptoms that occur when they feel afraid of how others will react to them, their brain is at work. The amygdala may be enlarged or overly sensitive to subtle changes in the faces of people. This means that when interacting with others, people with social anxiety will notice small changes that someone else might ignore. Plus, the oversensitive amygdala overinterprets negativity in others. It quickly generates an "Oh, no!" at the slightest change in the face it sees, and it triggers fear responses that set off the embarrassed, flushed appearance. If the socially anxious person believes that blushing will immediately cause social rejection, he or she will catastrophize that normal and minor interaction between people. Catastrophic thinking in this situation is coupled with an unspoken belief that there is no escape.

The success of technique #5 depends on using the left prefrontal cortex (PFC) to take control of the catastrophic interpretations of feelings/thoughts/situations and calm down the rest of the brain activity triggering such mental anxiety. Figure 7.1 demonstrates how the PFC can control thoughts and even automatic reactions, deliberately calming and eliminating them.

Technique #5 addresses various kinds of catastrophizing thoughts. Several different methods exist to interrupt catastrophizing and begin to control the way you think.

LEARN THAT A FEELING IS JUST A FEELING

If someone with any variety of anxiety begins to fear how the anxiety feels, remembering that "a feeling is just a feeling" can really help. It doesn't matter if the feeling is a racing heart, upset stomach, and dizziness, or if the anxiety causes red splotches all over the neck and face with heart palpitations and obvious sweating. These sensations of intense anxiety are not lethal. They are simply sensations. Are they unpleasant? Absolutely. Annoying? Sure. Unwelcome? Yes. Distracting? No doubt. But they are nothing more than that. The belief that these sensations cannot be tolerated causes more trouble than the actual sensations themselves, because the belief not only intensifies the sensations but creates a sense of helplessness that interferes with taking control. A primary goal of managing anxiety is understanding that a pounding heart, a sinking stomach, and a flushing face are all just *feelings*.

Panic Is Unpleasant but Not Lethal

Stop panic in its tracks. When sensations that are reminiscent of panic attacks begin, immediately stop catastrophizing that it is *awful*. Self-talk is important here, and you should repeat, "Panic is unpleasant. It is not lethal." It is vital to use that message. You can then add diaphragmatic breathing to calm whatever alarming sensations you're experiencing. Coming to believe that "a feeling is just a feeling" requires paying attention to outcomes. Even a full-fledged panic attack is eventually going to stop and leave you unharmed. When you can stop the catastrophizing belief that panic is awful and practice breathing exercises to manage the anxious body, this method becomes a very effective means of diminishing the feelings that are so troubling.

Dread Is Just a Feeling That Can Occur Even When Nothing Is Wrong

Sometimes the high levels of norepinephrine that contribute to hypervigilance end up causing a feeling in the gut that is a lot like the feeling you get when something is about to go wrong—that "uh-oh" feeling of dread. People who tend to be too tense are most susceptible to this. The *brain* of the worrier looks for reasons to explain the feelings felt in the worried *body*; a queasy gut may not be an urgent feeling, like danger, but it sends a signal to look out for something. It activates the thought process to scan, like a radar dish, recent experiences to find out what you ought to be worrying about. A hypervigilant worrier will definitely find something—as did Dayne, a 17-year-old catastrophic worrier. He described how this worked in his case:

> I was joking with friends at my locker before class, and then as I walked to class, I was struck like lightning with a bad feeling, and then my thoughts raced ahead. "Oh no! I made a joke about being fat. My girlfriend was right there. What if she thought I was sending a message to her? I don't think she's fat, but if I go to her and say the joke was not about her, then she will definitely think it *was* about her.

So now what do I do? There is no way to fix this!" And I felt sick with anxiety all morning. That is the way my brain works all the time.

If you can identify that the sensation of doom or dread actually precedes the thought that something is wrong, you can begin to ward it off by declaring to yourself, "A feeling is just a feeling. It doesn't mean that something is wrong." Then the goal becomes to stop looking, to distract yourself (see Chapter 8 for ideas to distract from worry), or to shift to breathing or mindfulness.

I have seen clients who fight this idea of distraction from the feeling. They often ask, "But what if something really is wrong and I ignore it?" The trick is to ask yourself if the feeling *preceded* the need to look for something. If the answer is yes, then attempts to distract from the feeling are in order. "But," you might object, "what if I *should* be feeling dread about something about to happen and I ignore it?" I would answer, "If you have a real problem, you will not forget you have it." And, I would add, *real trouble* is not so elusive that you have to go looking for it. Real trouble usually presents itself without equivocation: we get a document by mail or the Internet that clearly spells out the trouble, such as an overdue bill, or we are blasted by someone complaining about what we did (or didn't do), or some other very clear sign that we are in trouble. Also, it's fairly common that once we get adjusted to the need to fix the problem, we feel better. A real problem that is in the process of being solved is less anxiety-producing than a potential problem.

I don't want to minimize dread, however. There are times when dread is the signal of a situation we ought to pay attention to. In those cases, your unconscious mind is noticing trouble and you physically feel it faster than your conscious, thinking brain can recognize it. This is what psychotherapy will help sort out—whether the problem stems from unfounded feelings of dread or whether the unconscious mind is picking up on real trouble. That said, people with anxiety are usually so overfocused on that physical "uh-oh" feeling that they rarely overlook signals of trouble. As you learn to identify all the different kinds of sensations that accompany emotions, you will get better at reading your body and will not confuse anxiety with other emotions. Then, if dread is a true warning sign, you will pick up on it and will not be confused about whether you should feel it.

Until that is sorted out, it is safe to assume that the "uh-oh" of dread is more like a brain glitch, a sort of mental short circuit. Stop catastrophizing this dreadful feeling by responding to it with the statement, "Dread is just a feeling that can occur, even when nothing is wrong." Then immediately distract yourself from these feelings. Catastrophizing about hypothetical problems never does anyone any good.

Embarrassment Is Just a Feeling

The flushing, trembling, sweaty feelings that social anxiety sufferers experience when they are in public are very hard to control. Stopping the catastrophizing about these symptoms entails disputing what you believe will happen and then ignoring the physical sensations. Tell yourself, "Being *noticed* is not the same thing as being *rejected*." It is true that typical signs of embarrassment—blushing, sweating, shaking—are obvious and that people can notice them if they are looking at you. What is *not true* is that others care about whether you are red or sweaty. It is *not true* that they will dislike you, or reject you, or laugh at you. Most people have been in situations in which they have seen someone look embarrassed, and they just ignore it. Most likely, they will feel some sympathy for you, especially if you appear troubled about it. The only real exception to this is adolescents, who are often unkind to each other and may indeed make a big deal out of flushing or sweating.

Several women in my practice have used the strategy one of my clients, Ingrid, used. In our first session, Ingrid preempted any discussion about her splotchy, flushed neck by saying, "You will notice that my neck gets all red when I talk about things that I have feelings about, but don't worry about it. It doesn't mean anything. My mother and grandmother had that, too." She completely decatastrophized the splotchiness by telling *me* not to worry, and in that way she stopped herself from worrying about it as well. Her neck got red, but I already knew she knew and accepted it without difficulty, so

I could ignore it. Her plan was to just announce it would happen and be done with it.

Men seem to have more trouble announcing that these symptoms may happen before they actually do. It's easier for women to declare a foible in advance, because women often bond with each other over trouble or embarrassing situations. Men usually feel safer when they know where they stand in the hierarchy, and they don't like to acknowledge any possible flaw that could make them seem weak in the eyes of another man. If this is the case, they can minimize their distress by deciding they are going to ignore their symptoms if they happen. (Chapters 11 and 12 discuss ways of stopping fear and controlling physical signs of social anxiety.) They can remind themselves that flushing, sweating, and shaking aren't the end of the world, and that using breathing to stay as calm as possible will help greatly.

Blushers who are in middle school or high school may have to go further than simply planning what to do if they experience these signs of embarrassment when others are around. They need to desensitize themselves to feeling the fear of being embarrassed. Techniques #9 and #10 (in Chapters 11 and 12) will help by explaining what to do to control physiology and reduce the fear of being embarrassed. In the meantime, repeating the mantra "A feeling is just a feeling. It doesn't mean that something is wrong" will minimize the symptoms.

To recap, remember that:

- Panic is just a feeling. It is unpleasant but not lethal. Remind yourself of this at the first sign of a panic sensation. Then practice diaphragmatic breathing.
- Dread is just a feeling that can occur even when nothing is wrong. Reinforce that mental statement. Then distract your attention away from the dread.
- Embarrassment is just a feeling. Plan for what you will do if you show signs of embarrassment. Repeat to yourself that being noticed does not mean you will be rejected.

DEBUNK THOUGHTS ABOUT DYING, GOING CRAZY, OR LOSING CONTROL

"I am dying!" "I am going crazy!" "I am losing control!" It never ceases to amaze me, even after all these years of doing therapy with people who have anxiety, that these thoughts trouble nearly every panic sufferer. It would be great if it were as easy as just telling people they are not dying, going crazy, or losing control. The problem is that they already know that. Their left prefrontal cortex (PFC) is already aware that they have gone through this many times and have not yet died, gone crazy, or lost control. But their right brain is still waiting for that catastrophe to happen. The left brain just can't connect with the right brain's emotionality of the terror when it is happening. The emotion is far too powerful and convincing. One young woman, Makayla, came to treatment only when the cardiologist who evaluated her symptoms not once, but three times, told her she could have no more evaluations unless she had psychotherapy first. Makayla would not believe her physician, much less her own PFC, without some strong reinforcement, which, finally, therapy was able to provide. But even people who had at one time "conquered panic" can fall into catastrophic fears of dying. I was reminded of this when Isaiah, a competent, intelligent man I had seen for panic, had a panic relapse and took himself to the hospital. He said to himself, "I know it is probably just panic," but he believed the catastrophic fear that this time it *was* a heart attack. Thousands of dollars and many medical tests later, his right-brain limbic structures finally believed his left prefrontal cortex and settled the panic down.

Step #1: Search for the Exact Image or Thought

So, what works to stop the catastrophizing of a panic attack? Psychotherapy will probably be needed, because people who have been panicking are not usually able to identify their thoughts during panic. It is essential to get very specific about what people are envisioning when they declare, "I am dying!" "I am going crazy!" or "I am losing control!" Searching for this exact image is the first step in debunking these panicky thoughts.

Let's begin by looking at "I am dying!" Start by identifying the exact physical sensations that are the most troubling, such as shortness of breath, pain in the chest, pain in the arm, tingling, or nausea. Then, find an exact image, played in the mind like a movie, of what you fear, such as collapsing in the street or being in the ICU at a hospital. Most people don't have any specific image of dying. Even if you imagine collapsing, that is not the end of the situation, so don't stop there. Ask yourself, "What happens next?" This question is very important and may be difficult to answer at first. But it is important to keep pushing to imagine how the full scenario plays out. At every step in the process of imagining dying—"They hook me up to machines" or "My chest hurts worse" or "I am blacking out"—keep asking, "Then what happens?" until you get to "Then I die." And then *ask again*, "What happens next?" At this point, most people laugh and recognize that the panic would at least be over. But your answer to this question will lead to a better understanding of your relationships, your hopes and aspirations, and even what the panic means to you.

For the person who fears losing control, again, getting the image is an important part of beginning to stop catastrophizing the panic symptoms. Ask, "If someone were observing you, what exactly would you look like? What would you be doing or saying?" Go step by step through what it would look like to an observer. This should be done in detail. For example, if you are talking about what would happen if you lost control in a public place such as a bus or restaurant, you might report, "Well, I would look like I was frightened." But that is not enough. You need to go all the way through to the end of what you would look like, and what you would do, asking yourself, "Then what?" Most people need to learn this by working with a therapist who can guide them to clarify their images of losing control.

For example, when I asked one of my clients, Shirley, to describe what would happen if she lost control on the bus, she said, "I would look scared!" So I asked, "Then what?" Shirley looked confused, as if she didn't know what I meant, but then replied, "I don't think I would *really* scream at the driver to let me off in the middle of the block. He would have to pull over anyway, so I guess, in reality, I would get off the bus as soon as I could." So

I pursued with, "Then what?" Shirley considered this seriously, and said, "People might look at me just standing on the street." To which, of course, I asked, "Then what?" and she went on to say that those people would quickly be out of sight as the bus pulled away. And (you guessed it) I asked, "Then what?" At that point Shirley burst out laughing, "I would be stuck paying for a cab if I wanted to get to work on time!" She realized that her fear of losing control disappeared when she followed the image of panic all the way through to the end of the scenario.

Of all the fears, that of "going crazy" is least likely to have a vivid, realistic image. It is more often an expression of the fear that having a panic attack means you already *are* crazy. But sometimes that is not the case, and it is wise to follow it through to the end of the image: "What does going crazy look like?" This can be done in the same way that the images for the other two fears are explored. I did this with a client named Norman, who described his fear of going crazy by saying that he imagined himself pacing around, saying things that had no meaning, and waving his arms. He imagined that other people would be frightened of him and he would be carried off to a mental hospital. This sounded like a pretty clear picture of being "crazy," and it described much of how he thought he looked when he panicked. So, we moved on to step #2 to fully debunk his catastrophizing thoughts.

Step #2: Ask Yourself If This Is Like Any Other Experience You Have Had

Remembering a real experience allows you to logically compare your panic to the feared catastrophe. For example, you have the catastrophic fear "I am dying." This is typically triggered by specific physical symptoms, such as chest pain or shortness of breath. Figuring out which symptom triggers your fear of dying will provide useful information about what the cause of that fear really is. It often relates to the illness or death of another person. For instance, a woman whose father died of a heart attack in front of her may indeed fear that her chest pain is the same as her father's. A mother who rushed her child to the hospital with asthma may immediately feel helpless when she has shortness of breath. Understanding what you associate your experience of panic to will help you desensitize the fear.

For example, when I asked Norman what other experiences his panic attacks were like, he replied that they reminded him of his uncle, who was schizophrenic and had lived with Norman's family when Norman was young. The uncle was often irrational and paced a lot, and on more than one occasion he had been removed from the house when he "went crazy." This was scary to young Norman. By talking through the image of going crazy, Norman realized he was not his uncle, and his fear of going crazy disappeared.

When the Catastrophic Fear Is Rooted in a Trauma

Sometimes the catastrophic fears of "I am going crazy, losing control, or dying" are rooted in a traumatic experience from childhood, and the person who has these fears may not recognize triggers in the environment or in relationships that set them in motion. You can explore what could be triggering fear by following these steps:

- Keep a panic diary with careful attention to the details of what preceded the panic attacks.
- Identify a pattern either in the emotional state or in the events that precede the panic.
- Then, look for the earliest experience of such a feeling or event.

Discovering the trigger for panic can help you to avoid the panic attacks altogether. However, discovering the trigger may not be enough, and a person with a history of trauma should probably explore the impact of the original trauma in psychotherapy. The therapist's approach to resolving the underlying trauma will depend on his or her training and experience. If the trigger to panic cannot be discovered, a psychotherapist will have suggestions for working on that in therapy.

To recap, you can debunk your panic thoughts about dying, going crazy, or losing control by following these steps:

1. Identify *exactly* how you envision this fear playing out.
2. Find out if this fear has a basis in reality—is it like any other experience you have had? Logically comparing your experience of panic to the feared catastrophe may be enough to end your tendency to catastrophize.
3. If step #2 does not debunk the panic thoughts, identify the first experience of this fear or idea and determine whether it has roots in an earlier traumatic experience.
4. Psychotherapy may be needed to identify and resolve the panic trigger.

PREVENT PANIC: PREDICT, PREPARE, AND PLAN

This method is simple—it is a protocol that fits any situation in which you fear you may panic—and will help you successfully return to doing the activities you did when the panic attacks first occurred. In the previous paragraphs of this chapter, I outlined finding the trigger. That is the "predict" part of this protocol.

Prepare to Be There Without Scare

You will then prepare to go into situations in which you fear you will panic or in which you previously panicked. This is important because it is easy to become afraid of the things you were doing when you felt panic, even if the situations themselves didn't cause the fear. The mind is so swift in making connections and so profound in the way it constructs symbols that if you panic while you are driving on a highway in the rain, the next time you drive in the rain you are likely to feel afraid of panicking. Subsequently, you might panic not only when you are driving on the highway in the rain, but also anytime it rains or anytime you drive, no matter how dry the road is.

It is only natural for people to avoid any activity in which the panic might come back. Avoiding driving is common, but other common situations that people avoid include being in crowds, at parties with a lot of people, or in grocery stores at high-traffic times of day. These are not symptoms of social anxiety but rather a fear of panicking when escape is not possible. So prepare to be there without the scare. That involves assessing what you will need to stay calm. Preparation involves simple steps.

1. Learn to breathe away panic (technique #2).
2. Review each aspect of the situation or scenario that you have been avoiding. What do you know about how to handle it calmly?
3. Desensitize every aspect of the situation that you fear could trigger you. Note any aspect of the activity that caused you to feel nervous and apply a method to calm down while imagining it. Systematic desensitization, EMDR, energy therapy, and other methods can help you to imagine the aspect of the situation that makes you feel panicky and calm down prior to going into it. (See the Resources section for more information on these therapy methods.)
4. Practice. Try a mini-version of the event or activity. For example, plan to get on a short stretch of highway at a time when it is not too busy and you can get off and go back home or continue on to your destination without using the highway. Stop the practice session at the planned end time, even if it is going well.

This method worked very well for a teenager who was asked to be the maid of honor at her sister's wedding. She had previously had panic during a church service, and she feared panicking during the wedding. However, she had never been to a wedding previously, so learning what would be expected of her, knowing there would be a rehearsal, and knowing where she would sit and who would be around her were very helpful. She knew that sipping water or having a peppermint handy might help her, so she prepared by placing a water bottle at her chair before the service started. When she was at the rehearsal, she noted exactly what was expected of her and affirmed that she could do it all without trouble.

Plan to Panic

In addition to preparing *not* to panic, planning *to* panic and cope with it becomes a safety net for these situations. It is unlikely that you can avoid every potential panic trigger in a situation in which you have previously panicked. So, just plan on panicking.

1. Write down exactly what you will do if and when you panic. Will you breathe? Think a specific calming thought? Where will you go if you don't stay in the situation? Will there be a person present who might be supportive? Carry your plan with you. Putting a note to yourself in your cell phone can be a good idea.
2. Review your plan before you go into the situation.
3. Try a practice session, knowing that if you panic, you have a plan that you can turn to.
4. Later, evaluate how it went. If you did it, praise yourself. If you did less well than you hoped:
   - Commend yourself for handling difficulties
   - Praise yourself for entering a situation that you were afraid of
   - Decide how to amend your plan if you had a problem
   - Notice that you lived through it no matter how it went

My teenage maid of honor used energy tapping to calm anticipatory anxiety and practiced diaphragmatic breathing until she was competent at it. She had no history of trauma, just a history of panic attacks. She felt capable of calming, but in addition, she scouted out an escape route via doors at the front of the church just in case she needed to leave quickly but without drawing attention to herself. She even asked a relative to follow her out in case she left during the church service so she wouldn't fear being alone.

LEARN TO KNOW
(AND CHOOSE TO SHOW) ANGER

The goal of this method is to stop catastrophizing the feeling of anger. Usually when people think of anger as a problem, they think of needing to calm their anger down and learn anger management. But sometimes anger is so anxiety-producing that people don't even recognize feeling angry about something—they feel the physical arousal and go straight to anxiety. They find it hard to dispel that sense of anxiety because they don't know what they are anxious about and, despite their assumptions about why they are so anxious, nothing seems to work to diminish it. This is because the anger causing the perception of anxiety is unrecognized.

People *can* face genuine risks if they show they are angry. In the past, you may have been hurt or abused or emotionally rejected such that the memory of anger causes fear. You may run similar risks in the present—you could risk being hurt or losing a relationship or job if you show you are angry. In these situations, not even knowing you are angry becomes a good mechanism for staying safe. Unfortunately, however, the anger manifests in other ways, contributing to your anxiety. It thus becomes important to identify it.

Even after you know you are angry, you may not know *how* to be angry. If you've had no good experience with being angry in your past, you may not have had much practice with appropriately expressing anger. You may be too quiet or, alternatively, blow up in anger, both of which are ineffective. If you know that you are prone to excessive anger (anxiety can prompt some pretty startling displays of excessive anger), you can use anger management books to help you learn to tone down angry expression. There are also excellent books on assertiveness, which are helpful for both people who are prone to excessive anger and people who are reluctant to express anger.

Six Steps for Decatastrophizing Anger

This method is not about *showing* anger; it is about *knowing* anger. And this is where the method starts, with reassurance that knowing you are angry is not the same thing as showing you are angry. It is a symptom-control method intended to decrease tension while raising conscious awareness of anger.

The method is simple. When you are in the grip of strong sensations of tension, worry, stomach-squeezing doom, and so on, look for unrecognized anger underneath the anxiety.

1. The next time you feel strong anxiety, immediately sit down, and in single words or brief phrases, write as long a list as possible in answer to this specific question: "If I were angry, about what might I be angry?" The hypothetical nature of the question is a key feature. You do not have to feel committed to being angry about anything on the list—you are only being speculative about it.

2. Reflect on what it felt like to write the list down. How does it feel to see what you have? What happened to your anxiety level?

3. Review the list. Is there anything on the list that needs action? What can you let go?

4. If something requires action because you are being hurt, taken advantage of, ignored, or worse, talk over your intended action with someone so that you don't put yourself at risk with a badly handled situation. After all, you were feeling your anger as anxiety, so there is a good chance you might not be good at handling anger.

5. Skill-building for expressing anger might be very useful. Learning to be assertive instead of aggressive is a good start for people who are either reluctant or excessive in their anger expression.

6. You can then destroy the list or discuss it in therapy. I ask my clients to discuss with me their reactions to writing this list, and if they feel comfortable, it can be helpful to hear the whole list. When they do review the list and their reactions to writing it, they gain insight into the connection between anger and anxiety. This opens the door to deeper levels of psychotherapy to resolve psychological problems with being angry.

CONCLUSION

Stopping every sort of catastrophizing will take you a long way toward managing your anxious mind. Thoughts of "Oh, no!" "Uh-oh," or "I'm going crazy!" in any situation can trigger anxiety that ranges from uptight tension to intense panic. When you practice the methods of decatastrophizing outlined in this chapter, you will be able to sidestep experiences of anxiety before they start.

EIGHT

Technique #6

Stop Anxious Thoughts

———————————

"What will happen if I panic?" "How will I stop these worries that go through my mind?" "How can I face other people without making a fool of myself?" If you have anxiety, you don't just face the problem once and in the moment it occurs. An anxious mind challenges you to cope over and over with the very things you fear, and the circular nature of anxious thinking affects people with any type of anxiety. Learning to cope with anxiety and diminish it requires every anxious mind to master the methods in this chapter for stopping anxious thoughts and interfering with their return.

WHY DO I HAVE SO MUCH TROUBLE STOPPING MY ANXIOUS MIND?

Recalling some of the brain and neurotransmitter information from Chapter 1 may help you recognize what is going on with hard-to-control thoughts and may explain why the thought-stopping methods in this chapter are going to work.

Worry has a purpose. When people are in ambiguous situations, they feel anxious. They begin to ask themselves, "What is going on here?" or "What if I do this (or that) about it?" or "What if this happens next?" And when they can figure it out, the ambiguity goes away and so does the anxiety. When people feel anxiety first, they want an answer and go looking for it with the what-if thinking that is basically worrying. But the worry is maladaptive. It doesn't help you figure out what is going on when the anxiety precedes the situation. When the anxiety is an outcome of neurobiology, what-if thinking becomes worry that makes the anxiety sensations worse. So, the first bit of helpful knowledge is that at times the anxious sensation can exist without a genuine problem, and what-if thinking (worry) is an attempt to get rid of it that won't work because there isn't a real problem.

Another factor of how the brain operates is that any thought or action you repeat is recognized as important, so if you go down a worry path and repeatedly think a negative thought (e.g., "What if I fail?"), it's as if your brain says, "Whoa! You are repeating it so often, it must be important. I'm going to help you out." And your brain literally starts supplying that neural pathway with more blood and more white cell support to speed up the processing. Now a worry pathway in your brain has become a worry super-highway, and there will be plenty of on-ramps to the worry highway. What else may be happening?

- Ruminating worry or getting mentally "stuck" stems from anterior cingulate cortex (ACC) overactivity. The ACC may be stuck due to structural problems, insufficient neurotransmitter activity, or lifestyle factors such as lack of sleep. It becomes necessary to use the prefrontal cortex's (PFC's) decision-making power to take charge and say, "Stop!"
- The amygdala, a part of the limbic system, is specialized to pay attention to any stimulus that presents a potential danger or threat. The amygdala may start causing problems for worriers early in their lives by shaping its own tendency to screen for the worst. When the amygdala reacts to a potential threat and the person's nervous system responds with alarm, then the PFC may well interpret the alarm as proof of threat. Now, in that circular way, the amygdala recognizes threat and will respond in the future as if the signal is in fact a sign of threat.
- Hypervigilance to mistakes, to onset of panic, or to potential rejection or humiliation is probably the result of elevated norepinephrine (NE) or overactivity in the basal ganglia (Pliszka, 2003). The brain is in a radarlike scanning mode, examining

all incoming stimuli for signs of a problem. Stopping the "scan mode" requires intention to divert it, planned ahead by the executive brain (PFC), which is what this technique is all about.

- When the limbic system is short on serotonin (SE), it readily contributes to worry in the anxious brain by focusing those structures on what is wrong or difficult or bad.
- Serotonin (SE) deficits contribute to rumination, despair, and anticipating trouble.

THOUGHT-STOPPING AND THOUGHT REPLACEMENT

When you have a worry superhighway ready for you to speed down it, your best option is to erase the trace of worry. That means no longer repeating the worry thought (or action). Your brain will quickly stop supplying the extra blood vessels and white cells and the highway will revert back to a pathway. There are two elements to the technique of stopping anxious thoughts: (1) thought-stopping and (2) thought replacement. Thought-stopping is critical, but it is insufficient on its own. You must also divert your attention to a preplanned thought replacement. Your brain makes a decision that the thoughts are unnecessary and then exerts control over them. When the executive brain (prefrontal cortex, or PFC) consistently takes charge to interrupt and divert anxious thoughts, several things happen over a fairly short period of time.

- The blood supply and white cell support are diminished.
- The anterior cingulate cortex (ACC) that ruminates and worries cools off.
- The limbic system becomes less active and thus less negative.
- The stress response becomes less reactive to worry.

The Easiest Method in the Book: "Self! Stop It!"

Why do we need thought-stopping? Any thought we think repeatedly makes a neurobiological rut in our brains. Once a neuron pathway is set, it takes only a little time to change that worry highway, but stopping and then interrupting thoughts must be done repeatedly and consistently to eliminate the worry. Consistency is the hardest challenge.

Worriers have all heard, "Stop worrying! Relax!" If a person could stop worrying, he would! But this statement is a necessary first step to replacing negative thoughts. When you have out-of-control anxious thoughts, say to yourself, "Self! Stop it!" Truly, it is that simple. It is just not easy to do. This is where the next step—thought replacement—comes into play.

Replace Negative Thoughts

Thought replacement is the key to successfully interrupting the anxious cognitions that burden the worried person. The replacement thought has to match the intensity of the negative thought, and *it must be planned ahead*. A worrier can't wait until she is stuck in the middle of a rumination to figure out what to think about instead. What you choose for a thought replacement will simply be based on what works best for your style and personality. Basic replacements come in several categories:

- *Substituting a negative obsessive thought with a positive obsessive thought.* This is useful if the worry thoughts are very obsessive. In this case, the replacement should be fairly simple and often repeated. If you are going to establish a rut in your brain, it might as well be a positive rut. Try a scripture passage, an affirmation, a poem, or song lyrics that you can keep reciting over and over, out loud if possible. You want to completely edge out the negative thought, and saying the replacement aloud will add the dimension of speech and hearing to occupy more of your attention. Although it is best not to encourage rumination, there are times when you must counter intense, negative rumination, and an alternative, positive rumination may be needed to defeat the negative one.

- *Competing with the anxious thoughts.* Sing, talk, or recite something. Making the replacement thought take up more space in your brain will make it more likely to win your attention. Singing uses more parts of your brain, and singing out loud uses even more, as it adds the dimension of hearing to your positive thought. Speaking or reciting aloud likewise adds power to the replacement. Plan your songs or the recitation you want to use ahead of time.

- *Distracting yourself from the anxious thoughts.* After saying, "Stop!" immediately distract your attention to something that will help your brain hold its focus away from the anxiety. Watch television, play a video game, read, work on a hobby, call a friend (and talk about his or her life, not yours), or do anything else that can distract you. Many people use the computer for distraction— games, social media like Facebook, Pinterest, blogging, and so on. Keep an eye on this to be sure it doesn't become obsessive, consume so much time that the balance of your life is compromised, or contribute to anxiety (such as if you are using it to search for information as a way to reassure yourself).

- *Refocusing on the work or task you were doing when the anxious thoughts began.* Pay conscious, intentional attention to what you're doing. This thought replacement method may be the most effective at work, where singing or going for a walk may be out of the question and it would be to your advantage to stay with the task at hand. You may need to intentionally refocus repeatedly if the work-related tasks are not sufficiently compelling.

Again, the best way to stop anxious thoughts is to:

1. Say to yourself, "Self! Stop it!"
2. Replace the negative thought by

- substituting a positive repetitive thought,
  such as an affirmation, poem, or prayer
- competing with it by singing out loud or reciting out loud
- distracting yourself by watching television, playing a video game, reading, or changing locations
- refocusing on the work or activity you
  were doing when the anxiety hit

The "Two-Ps" Thought Replacement List for the Day

As you get better at thought replacement, it needs to become a habit ingrained in your approach to the day. Having a replacement ready works for daylight worries as well as for the worries that spring up during the night. The best habit to get into for persistently fighting ruminating worry is making a daily thought replacement list centered around the "two Ps": pleasant and productive. Anxiety is generally *un*pleasant and *un*productive, not moving you toward successful completion of any action or thought process. But you can use your prefrontal cortex (PFC) to plan specific thoughts to replace negativity and change your anxious mind in the direction of being productive.

This is how it works:

1. Every day, take 60 seconds to identify things that you could think about during the day—what books to take out at the library, what homework to do first, what order to run errands in after work, what phone calls to return first, what Hawaiian island to visit first on vacation, whether you would rather buy a Mercedes or a BMW if you had the money, and so on. Don't include any thoughts that aren't pleasant or productive. Record these pleasant or productive thoughts on a Post-it note or an index card, using a single reminder word for each thought. These thoughts will probably change daily, so each morning, for one minute, make a list.

2. You may prefer a paper note rather than an electronic one because you may not always be in an environment where you can pull out your phone, such as when you're driving, but that

Post-it note could be right on the dashboard, on the side of the cash register you're working at, or on top of the pile of books you're carrying. However you do it, put the list anywhere it is readily accessible.

3. As soon as you stop the rumination with thought-stopping, consult the "two Ps" list for a replacement to divert your attention.

4. Repeat this process daily until rumination is no longer a problem. The habit of calming rumination without giving in to it takes time. (This is the basal ganglia habit formation that you are tapping in to here.) This simple tool will help you stay effective without generating new ruminative thoughts.

This very important but simple method positively affects the entire brain by interrupting anxious thoughts. Remember:

- Negativity comes from the overactive limbic system.
- Rumination stems from the anterior cingulate cortex (ACC) being unable to move information to the prefrontal cortex (PFC) to be resolved.
- Suppressing negative, obsessive thoughts is a function of the PFC activities of planning and conscious attention. By making and using the list of replacement thoughts, you help the PFC deliberately shift the ACC away from the anxious thought, thus helping suppress the overactivity of the limbic system by allowing it to cool off.

Nonverbal Reminders of Thought Replacement

Not everyone is good at remembering what he or she was going to use as a replacement thought when anxiety crops up, and not everyone does well with a list. In these cases, nonverbal reminders are helpful. Here are a few ways to create reminders for how you want to replace worry once you say, "Self! Stop it!"

- *Flip chart.* Use a three-ring binder or spiral notebook to make a thought replacement reminder book. Every time you get a good idea, draw a picture, write a symbol, put a sticker, or paste or tape a cutout from a magazine or newspaper on a page of the notebook. When you need a thought replacement mental or physical activity, page through the notebook until you find one that can work right at that moment. This is great for kids as well as for people who respond better to visual cues.
- *Apps.* Which app is best depends on the age of the anxious person. For children, there is a charming app called Breathing Bubbles; the viewer watches bubbles of worry disappear into the distance.
- *Symbol cards* for the school or work desk. The idea of the reminder notebook with symbols or visual cues can be done on a simple card that you leave on or in your desk at school or work. For small children, stickers or symbols can be used—for example, Dad's phone number on the card can be a symbol not to worry because Dad is just a phone call away if things are rough, or a small picture of the family dog can be a reminder of something pleasant to think about, or a sticker of a book can be a reminder that the child could read a book for distraction. An adult version of those same kinds of reminders about friends, family, pets, and activities can work at workplace stations.
- *Pictures* that cue you to think happy thoughts (vacation spots, favorite friends or pets) can go on a bulletin board or desk or be attached to the refrigerator with a magnet.

These nonverbal reminders can be planned in therapy, done in consultation with teachers or parents, and so on.

Use Your Body to Change Your Mind

When your anterior cingulate cortex (ACC) is stuck (one cause of repetitive worrying thoughts), it is often a help to actually move your body. Moving, along with mental attention to the activity, can help to displace anxiety and let your mind change to another thought. Moving the body can be done in many ways. If you have to complete some work that allows you to move around, get up and do it. Or you can do something aerobic, such as go out for a walk or run, listening to music or podcasts for extra distraction. Music occupies the right side of the mind with its melody and rhythm and pulls you away from anxious thinking more completely. Turn on music and dance while you do chores like sweeping, vacuuming, or cleaning the garage. Or turn on music and just dance. Or consider using any currently popular video game that gets you moving for a few minutes of positive distraction.

Another way to move the brain around is to literally change locations. When you change locations, pay attention to where you are going and what you will do there. You can make something more compelling by consciously and deliberately paying attention to what you are doing in the moment, noticing every detail. In this way, you are practicing mindfulness as thought replacement. You could create conscious focus by acting as an "eye witness" with the intention of noticing everything around you as if something wonderful and important is about to happen and you are going to be called on to describe what everything looked like the moment before. This level of absorption is necessary to create enough pull to oppose the anxious mind.

Playing musical instruments requires you to move but is not always so active physically. Even if you simply get involved in creating a playlist, thinking about the music makes you want to move and produces a mental shift similar to moving itself, so it will work to shift you away from anxiety. Making a playlist of your favorite songs that you may want to share has the double benefit of cheering you with music and distracting you with the activity.

Moving the body is also a big help with children, who can show a great deal of opposition when they get anxious. Suggest it before you confront them about anything. Teenagers don't always have the self-reflection to undertake other methods, so movement works well with them, too. Find out how they like to move best. They may prefer music and video games that make them move. For kids and teens, try popular apps and computer games that encourage movement that they can bring up via computer or tablet. A current popular computer program is GoNoodle (www.gonoodle.

com). It is loaded with fun ideas for moving that can be used by a whole family or in the classroom. But what else do they like? Shooting baskets in the driveway? Riding their bike? Make a list for yourself or help your children or teens make a list of ways they can move when their minds are anxious. This method is even more important with kids than it is for adults because children and adolescents have more energy and need ways to discharge it when they are anxious.

The Second-Easiest Method in the Book: Do the Worst First

This one little method can do a lot to stop your anxious mind from fretting. The slogan "do the worst first" is a simple reminder to do what you do *not* want to do, but *must* do, as soon as possible. If you are going to worry all day long about what you have to do (like make a phone call you don't want to make or pay the bills), just do it first and save yourself the worry. What a relief!

This is surprisingly beneficial for calming the anxious mind in an ongoing way. When you have on your mind something negative that you have to do, the thought is persistently agitating you. Constant agitation sets your brain up to worry more and more. But when you get the worrisome task done, your brain can calm down. The longer you can keep your brain calm, the easier it is for your brain to stay calm.

This method applies well to day-to-day situations, such as calling a customer who might be unhappy or taking a broken item back to the store when you don't want to deal with the process. It can also be used for tasks like cleaning or doing homework or preparing a report for work.

Although this method is needed on a nearly daily basis for the small things that crop up at work and home, it is also useful for the truly significant, big issues. Most people will face issues of great importance over the course of their lives. Real problems will certainly require attention to the appropriate solutions, but people who are worriers are often quite good at handling real problems. It is indecision and ambiguity that inflame the brain and make anxiety worse. Weighty, worrying, dreadful things that need to be done, such as telling someone you have seen for a while that you are going to end your relationship, telling a friend you think he is drinking too much, confronting a spouse about lying to you, talking to your child about finding drugs in her room, and similar problems drag you down. They preoccupy your anxious mind and distract you from everything else.

Correcting your cognitions about doing the worst first helps to motivate yourself to do it. Try this process:

1. Can you remember a time when you were faced with a similar task and how good you felt when it was done? Bring that sense of relief clearly to mind. If you are dragging your feet about a chore, really remember completing it—for example, how much you like it when the bathroom is clean, how you felt lighter after you told your friend you were not going to the concert you didn't want to spend money on, or even just how relaxing it felt to do something you wanted to do with the work or the problem off your mind.

2. Figure out how many hours you have until you *absolutely must* do the thing you don't want to do. Seriously contemplate how much the task is going to weigh on your mind during *all those hours*.

3. Ask yourself, "Do I want to worry about it for all those hours, or do I want those hours to be hours of relief?"

4. If you do the dreaded thing immediately, pay careful attention to the benefits so that you can recall them the next time you have to remember why doing the worst first is a good idea. If you don't do what you dread or put it off until the last moment, pay careful attention to how many hours you felt bad, worried, or anxious. Notice whether the *doing* was as bad as you anticipated, and notice whether the relief of getting it done was worth the hours of unpleasant waiting.

Although you might need time to think about it, getting the worst out of the way makes it possible to move forward rather than sitting on the razor-sharp edge of anxiety, trying to be comfortable but hurting no matter how you position yourself. The sooner you get off the edge and take the action you have been dreading, the sooner that discomfort will leave and free your anxious mind.

Transfer Your Worry to Another Person

While this may seem like an odd suggestion, I know almost every reader has done this without realizing it. If you used an accountant or a computer program to do your taxes, you transferred your worry to that person (or software program) to make sure your taxes were correctly filled out and you got the most out of your deductions. Anytime a person with anxiety can reasonably consult a professional for advice, this may be wise. For example, seeking the advice of an attorney during a divorce or a court appearance may go a long way toward relieving anxiety.

However, I am also aware that people with anxiety may overconsult, especially in seeking medical reassurance. Or, you may be a person who immediately goes to the Internet to search for reassurance regarding any anxious thought you have. I will discuss the problem of reassurance-seeking in Chapter 9. But, at times, consulting experts is a very good idea, and the point is not that consulting should *always* be the case, but when you can't turn off worry or when you don't have the skill to handle a problem, then transferring worry to someone else is a good idea. Here are some examples:

- *Planning elder care.* There is a whole industry now for helping families find the best setting for care and the most cost-effective plan for that care. Most of us don't have the knowledge to do that on our own.
- *Post–primary care treatment for addiction recovery.* It is likely that families will not have the best ideas for how to help a person maintain a recovery program, so taking the lead from social workers, counselors, and medical staff regarding next steps can be a relief.
- *Individual education plans.* If your child needs an individual education plan (IEP), this is without a doubt a situation where you will want to utilize the knowledge of school counselors, psychologists,

occupational therapists, and all the other specialists who might be called in to plan when a student is in need of academic assistance.

There are many other kinds of special circumstances where you may be worried about your own ability to handle a problem or be worried about another person and how to help. The basic idea behind transferring worry is that in situations where you don't have the knowledge, skill, or clarity of thought to know what to do about a situation, you will want the assistance of someone who does know. Rather than worrying about it or mentally going over what you don't know how to handle, seek out a person who does know—a mentor, adviser, family friend, coach or favorite auntie, or whomever you trust—and get that person's input. Then follow their advice! Don't rethink it when you've already decided to transfer your worry about whether you know enough.

Make a List With Time Frames

Holly was sure she was having a panic attack. "I don't know how I will ever get it all done! It's making me so anxious that I'm having trouble breathing." She was finishing up grad school and getting ready to move to start her first full-time job. She still had to finish the work for a few courses as well as pack her apartment. There were also many small things to get done, such as turning in the paperwork for her degree and getting her robe before the ceremony. She was a self-described wreck. When I asked how much time she had to do these things, she exclaimed, as if it were only two hours, "A week!" I saw the need for a list.

Holly was experiencing what I call quality stress, which I defined earlier and discuss at more length in Chapter 10 about TMA (Too Much Activity). She had a task to do but didn't know how to do it. This kind of stress can only be relieved by building necessary skills. In this case, the skill was how to move. I knew that she would learn how to go about the task pretty easily by discussing its components, and I also knew that she would benefit enormously from time management help. *Managing time is one of the critical skills of stress management*. And timed lists are a great way to learn this component of managing stress. In this case, I wanted Holly to be specific in applying time management to appreciate the way she was getting stressed because she didn't know how to plan to move, and making a timed list was just what she needed.

List-making to calm anxiety goes beyond just writing down the items that need to be accomplished, but it does start there. List-making involves an accurate appraisal of how long each thing will take and what is most important. When you can accurately know how much is possible to get done in a day, you can have reasonable expectations of how it will get done. The decision of what to do at what time resolves the ambiguity of what is going to get done and resolves the anxious self-talk about not doing enough or not doing it perfectly.

I asked Holly to take a breath, handed her a pad of paper, and asked her to write down every single thing she needed to do. We worked on this list out loud, because I wanted to be sure that she was detailed enough. It turned out to be a good idea. "Pack the apartment" became a longer list:

- Put out the clothes I need this week.
- Put the rest of my clothes into suitcases.
- Pack my dishes, pots, and pans.
- Put the bathroom stuff into a box.
- Put my bedding and linens into a box.

We decided that some of her list would be errands she needed to run, and some would be things done at home, so she sorted her list into errands and home tasks, which would be useful later when she decided when and how to do the work. She then added the small and large tasks of finishing up the school-related details of graduation. She even remembered several more small tasks, like turning in keys, that would have come to her mind later— probably just as she started to calm down from her panicky mode.

The next step was to go through every item on the list and write down how long she estimated it would take her to complete each in minutes. "Turn in the keys" looked like an item that was inconsequential, but it would require 45 minutes to drive to her landlord and return home unless she found a way to combine it with another errand (which she subsequently did). She went on to estimate a time frame for each and every task on the list.

She then created a hierarchy of all the tasks from most important to least important. This is the anxiety-relieving step. If you have a limited amount of time, knowing how much you can reasonably do in that amount of time eliminates the pressure of the things that won't get done. If your major and most important task of the day is to finish your homework (or the work you brought home) and you know you need about 90 minutes to do it, you can relax about everything else. You can do something else without worrying about whether you are going to get the homework done, because you know you have 90 minutes in which to do it after dinner. Or you can relax your mind about other things because you know you have only 90 minutes, which is not enough time to also get another job done. Holly had more than one day, so once she made her list, she decided what time she had available each day and began to plug in the tasks, from most important to least. She had some set appointments to work around, and she remembered to put in time for taking lunch and other breaks. When she realized that she had about two days' worth of work and seven days to get it done, her panic disappeared.

A major premise of stress management is that people feel stress in direct proportion to the degree of control they believe they have. Even if they have a lot to do, knowing they can get it done feels as if there is some control. And Holly got two benefits from developing a sense of control: the knowledge that she really did have the ability to plan and execute a move (quality stress got relieved) and she knew she had time to get it done (quantity stress never took hold). She had been so overwhelmed by the number of tasks that she thought moving entailed that she couldn't get past that. She would have been less efficient working in that state of upset. Now she thought about how she was going to be able to enjoy her last week before starting the new job.

Most of the time, when people do this for a day's worth of work, they get a very different outcome than Holly's extra time. This was the case for John, who had a situation I call quantity stress. He knew how to do everything on his list, from packing to mounting the bike rack on his car, but he had too many things to do. To get a handle on quantity stress, he made a timed list of what he needed to get done to leave for the family vacation.

He discovered he had 10 and a half hours of work and about eight hours in which to do it, so he had to trim his expectations by two and a half hours. He then decided what tasks on his list were absolutely necessary and what tasks could be left undone. So, instead of anticipating a day full of pressure that would aggravate his mind, he felt calm, knowing he had time to get things ready for his departure. If something didn't go as planned, he would add the amount of time it actually took to his list and revise his expectations about what would get done. But unless that happened, he could perform his tasks without that under-the-gun feeling that makes days like this anxiety-provoking.

Priority Lists

What is important is seldom urgent, and what is urgent is seldom important.
—General Dwight Eisenhower

If you are a busy person, your anxiety may well be spurred by the fear that you won't get everything done, and then you may have to face fear of failure, fear of judgment, or just plain too much stress. General Eisenhower opened the path to an important way to prioritize tasks that can be extremely beneficial to people who have multiple tasks across their home and work arenas. This "path" is the Eisenhower matrix, into which you can enter your tasks in the categories of urgent/important, not urgent/important, urgent/not important, and not urgent/not important. See Table 8.1 to see this as a grid. You can download a grid to cellular devices or phones that you can even integrate with your calendar and with a timer to keep you on task. Two of these can be found at Eisenhower.me and Focus Matrix, which is an app for Apple IOS systems. These matrices are excellent for establishing a sense of control when quantity stress is a prominent component of your stressful life.

Making lists is also a great way of preventing the common anxiety-producing problem of running late for an appointment, meeting, or social event. The list can be done mentally in just a minute or two to figure out if you really do have time, for example, to stop at the grocery, the dry cleaner, and the pharmacy on your way to pick up the kids after their baseball prac-

Table 8.1 Urgency and Importance Grid

	Urgent	Not Urgent
Important	urgent/important	not urgent/important
Not Important	urgent/not important	not urgent/not important

tice. Even if you realize that you have to skip one of the tasks, you will be less agitated, and limited agitation is good for calming the anxious mind. Mentally visualizing the urgency and importance grid can also relieve a lot of anxiety about whether the choice is even important enough to worry about.

To recap how to stop anxious thoughts by making a list:

1. List every single task you have to get done.
2. Estimate the time (including driving/walking/bus time for errands) each task will take.
3. Prioritize the list (use the Eisenhower version of prioritizing)
4. Eliminate tasks you can't fit into your time frame

Making the Thought-Stopping Technique Work

The watchword for stopping thoughts is *persistence*. Symptoms are usually persistent, and the technique works only when it is applied persistently. Therapists working with clients who have generalized anxiety will cover this ground over and over to pick up on all the subtleties of their thought processes and to reinforce thought replacement methods. This does not work fast. Improvement can be noticed almost immediately, but it can take many weeks or even months before the anxious mind is persistently calm.

The key to making thought-stopping work as quickly as possible is also to be very consistent in trying to divert thoughts. Progress will be slow if the thought-stopping methods are only occasionally applied. When you start to practice thought-stopping, you may also see that the anxious thoughts increase very briefly (this is more likely to happen when the thoughts are both persistent and consistent), but this period will be followed by a rapid decrease in worrying. There is a direct correlation between consistently applying this method and decreasing the brain's overactivity.

Janis, one of the hardest workers in therapy I have ever seen, is a good example of the need for persistence. Beset by anxious thoughts, Janis practiced every method I suggested over the course of therapy—quite an unusual client! She was having persistent and extremely disturbing ruminations about whether her cancer would recur. After learning to calm her body, she was ready to use thought-stopping to interrupt these thoughts. After just a week, she reported success at cutting the thoughts way back, and she told me that the key to making it work was that I had warned her how hard it would be to stay persistent. She said:

> I thought you were kidding when you told me I would have to thought-stop every time the cancer thought occurred, even if it was a thousand times a day. If you hadn't warned me, I would have given up in despair after about a hundred times that first day, thinking this method would never work for me. But you said a thousand times a day, so I figured I had better keep at it.

What an example of persistently stopping persistent anxiety!

CONCLUSION

Progress with calming mental anxiety begins before thought-stopping. It starts with learning to calm the anxious body. The bad news is that unlike physical calming, which can work immediately, calming the anxious mind and stopping anxious thoughts takes time and practice. The good news is that the high energy of the anxious brain can be tapped to effectively avert anxious thoughts and replace them with positive ones.

NINE

Technique #7

Contain Your Worry

Everybody worries, but people with generalized anxiety elevate worry to an art form. They take normal worries and develop them into monstrous impediments to clear thinking, enlarging them out of proportion to reality by excessive rumination. The anxious mind can find odd things to get stuck on, too: breaking laws, germs and contagion, poisoning, hurting others by accident. This exaggeration of normal worry might even achieve a state of paranoia or delusion, causing people to fear they are going crazy.

This kind of worry is hard to control; it becomes an anxiety disorder when a person is so preoccupied by it that it robs life of joy and interferes with attention to the details that enrich or inform life. When a person is no longer able to shrug off worry, it is time to take charge and learn how to manage it. No one can *avoid* worry altogether, but anyone can *contain* it. This technique acknowledges that at times people cannot just "stop worrying about it," as their family and friends tell them to do. They instead have to learn strategies to contain their worries.

The strategies in this technique will not only provide immediate relief from worrying but also change the likelihood of future worry by calming down the overactive limbic system that overreacts to indicators of trouble with excessive worry. You might recall the example of the car with a stick shift describing the role of the anterior cingulate cortex (ACC). In this technique, you will learn to "put in the clutch" and get some space in your thoughts and your behavior. Then you will get ideas for how to "shift to a different gear," that is, to find a new perspective to reengage more fruitfully with the problem that is on your mind. And you will learn ways to let worry go on its way without sucking up your mental energy. As with all of the other techniques, the goal is to eliminate the frequency, intensity, and duration of anxiety symptoms to give your anxious brain a rest. Freed of anxiety symptoms, your anxious mind will recuperate from its agitation and generate less anxiety.

WHAT'S MAKING YOU SO WORRIED?

It's that darned negative, limbic-generated worry getting stuck in the anterior cingulate cortex (ACC) that can't shift to a new thought! The prefrontal cortex (PFC) is too tired to take charge, perhaps because of low serotonin levels that increase negativity, increase agitation, and decrease the energy to contain worry. These brain structures get overly active when you've had shortened sleep for weeks or months, and they recuperate when you get better sleep, but not overnight! That lifestyle change can really matter. Stress plays its role in generating excessive reactions—including excessive worry—whether you are worrying about what is stressing you or you have been under stress so long that it's hard to turn off worry and anxiety. Even when your thinking brain is temporarily distracted, worry comes back to trouble you, like your tongue trying desperately to get rid of a raspberry seed in your molar. Like shifting gears in that car with manual transmission, the PFC needs to do a manual override on that automatic process, which is what this technique is all about.

Psychotherapy is very useful when people worry like this, because worry seems so real to the people who are stuck. They lose sight of all the reasons why it is safe not to worry. Needing help getting out of their rut is not unlike needing a tow truck to get a perfectly running car out of a ditch. There is nothing wrong with the car except that it cannot steer or move forward when its wheels are just spinning. Once the car is freed from the rut, it can go back to handling the road well. Containing worry allows the brain to do its work without spinning its wheels.

Carrie was so good at worrying that she could take the slightest threat and spend a whole day on it. A college senior, Carrie was applying for jobs and needed to squeeze in interviews between work and classes. She scheduled one interview that was a long drive from her campus, but she thought she could make the trip and return in time for her senior seminar—a once-a-week class she couldn't miss without it affecting her final grade. When she overheard two classmates agitatedly discussing construction starting on the highway she would need to drive, her amygdala picked up on the agitation and signaled a warning that her thoughts immediately went toward: "What if the trip takes too long?" Then her brain got stuck on the fear that she would be late for the interview. When she shook that off, it would switch to worrying about being late getting back. Her logic never stepped in to consider what the actual consequences would be because she just assumed they would be terrible. She finally mentioned to me that she was stumped about what to do; she had been worrying for a week. She was thoroughly agitated and becoming less able to control or correct her worries. Part of her worry could be handled by planning, but part could not. It was entirely possible that she would be late for the interview or class—even if there was *no* construction, as highway slowdowns due to accidents or weather are unpredictable. Any reassurance that there would never be a delay was pointless because it would not be true. She needed to learn to contain her worry.

GET THE RIGHT REASSURANCE

People may try to cover up or get rid of ruminating worry without dealing with it directly. One common way they attempt to do this is by seeking reassurance that their worry is unfounded. If they can just hear the right information, they believe that this reassurance will rid them of their worry. They endlessly ask other people for reassurance that they have no reason to worry. They want to be reassured once and for all, and sometimes they hear information that gives them relief—for a moment.

Ultimately, however, the anxious mind will find a flaw in the reassurance because there will always be something that makes the reassurance suspect or ineffective. The anxious mind will then start off on another search for reassurance. This is why Internet searching has become such a time-consuming pastime for worriers. They can search and search without actually bothering their families and friends for reassurance. Reassurance-seeking is a trap that makes worry worse and does not teach you how *not* to worry in the future.

Worriers like this may also have odd thoughts that they know are bizarre but can't shake off. They can't get reassurance unless they mention these thoughts in some way, but they don't want to actually tell anyone what the nature of their (irrational) worry is. Let's say that a worrier is afraid she has been exposed to a virulent form of tuberculosis that was covered in the news when a man traveled internationally knowing he had it. The worrier may try any of the following ways to seek reassurance:

- She may joke: "I am going to put my boarding pass in my safe deposit box, because when it comes out that I have that TB, I want to be sure I can prove I was on his airplane and get in on the class action suit."
- She may make a quip: "I bet I sat next to that guy—the passenger next to me coughed all the way. That will teach me to wear a surgical mask on the airplane!"
- She may ask a question: "There is no way the airline wouldn't call to tell me he was on my flight, is there?"

What the worrier hears back may provide some relief or start a cascade of new worry. For example, a person searching the Internet for a possible explanation for his persistent headaches might discover many terrifying possible causes that generate a whole new set of worries for him. One woman I worked with tracked her Internet searching and saw it escalating. I thought she would do it less when she really saw that she always felt worse after searching. When she observed her feelings before, during, and after searching, she saw that she did feel worse. But she also realized that *while she was searching* she felt good; the belief that she might feel reassured by what she found made the search itself reassuring—and downright addictive.

The *right* reassurance is reassurance that the worrier is competent to handle problems. The *wrong* reassurance suggests in some way that "everything will be all right," which the anxious mind will only believe for a moment before moving on to new worries. Brandon is a good example of this. He had a fear that he had an STD because he had some chafing marks at the juncture of his hip and leg after a long bike ride. He knew he had not had the marks before the ride, but his mind created all kinds of reasons why this could be a sign of STD trouble. He thought if he just called the toll-free number for STD information, he would get information that would let him stop worrying. Sure enough, when he called, he was told that the symptoms he was worrying about had nothing to do with an STD. His PFC sent the calming message down to his limbic system, "Wow! Relief!" But then the helpful person on the other end of the line told him that sometimes STD symptoms don't always appear right away and might not be visible in a sexual partner, so if he had sexual contact with someone who could possibly have had an STD, he should see his doctor anyway. His amygdala then screamed at him, "Red alert! I can have symptoms and *not even know it!*" It didn't matter what his actual risk was; what he got was the wrong reassurance. In seeking reassurance about his chafed skin, he heard something that triggered another unnecessary worry. This commonly occurs when worriers try to escape anxiety by looking for reassurance for each and every worry.

What Brandon needed was the right reassurance. The right reassurance involves:

1. *Getting the worry out in the open to determine if you have a real problem.*
   Good worriers typically can't tell the difference between their worry and the real thing. Actually, they do know the real thing when it is in front of them, and they usually respond very well. But they can't tell when a worry is *not* the real thing. The first part of Brandon's experience wasn't so bad. His worry stemmed from not being able to ascertain if he had a genuine problem, so he called the hotline to get his worry out in the open and ask if there was something he should do about it.

2. *Affirmation that you are competent to handle the consequences of the possible problem.* This is where things fell apart for Brandon. Instead of being told that even if he did contract an STD, he would be competent enough to figure out what to do about it, he was told that he was not even capable of *knowing* that he had a problem.

He needed to hear that he could determine a course of action that would allow him to (1) identify an STD and (2) obtain treatment.

3. Most important is *getting the reassurance that you know how to stop and contain worry*. If Brandon had managed his worry better, he would have contained it for a day or two, which would have allowed the chafing to go away and not allowed his anxiety to take over.

The Right Reassurance for Panic and Social Anxiety

The right reassurance for panic and social anxiety—as opposed to generalized anxiety—is a little different. When people are worried about whether they are going to panic or blow it in a social scene, they do need to address the worry directly, because it is almost always about whether they will show their symptoms and how people will react. They will benefit if they can get that fear right out on the table. It can help them to hear their own acknowledgment that they fear how they will look or what they will do if they have symptoms. This is a worry that can be directly handled with reassurance about competence to cope with the anxiety. The right reassurance for panic involves:

1. Acknowledging that the fear is a fear of experiencing panic.
2. Reminding the person who is panicking (or reminding yourself, if you are the one panicking) of skills he or she already has to cope with it.

The fear of having a panic attack can be intense. It is what leads people to avoid situations in which they might panic. And it can help to hear the right reassurance. Instead of saying, "Oh, you won't panic," try, "Even if you panic, you will get through it." Or, "Even if you do panic, once it is over, you can go on with what you were doing." Or, "If you should panic, even if it is a lot of panic, you have all the skills you need to cope with it." Of course, if you are going to use this last example, the person really does need to have the skills to stop panic, such as diaphragmatic breathing and cued relaxation.

People with social anxiety are also inclined to fear the feelings of anxiety, especially those that others might notice. The right reassurance for social anxiety is to:

1. Get the worry out on the table. What exactly does the person think will happen?
2. Make sure the person is competent to handle the anxiety regarding the things she or he fears.
3. Make sure the person has skills to handle the situations she or he fears. For instance, if the fear is about doing something new and looking afraid while doing it, two levels of competency are needed—skills and anxiety management. Make sure the person has the skills to handle the situation. People with social anxiety often need to learn social skills they missed growing up. They can't believe they will handle anxiety if the social situation is beyond their skill and practice level.
4. Reassure the person that she or he has the competence to handle the fear and to handle the consequences of feeling afraid.

Reassurance should only happen one time for any situation. If a person repeatedly raises the same concern, it is a disguised form of worrying. "One time through" should be the rule for any specific worry or situation that a person brings up. For example, if a woman has trouble responding to criticisms made by her mother-in-law and brings up the issue over and over, she is probably seeking reassurance. She may seek reassurance for how to handle her mother-in-law's criticism of her Thanksgiving dinner and then the following week seek reassurance that she can handle it if her mother-in-law criticizes her birthday party hosting. This is the same worry, and it does not need reviewing again. After a situation has been reviewed according to the steps offered earlier, it should not be repeated. If the worry comes up again, reassurance is simple: "You know what to do about anxiety, and you can handle being worried or afraid."

To sum up, below is a list of the right reassurance for the three types of anxiety:

For general worries:

1. Get the worry out in the open to see if it is a real problem or a worry.
2. If it is a real problem, make a plan, which reinforces a sense of competence to handle the problem.
3. If it is a worry, stop and contain the worry (addressed later in this chapter).
4. Reassure the worrier, "You are competent to manage your anxiety."

For panic:

1. Acknowledge that the fear is a fear of having panic.
2. Remind the person of his or her skills for coping with it.
3. Reassure the worrier, "You are competent to handle your panic and the consequences of panic."

For social anxiety:

1. Get the worry out on the table.
2. Make a plan to handle whatever realistic components there are, including learning additional skills if necessary or practicing skills.
3. Review the methods for handling pre-situation anxiety and during-situation anxiety to be sure all the management skills are in place.
4. Reassure the worrier of his or her competence to handle the fear and to handle the consequences of feeling afraid.

For all forms of anxiety:

After a situation has been reviewed, it should not be repeated. If the worry comes up again, reassurance is simple: "You know what to do about anxiety, and you can handle being worried or afraid."

PLANNING IS AN ANTIDOTE TO WORRYING

Worry is defeated when people confidently take action to solve their problems. I have found that people who worry about things going wrong are often competent at handling things when they *do* go wrong. It is the ambiguity of potential problems that is so hard on people with anxiety. The rule is, "If you have a real problem, you will not fail to notice it." And remember, real problems have real solutions, so they don't stimulate anxiety about what to do about them. A clear plan of action is a godsend to an anxious mind.

Even though people with anxiety might do better facing real problems than facing worries, they may not be very good at planning. They also may not see how to use a plan to relieve worry. Planning is a simple but often overlooked skill that can make a big difference in calming a ruminative mind. If you don't have planning skills, you will be at a loss for how to get relief. If you are worrying about an upcoming situation, examine whether you can make an action plan for it. A typical situation would be a "what-if" type of worry. "What if my car breaks down on vacation?" "What if I fail the test?" "What if no one asks me to the prom?" "What if I don't get this job I applied for?" All of these situations have a common element—if they do happen, a response will be in order, and in each case, a plan could be made. Worriers get confused between what might require action and what is just a worry.

An excellent response to "what-if" syndrome is to make sure you know how to make a plan and then to see if the situation is something for which a plan can be made. Lots of materials are available that teach problem-solving and planning skills. (An Internet search for books on problem-solving and planning skills quickly pulls up a long list of resources for different age groups and different kinds of environments.) One of the first things a plan always addresses is how to clarify the problem. If you can't identify a specific problem that can be solved, then it is probably just a worry, and thought-stopping and thought replacement will be sufficient.

If you can identify a problem, going on to make a plan will be a relief to the anxious mind. "What-if" thinking is anxiety-provoking. The goal of thought-stopping is to eliminate the arousal of constant anxiety and cool off the anxious mind. Therefore, figuring out what to do *if* a problem comes up

becomes a part of the overall plan to stop thinking about it at all. Once the "what-if" cognitions are identified and resolved into action plans, the idea is to never think about them again unless the "what-if" scenario actually occurs, in which case the anxious person has a plan all laid out. If you *do* find yourself continuing to worry, control it by saying, "Stop! I have a plan!" and then, without reviewing the plan, replace the "what if" with a planned-ahead thought replacement (Chapter 8).

The process of making a good plan includes:

1. Concretely identifying what the problem is, including at what point it will be a problem and how you will know if it needs a solution
2. Listing (brainstorming) options for solving the problem
3. Weighing the options (you may need a pro/con list here)
4. Selecting one option or plan
5. Writing out the steps you will follow for this plan
6. If the time comes to exercise the plan, starting the plan and carrying it out
7. Evaluating how the plan worked

It is helpful to write out the plan on paper, because the anxious mind will remember it better. Seeing the list in writing puts the information back into your mind through a different pathway.

Let's look at these steps more carefully.

Identify the Problem

Good plans start with a description of what the problem is. That may seem too obvious to mention, but actually it is the most important step. "What ifs" can go on endlessly in the mind because the problem shifts as you worry. For example, "What if I don't get asked to the prom?" can transform into "What if I get asked by someone I don't like?" "What if I ask someone who says no?" "What if I say yes to someone because I'm afraid no one else will ask me and then I get asked by someone I really like?" "What if I end up having no one to go with two weeks before, a week before, two days before . . . when do I do something about it?" This can go on endlessly. At this point, *stop!* Define the problem.

In this example, even though all the "what ifs" seem worthy of discussion, they are only problems if you *do* get an invitation to the prom. The answer is to handle "What if I *don't* get asked?" with a plan. "What if I *do* get asked?" is a question you can handle with "I will stop and make a new plan."

Brainstorm Options

After you know what the problem really is, it is time to brainstorm. Brainstorming means quickly thinking of many things you could do if you faced the situation. Don't censor yourself during this stage; write down everything you think of, even if it seems silly or outlandish. This is the time to get your brain busy and stimulate creativity. Remember how the anterior cingulate cortex (ACC) gets stuck? This part of problem-solving, finding as many solutions as possible, is an intentional (prefrontal cortex, or PFC) way to get unstuck. You may even want to ask someone to help you—that person's point of view will be different, and he or she may be able to stimulate new ideas in you as well. After the list of options is as long as you can get it, begin to weigh them each with a pro/con list.

Select One Option

In addition to helping the ACC get unstuck, listing every option, even the silly and outrageous ones, helps make the process of selecting the best option easier. Seeing the obviously wrong choices makes the right choice easier to identify and accept. For example, suppose you are fed up with your job and have brainstormed what to do. Even though you know it's preposterous, you've listed the option of "quitting today." "Of course I can't quit," you say. "I need the money I earn." But in reality you *can* quit, and this is what putting everything down shows—that you do have choices. Knowing that *staying* is an actual choice somehow makes staying seem easier. And it clarifies what all of your other options could reasonably be. A final reason for listing everything is that sometimes the wild ideas sow seeds of solutions that can work.

It is usually fairly easy to see a few "best" options. Identifying the best of that group, however, may require a pro/con list or a cost/benefit analysis. Again, putting this in writing helps to make the choices evident. Also, the anxious mind has trouble concentrating, so putting something in writing will help you focus on what the most salient aspects of the solution are without wandering off into the territory of more anxiety about what to choose.

At this point, you may get stuck for another, very common reason. The anxious mind wants to believe in a perfect choice. If you can find the perfect choice, then you won't have to worry, right? (Remember how perfectionism is an attempt to ward off anxiety? This is another version of it.) Remind yourself, "There are many good choices. There are no *perfect* choices." Then, pick one of the good choices and carry it out.

A small but important point here is that once the plan is selected and steps are written down for following the plan, the process of planning is done on that problem. The "what-if" worrier can easily make a transition to "What if I didn't think of everything?" and go on worrying by replanning the plan she or he just made. When this happens, you must immediately say, "Stop! I have a plan!" and then divert your thoughts without reviewing the plan for any reason. Even reviewing the plan to reassure yourself that you have one is a subtle version of "what-if" thinking, and must be avoided if you are going to calm your anxiety.

Evaluate How the Plan Worked

The amygdala, the part of the brain that is on the lookout for trouble, needs opportunities to learn that some things are not scary (as anticipated) and that not all experiences are like other times that were anxiety-provoking. Setting up a plan provides an opportunity for the amygdala to observe how a new situation is different from an old one. Taking time to evaluate the outcome of a situation can help the process. Bringing conscious attention to the outcome is a prefrontal cortex (PFC) decision to analyze all of the information coming from the senses and the body through the limbic system.

This involves the processing function of the anterior cingulate cortex (ACC) and the integration of the orbitofrontal cortex to take note of the motivational information from the basal ganglia. The whole brain gets in on the act. The amygdala will have learned something whether you take the time to analyze or not, but it learns much more when the process is deliberate. (See Part IV for a description of the more intentional process called memory reconsolidation.)

Recalling all the aspects of the situation is a way of reliving it. Reliving it helps reinforce the memory of it, and focusing on positive outcome reinforces the desensitization of fear that occurs when something goes as planned. Even when the outcome is not 100% positive, noting which parts of the solution worked and which did not provides the opportunity to really feel and analyze what worked so that it doesn't get lost in the anxiety of what wasn't perfect. Many anxious people dismiss what wasn't perfect as no good at all. Evaluating outcomes helps to avoid the notion of perfectionism to see that a lot of good can exist among the few not-so-good aspects of a solution.

If a solution to a problem and its action plan went unused because the problem never came up, that outcome ought to be noticed as well. This reinforces the knowledge that most of what we worry about does not ever happen. Those "what ifs" are just potentials, not realities.

To recap planning:

1. Look for the "what-if" thinking that could be solved with a plan.
2. Identify the problem.
3. Generate a list of solutions and select one good one—there is no perfect one.
4. Write out the action steps you will follow if necessary.
5. Stop "what-if" thinking by telling yourself, "Stop! I have a plan!"
6. Immediately practice thought replacement.
7. Do not replan the plan.
8. Put the plan into action if the time comes to use it.
9. Evaluate the outcome whether or not you put the plan into action.

WORRY WELL AND ONLY ONCE

Noelle was seriously worried about losing her job. She was constantly alert to her boss's moods and reported to her sister on an almost daily basis about the status of her job security. "Well," she would say, "he looked at me funny when I told him I wanted Wednesday night off, and I'm sure he is just waiting to see if I will be willing to work overtime to make up for that. If I can't, I know I will be in big trouble." Sensing that Noelle was suffering from anxiety, her sister recommended she seek therapy.

As Noelle described her problem to me, I began thinking about possible causes for it. She could be having trouble with self-esteem, or with reading other people's emotions. She could be overreacting to small signals from her boss that her request was causing him a problem. In the absence of a personality disorder, Noelle might have been showing hypervigilance, perceiving her work situation as "precarious" when she was the one who was unclear about what her boss's attitude was. She could have been worrying in the absence of evidence that worry was called for. However, worrying about a job loss is not unreasonable if there is a real threat. It was impossible for me to know for sure whether her boss wanted to fire her, so any attempt to convince her to just stop worrying was not going to be effective. Also, thought-stopping alone wouldn't be enough because every day could potentially bring a new threat. Noelle needed to learn how to manage her worry about her job once and for all if she didn't want to carry the anxiety around with her and didn't want to wear out her sister. This was the time to teach her how to "worry well and only once."

This is a strategy that takes worry seriously one time and one time only. It sorts out what is a real problem from what is unfounded worry. It involves examining what you can control versus what you cannot control and what you can do something about versus what you can do nothing about. And it helps you make arrangements for when it would be a good idea to worry again.

Worrying well and only once should have a time limit. Usually 10 to 15 minutes will do the trick.

1. Begin by making a list and outlining all the things that you could be worried about. Brainstorm to make sure every worry is identified and none is held back for you to reworry about later. Tease out every aspect of each worry.

2. Do anything that must be done at this time and do not delay. Make phone calls, talk to someone, write or make something, repair, clean, or take any action that will improve the situation.

3. In some cases, actions are necessary only *if the problem should occur.* This is where planning skills can come in handy, because making a plan is the intermediate process when you cannot just set a problem aside. Review the problem and make a plan for what you'll do if it actually happens.

4. Ask yourself, "Is there anything I else I need to worry about regarding this situation?" If the answer is yes, apply the steps of whether it is a real problem that needs a plan and a date. If it doesn't, it goes into the category of worry without a plan. With these worries, it is helpful to set a date to review the worry to see if it needs worrying about later on. Continue with this step, asking, "Is there anything else I need to worry about?" until the answer is no. This is the only way that the worried brain will be able to move on. This step prevents later reworrying by ensuring that all the possibilities are covered. Your brain has to believe it when you say you *already* worried, and it will believe you more easily if you have asked this question deliberately while you are *worrying well.*

5. Set a time when it will be necessary to think about the worry again, and write it down somewhere: "If *x* happens, I will do *y*. If *x* does not happen, the next time I will review this worry is on March 15." (You can also note this on your calendar: "Worry about *x*.") This will relieve your anxious mind of trying to remember when to worry, which it would otherwise bring up frequently. When a "worry date" is written into the calendar, you can say, "I know when to worry again, and I don't have to worry now."

6. Whenever the worry pops up again, immediately declare, "Stop! I already worried!" and divert your thoughts as quickly as possible with thought replacement techniques.

With Noelle, the challenge was not to worry about how to change her boss. It was to say, "Okay, let's worry about what will happen if you do lose your job"—to get it right out there as if it had happened.

We began by outlining all the things she could be worried about. At first, it seemed that her only worry was "What if I lost my job?" but eventually she was able to break down that worry into several components:

- How will I pay my rent if I lose my job?
- Where would I look for another job?
- What if I never get another job?

We then moved onto step 2, do anything that must be done and do not delay. Noelle decided to call her boss and tell him that she could work on Wednesday night. She also decided to set up a firm schedule for future work and discussed this with her boss. But this only partly resolved her fears about being fired. We then needed to move onto step 3, making a plan.

To address her worry about paying her rent if she lost her job, Noelle came up with two ideas. First, she would ask to borrow money from her mother. Second, she would apply for a job at the local convenience store while she looked for another job. We continued to talk about all her worries until she had a plan to resolve them.

I then asked Noelle, "Is there anything else you need to worry about?" She thought for a few moments. "What am I going to do about losing my insurance if I get fired? I can't go around without health insurance!" Again, we discussed a plan to resolve this. Noelle researched COBRA's continuation health coverage and figured out what she would need to do to apply for it.

Next, Noelle set a date to worry about this problem in the future and wrote it down on her calendar. She decided it was reasonable to review her worry about keeping her job once a month in case her boss's attitude shifted in a noticeable way, and she wrote down that on the 15th of the month, she would worry about whether she was going to be fired.

Finally, after all this planning, Noelle felt that she had worried sufficiently about the problem, at least for now. When her anxiety cropped up again, she told herself, "Stop! I've already worried!" and reminded herself that she'd set a date to reevaluate the problem on the 15th. She then distracted herself with thought replacement techniques.

The idea behind the "worry well and only once" method is to address the tendency to come up with new thoughts that keep the worry in place. Taking the time to uncover all the aspects of a situation so that they can be evaluated ("Do I need a plan or not?") and resolved ("When or under what circumstances do I review my worry?") is using the PFC functions of analysis and decision-making to their best advantage. When doing thought-stopping on the problem later, the whole brain will respond by settling down faster because the cortex has deliberately modulated the worry and will remember doing it. Thought-stopping and replacement will calm the rest of the brain activity about the problem over time.

Health Anxiety

When applying "worry well and only once" to health anxiety, there are a couple of specific challenges, especially the truth that serious health problems, like cancer or heart disease or MS or an aneurism, could be developing and not yet be noticeably symptomatic. People with this kind of worry-related anxiety are overusers of health care. They visit a primary care physician on average four times more than other people. And CBT methods, such as those in this chapter, are very effective to reduce doctor visits. There are a few specific situations and some ideas for using this method to reduce health anxiety, but most of these are precursors to using the "worry well" method for genuine health-related concerns.

1. The first situation: waiting for medical results. Here the possibility of bad news exists, as does the possibility of good news.

The basic additional step here is not to worry until the results are in. Internet searches on treatments are anxiety-provoking and fruitless unless you know the outcome of the test. So when the worry about the test comes to mind, say to yourself, "Stop! I will worry well when I know what to worry about." Then thought-replacing is in order.

2. The second situation is when there is a noticeable symptom. This is when "wait and see" precedes "worry well."

   • When people have symptoms that might be a virus, the general rule is to wait for seven days. Most illness of that type resolves in a week. Even the sort of never-ending colds that go around in the winter are usually notice-ably better, if not over with, in that amount of time.

   • A common health anxiety escalator is a rash or skin mark that looks inflamed, such as a bug bite. People who are very good at worrying might immediately decide it is a poison-ous spider bite or a flesh-eating bacteria. In this type of sit-uation, the question is, "When should I worry?" If you are worrying about a quickly changing situation, then checking on the inflammation or rash is not a bad idea, but sitting and watching it is not a good idea. Ask yourself, "How long could I wait to see what develops?" That might be 30 min-ute or an hour or two hours or more. Then cover up the area and don't look at it again until the time elapses. Handle the intervening worry with, "Stop! One hour!" I know peo-ple have drawn circles around a skin irritation to make sure it isn't spreading or even taken a picture to compare. The real point here is to push off worry for a reasonable amount of time in order to determine the severity of the situation and whether you just need some soothing skin cream!

3. When should you worry if the problem is a developing symptom over long periods? Let me offer an example: Penny was worried she had MS. Her father had had it, and she knew there is a genetic

component to the disease. Just before Thanksgiving, she realized she had some dizziness. It could have been her anxiety—or MS. Or so she worried. She told me she just wanted to get through the holidays without dealing with medical tests and appointments too. I didn't want to get into "worry well and only once" at this point. So, asking her to use her knowledge about the disease, I inquired whether, if she indeed had it, it would be critical to diagnose it this week and if it would matter if she waited six weeks. She had had a neurological exam earlier in the year with no findings, and she felt certain that delaying diagnosis would not affect the prognosis or treatment in any way. I asked when she wanted to assess her dizziness and decide if she wanted to consult a neurologist. She chose January 15 as the day to assess it. Now, for the next six weeks, the worry "What if I have MS?" was answered, "January 15!" and followed by thought replacement. When January 15 rolled around, her anxiety had improved, her dizziness was gone, and she had no symptoms to consult a physician about. (For those of you who are worried that I acted as a neurologist or took a chance that an important diagnosis might have been missed, please relieve your worries. My client also was instructed and was competent to follow the obvious. *If something changes, you can reassess!* But remember, you don't need to be constantly assessing. This is the corollary to "If there is a real problem, you will not fail to notice it."

4. Then there is the sad but very common worry, felt even when there is no symptom to focus on, "But what if I get sick someday?" While psychotherapy is going to help figure out whether underlying causes are at play and will address those over time, start with the mindful, "At this moment, all is well." I ask people to say that out loud, watching their body response and verbalizing the immediate thoughts that occur. I can then often discover what other aspects of illness may be troubling a health worrier. Those set up a discussion to resolve life history issues or self-efficacy issues or even life purpose issues.

To recap:

1. Worry through all the issues involved in the situation.
2. Do anything that must be done at this time to alleviate the worry and do not delay.
3. Make a plan that might be called for if certain aspects of the problem crop up at a specific point.
4. Ask yourself, "Is there anything else I need to worry about?"
5. Set a time to think about the worry again.
6. Then, whenever the thought pops up again, say, "Stop! I already worried!"
7. When the problem is health anxiety, use the precursors to worrying well, especially, "When should I worry well?"

DITCH YOUR DREAD

The sensation of dread can precede any idea that there is actually something to feel dread about. Sometimes this is referred to as "free-floating" anxiety, but it can be recognized by the pit-of-the-stomach unease that all people associate with dread. High norepinephrine levels that affect many anxiety sufferers cause the brain to go into a scanning search for what the problem could be. Like doing an MRI on a person's life, the brain scans every aspect of life to see if there are identifiable problems to be solved. This is foolproof for worriers. If they look for trouble, they will find it. Some problem or potential for a problem will present itself as the reason for the dread, and with an explanation, a switch is made from unease to worry. The circle of dread is shown in Figure 9.1.

However, when worriers learn that the sensation of dread can develop for no good reason, often as the result of brain activity, they can monitor this in themselves. High levels of norepinephrine in particular affect the autonomic nervous system and can create a sensation of arousal that feels just like dread. Also, people who have trouble with falling blood sugar levels may experience feelings of dread from out of nowhere. *But this is just a feeling.* Reminding yourself of this is essential: "Feelings are not facts!"

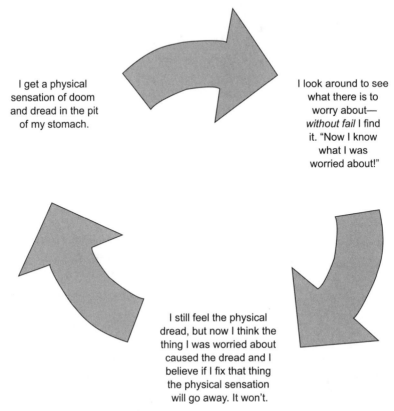

I get a physical sensation of doom and dread in the pit of my stomach.

I look around to see what there is to worry about— *without fail* I find it. "Now I know what I was worried about!"

I still feel the physical dread, but now I think the thing I was worried about caused the dread and I believe if I fix that thing the physical sensation will go away. It won't.

Figure 9.1 The Circle of Dread

At first, however, it may be hard to tell the difference between dread for no reason and dread *for* a reason, because the mind is involved in explaining why the sensation is there. Containing the anxious mind means using mental strategies to identify the dread and ditch it. The method is fairly simple. The first step is to come to believe that you will not fail to notice a real problem. Ask yourself, "Have I ever had a real problem that I failed to notice?" As discussed above, this applies to physical health (a common worry for people), problems at work, problems with children, and so on.

If you *do* think that you have a tendency to overlook or ignore problems, some therapy work on that thought or belief will be necessary before you can use this method to contain your worry. For example, when people are raised in families with parental addiction, they often distrust their own perceptions. They may have been taught to ignore their own needs and even been directly primed to not believe what they see, hear, or think. Give Claudia Black a read. Her book *It Will Never Happen to Me* does a great job of explaining how that doubt of one's own perceptions develops. It is necessary to address that in therapy over a series of discussions, even if just to start looking at ways of learning to trust one's perceptions.

Usually, however, people know when a problem is real. If you are really sick, for instance, you have a fever or a cough or you bleed or have obvious pain. (Knowing you have a problem, by the way, is different from knowing your diagnosis. This question about failing to notice problems is about the ability to *recognize* a problem, not about the ability to solve or diagnose it.) Being full of dread when there is really nothing to worry about, however, is common in people with generalized anxiety, and this kind of dread needs to be eliminated.

Next, it is necessary to notice that the dread occurs *before* your brain comes up with a reason for it. Instead of asking what the reason for the dread is, ask whether this is a sensation of dread for no obvious reason. It is common to believe that if you have this feeling, there *must* be a reason for it, so education about how neurochemical changes can create the sensation in the body without any real reason will help you believe that your body is creating this without cause. Claire, age 57, told me she would feel a sinking feeling, just as if something was really wrong. Then she would ask herself why she felt so bad. And of course she found many possibilities. As she mastered noticing that dread preceded anxious thoughts, she said it felt as if she was making a *physical* movement to pull her thoughts away from the gut awareness to think on something besides what could be wrong. But she absolutely believed that her gut preceded the worrying, so she made the effort until it became fairly easy to do.

Pay attention to how you know you feel dread. It will almost always be noted as a sinking sensation in the stomach, plus various other, less significant physical indicators. But again, a feeling is just a feeling. You will not fail to notice a real problem that needs a solution.

One way to stop the physical feeling of dread is diaphragmatic breathing. With just a minute to breathe and induce muscle relaxation, the body can relax and begin to let go of the dread at the physical level. (See Chapters 2 and 4 for a discussion of the breathing and muscle relaxation techniques.)

As the relaxation is initiated, the thought-stopping process allows you to notice that the sensation is physical. After thought-stopping, it is helpful to reiterate, "I will not fail to notice a real problem." Then, immediately use a distraction or other thought replacement method. But even as the sensation of dread settles down, the niggling sense that you ought to be scanning for trouble may stick around, and you may need to repeat this step. Don't be tempted to scan if the niggling sensation doesn't disappear. This is not a sign of a real problem; it is a sign that you have not eliminated dread. Don't be tempted to go back and review. If you have let it go, then let it stay gone.

Again, the steps for ditching your dread are:

1. Ask yourself, "Have I ever failed to notice a real problem that needed to be solved?" Work on believing that you will notice real problems and respond to them when necessary.
2. Notice whether the dread is present without an obvious cause; notice that it has preceded a reason to have it.
3. Tell yourself that a feeling is just a feeling.
4. Immediately breathe for a minute and do muscle relaxation.
5. Practice thought-stopping and tell yourself, "I will notice if I have a real problem"; immediately use thought replacement.
6. Ignore the temptation to go back and scan for a problem.

CLEAR YOUR WORRIED THOUGHTS

Sometimes you just need to get everything off your mind—to clear away the tangled thoughts and focus on something else. Sometimes you need to empty your mind to rest and then pay attention to what is really important at the moment. All the worried thoughts buzzing around in your anxious mind distract you from thinking clearly about just one thing at a time.

Contain Your Worry

This method of clearing worried thoughts can be done in several ways. Basically, the method is to list all the thoughts, worries, and concerns that occupy the mind and clear the way for selected thoughts to take their place. This can be done as follows:

1. Imagine a container sitting in front of you. The container can hold all your concerns. It has a lid, but right now the lid is off.
2. Next, create an image of all that concerns you in your life on this day. Without thinking them over, see and name those concerns and set them into the container.
3. When everything has been named and put into the container, put the lid on the container and set it aside.
4. Then, in the space you just cleared, invite thoughts about what most needs your attention *at this time* to come to forward.

Some people are imaginative worriers but don't appreciate using imagery such as the container. There are many ways to use this method without the image of a container. For example:

- Write down your worried thoughts in the form of a list. Be very brief—this is not like journaling. Use one or two words to list what is going on in your life that occupies your thoughts. Then put the list in a drawer or briefcase or another place where it will literally be put out of sight (and out of mind).
- Another version of this method is Al-Anon's idea of a "God box" to hold slips of paper, each of which have a worry thought or a problem that is to be turned over to God.
- Children can write or draw a picture of their thoughts or worries and put it into a backpack. With an adult, they can periodically open the backpack and see what's in it. This allows them to see which of the things that worried them actually happened and

how they coped with them. All the things that were unnecessary worries that never happened can be thrown away. This is a practical and concrete way to show children that most things they worry about never happen and just waste thought and time.

- There are small dolls in a box or bag from Guatemala that can be purchased from global marketers or import stores. The legend is that a person can hand the concerns or worries of life over to the dolls and the dolls will take the worries away. The lid is literally put on the box so that the dolls can carry the worries away and ready themselves for the next batch of worries.

Once the mind is cleared, attention is free to focus on the activity or thoughts that are most important at the moment. A student might clear his mind before taking a test; a manager might clear her mind before a conference call or staff meeting; someone who wants to contemplate a solution to a problem might want to think about it without the confusion of many other thoughts. Clearing your mind of worries before going to bed can help you get a more restful sleep. If you do this, invite a peaceful thought into your mind after clearing the worries away.

A similar method of clearing the mind prepares people to work in therapy sessions or to focus on specific concerns, even if working alone to gain insight. This psychotherapy method, called "focusing," was created by Eugene Gendlin (1998) and developed further by Ann Weiser-Cornell (2013). (See the References for more information on these readings.) The complete process of focusing is an excellent therapeutic method for becoming aware of all the implications of an issue. It is especially powerful for people whose physical symptoms cloud their thinking. Because people with anxiety misinterpret physical and emotional sensations as anxiety, they miss other, important information that would cause them to make different choices if they were aware of what they were missing. With focusing, people learn to listen nonjudgmentally to their body's message and don't misinterpret sensations as anxiety. Learning to read the body relieves much anxiety on a permanent basis.

Contain Your Worry in Time

There are situations that you will worry about when you probably should worry. No, really. There are things not under your control, things you can't plan for and that are so important it would be impossible *not* to worry. For example, what if someone you love is in danger? Perhaps she is in the military, a firefighter on duty, doing a stint in Doctors Without Borders, or another kind of worker in a war zone or health-risk area. What if you are letting an adult child live outside your home after having that child with you while recovering from drug addiction? You are going to worry about relapse or safety. What if someone you love is suffering from cancer or has a life-altering disease? You must feel worried about their survival and well-being! Other situations may fit this issue too. But what should you do? Here I am telling you to worry. Yes, worry, but do it for a brief time every day. Containing worry in time works—surprisingly quickly—to free your mind from worry for the rest of the day.

Here is how the method works: You are going to pick a 10-minute time that you can spend worrying at the same time every day. Sit in the same place every day. Make the worry time as much of a ritual as you can. Ritual is profoundly helpful to centering a person in the goal of the ritual, and its various aspects will anchor you in positive ways. Ritual engages the basal ganglia activity for habit formation, because in ritual, repetition of words and actions, often in response to a cue, become automatic after some practice. If you have participated in any religious practice, you may know that certain words spoken by the leader of the ceremony always elicit the same words from the participants. The songs or words of prayers can be spoken (perhaps unfortunately) automatically. The components of ritual are very similar, no matter what type of ritual you are creating, and they can be readily applied to contain your worry in time.

You will want to pick the focus of your ritual as the person or situation you are worrying about. For example, Craig was worried about his mother, who had just been diagnosed with cancer that was very far advanced and from which she was not going to recover. He decided to worry every day before he left for work. Since she loved the outdoors, he wanted to sit where he could see greenery, and he put a favorite picture of her on a table near the chair to focus his attention only on her. For many people, this is an opportunity to pray for the well-being of the one they are worried about, and I encourage them to use the time for that, incorporating standard prayers and using articles of faith such as rosaries, crosses, prayer shawls, incense, or whatever is religiously meaningful. Craig was not a person who prayed, but he had practiced some meditation, so he decided he would start his worrying by striking a singing bowl. He also needed to think about how to worry, and he decided that he wanted to transform his worry in some way to a more positive activity. He would imagine that his worry could operate as a protective force, sent to surround his mother with protection from fear while she faced the end of her life. He set a timer for 10 minutes, and when it went off (it would clearly signal time to quit), he would strike the singing bowl one more time. This example is unique to Craig but demonstrates one way to do this. Containing your worry in time is always adapted to the worrier's spiritual stance, but ritual has the same components for everyone:

1. *Regularity of time and place.* For Craig, it was the green view and before work. Set a timer, especially at first. Your brain is already in the habit of interpreting the ding of a timer to mean that you are done.
2. *Starting with a specific signal.* For example, this could be saying the same words, saying a prayer, lighting a candle, or bowing the head or the body. Craig chose the singing bowl.
3. *An object that represents the person or the situation.* Craig chose a picture, but you could use any object.
4. *Religious articles that are meaningful.* Craig was not someone who prayed, but he felt this time was important to value his mother. He chose the singing bowl to represent that.
5. *Ending with the same closing consistently.* Snuff the candle, say a closing prayer, or strike the singing bowl as Craig did.

6. *Freedom from worry*. Then, for the rest of the day, when the loved one crosses your mind, say to yourself, "Yes! And I will worry about this again tomorrow!"

Craig, and others who have used this method, have found that they are almost immediately able to contain worry in the worry time and then focus on other parts of their lives, such as the work they have in front of them. As it becomes a habit (and they do it until the situation is resolved), they may end up using it for any worry that is important and persistent.

These and other ways of putting worries away have positive effects on the brain. They stop the rumination of the anterior cingulate cortex (ACC), slow the overactive limbic system, and make it easier for the prefrontal cortex (PFC) to direct attention to whatever is most important at the moment. They take advantage of the power of habit to keep worry in its place and not let it bleed over into every other part of life. This method works to turn off the ruminative mind, giving it a chance to rest the feverish overactivity in the brain. Done habitually, such "cooling off" of the anxious mind makes it less likely that the brain will be preoccupied with worries.

CONCLUSION

Control over the worried mind is won slowly, purposefully, and persistently. Doing it requires a willingness to put in effort, but the payoff is a calmer, quieter, less anxiety-generating brain. Using the prefrontal cortex to change the brain is the basis of thought and worry management techniques.

PART IV

MANAGING YOUR ANXIOUS BEHAVIOR

Many skills must be learned and interwoven for the best success in recovering from any anxiety problem. We have already covered calming the anxious body and managing the anxious mind. Now we turn our attention more fully to changing anxious behavior, the final component in successful anxiety management.

As you already know from earlier chapters, avoidance is the behavioral hallmark of anxiety. People who panic do everything they can to avoid situations that might provoke it. They develop the belief that they can avert panic with careful avoidance of any panic trigger, so they avoid driving, airplanes, enclosed spaces, crowds of people, and so on, and their lives are inevitably diminished as a result.

Worriers, too, try to avoid anything that will make them worry. They hold themselves back from situations that seem too stressful and avoid interactions with new people or new activities. They may also try to avoid worry by doing everything they can think of to prevent a problem. Worriers typically have high drive, hence their tendency to avoid worrisome things with lots of activity.

Socially anxious people are perhaps affected most, avoiding being in the limelight. They do not promote their own skills, they often do not fully develop their talents, and they avoid new people or situations that would enlarge their scope and help them make good connections. As a result, they miss out on the richness of life that comes with experiences and interactions with other people.

Anxiety is sometimes more troubling for what it takes away from a person's life than for the trouble it adds. When avoiding thoughts, situations, or feelings, a person is less engaged in life. People may not develop their talents, interests, or skills for fear of failing or being embarrassed or rejected. If they have had a bad experience of humiliation or panic, the tendency to avoid similar situations is even stronger. Recent research about changing memories of such experiences has given clear direction about how to rob those previous experiences of their power to hold people back. Therapists can now create very potent exposures to literally change the prior bad memory. This process is called memory reconsolidation, and I will explain it fully in Chapter 11.

It is also necessary to manage the impact of stress. As described in Chapter 6, there are four arenas of stress management vital to relieving the anxiety that stress kicks up, including eliminating stressors, managing one's time and environment, managing one's attitude, and relaxing the body. Chapter 8, "Stop Anxious Thoughts," addressed time management, and Chapters 10 and 11 will tackle methods for managing one's environment and one's attitude.

Changing anxious behavior is the culmination of learning all the techniques and putting them into practice. Sometimes behavior changes in a quiet, almost unremarkable way as a person worries less, panics less, and feels less inclined to avoid a problem. Sometimes the change is dramatic, as when a shy person asks someone for a date and feels thrilled about it. Whether the change in behavior is quiet or dramatic, the person's life is richer for their being able to connect with others and accomplish activities that previously felt impossible. The feeling of accomplishment a person has after finally doing something without fear is unparalleled. The techniques in this section for changing behavior can offer relief, connection, and success—and hopefully all will be more apparent in your life.

TEN

Technique #8 Control TMA (Too Much Activity)

People who have anxiety typified by tension, worry, and high-drive activity make their anxiety worse with too much activity (TMA), developing a nonstop lifestyle that they then seem unable to change. Those with a sensitive temperament who are easily overstimulated are more likely to avoid this lifestyle, recognizing the exhausting impact of TMA on their energy and attention. They suffer enormously from quantity stress, which is a typical state for those with TMA, and they especially need to manage the environment. They quickly notice how much more anxious they become when they try to do too much. However, the person with generalized anxiety—the worrier—often thrives on activity and is less likely to see its negative effects. Although people with panic disorder may also have TMA, it is the person with tension and high drive who is most likely to have TMA-related problems.

THE BRAIN AND TMA

Being unable to shift gears and let something go is the result of that "stuck" quality where the anterior cingulate cortex (ACC) is short on serotonin. Once on a track of getting something done, high-drive individuals don't seem able to decide that it can be let go. They can't see alternate ways of doing things well. This intensifies the likelihood that they will escalate their busyness rather than learning new skills such as delegation and prioritization. See Chapter 9 for a discussion of prioritizing.

The elevated norepinephrine (NE) so common to the tension and hyper-vigilance of generalized anxiety can lead to perfectionism. The need to avoid mistakes is a critical cause of TMA. In some cases, GABA, the brain's braking mechanism, may be insufficient or ineffective. This contributes to TMA as well, making it hard for the person to put things away mentally and keep things in perspective. This adds to difficulty relaxing. When GABA is not working effectively, worrying is hard to stop, and that makes perfectionism worse.

Overactivity in the basal ganglia (BG) often results in highly motivated, goal-directed behavior, and people who have that drive typically get a lot of work done in a day, no matter what the work is—washing windows, grading papers, writing computer programs, or doing a home repair project. This high activity is not just adult, work-related activity. It is seen in the elementary school child who never misses a homework assignment, the high school student with extra classes and three extracurricular activities a day, and the homemaker running a household with three busy kids and community activities that fill every spare moment. People with TMA are responding to their high-drive energy level, which can become a problem when it is not harnessed for the benefit of the anxious mind. The high activity level is probably not going to change, and people with TMA may not ever relax in the way a less driven person can, but they can change the way they direct their energy to achieve more balance, more fun, and much less anxiety.

WORK STYLE AND WORK VALUES

A high activity level is not perceived as a problem by people who are that active. Others around them may wish they would be less busy, but they themselves do not recognize a problem until something brings it home. Sometimes the feeling of being "burned out" from quantity stress will do it, as may occur when someone in their life gets sick and needs attention. The pressure from a spouse or the children to be more available may intensify, especially if the family member has a problem that requires the person's attention to solve it. If something blocks these high-drive people from working at their "normal" pace, they feel agitated, and if that interruption lasts too long, their anxiety skyrockets.

Even though they may be go-getters who get a lot done, people with high drive are easily thrown into anxiety when things don't go as planned. Harry was a good example of this. He traveled frequently for work, and he nearly always had a story about getting into trouble for loudly and rudely hounding the airline personnel when flights were delayed or canceled. He had trouble reorganizing emotionally in a way that would let him find a new solution or plan for his time. This was good evidence of a stuck anterior cingulate cortex (ACC) coupled with impulse-control problems. His prefrontal cortex could not generate enough energy to control his highly aroused limbic system when he was threatened with flight interruptions. His stuck ACC could not generate a new solution when under attack from limbic arousal without enough PFC to control it and talk him out of it. He appeared on the outside to be in a rage, and on the inside he was feeling out of control over not being able to follow a plan he had made. In that state, he couldn't soothe himself easily with some optimistic PFC talk, nor could he shift gears. Unfortunately, it took nearly getting arrested for him to put in the clutch and develop a new perspective. Only then did Harry decide he needed to take control of his anxiety.

Being forced to hold still or stop their work, whether for a brief period or a longer spell, can seriously intensify anxiety for people like Harry. Having an unexpected few hours of free time when a meeting is canceled can cause anxiety about how to use the time to their best advantage, and that stuck ACC can cause even more anxiety by preventing the person from finding a good alternative use of the time. I received a phone call one morning from a client whose office had unexpectedly closed because of a plumbing problem. My client was having a panic attack about what the right thing to do for the day was. He had so many ideas of what he ought to be doing that he couldn't even begin to choose the "best" one, and if he didn't use his time to his best advantage, he knew he would just get more anxious.

Sometimes being slowed down by injury or illness can cause anxiety to rise. If illness interrupts the flow of work, people may try to get back to work too soon and suffer relapse or even reinjure themselves, as I have seen with anxious clients trying to recuperate from a surgery or a muscle or bone injury. Holding still seems to build up pressure that is hard to release, and that pressure becomes a serious problem for health and relationships. It can raise blood pressure or blow up in bad temper, irritability, and outbursts of anger at inappropriate times or at people who don't deserve it.

HOW TO CONTROL TMA

Why would people with TMA from anxiety resist changing their behavior or activity? Because high activity diminishes anxiety. They believe that if they can just do enough, they won't have to be anxious, or they just know they don't feel anxious thoughts when they are preoccupied with the tasks that fill their days. People with TMA feel agitated when they *aren't* active, which is distressing to them both mentally and physically. When they hold still, especially when they have not planned how to use their down time, the feelings of anxiety crescendo to an overwhelming pitch. The following strategies provide ideas for controlling TMA.

Plan for Dreaded, Unexpected "Free" Time

This is a brief strategy but genuinely helpful to the overdriven TMA person. Life always produces unexpected times when people must hold still in one way or another. People who travel for work know they are going to face delays; they just don't know when those delays will occur. Or at times, social plans may be canceled, leaving an unexpected free afternoon or evening. People get sick and work meetings are put off, leaving a space of unscheduled time. Although most people long for a few extra hours in which to get things done, people with TMA can't think of what they would do if they ever had a free minute. Their anxiety spikes so fast about what to do with the "free" time that they become stuck and can't choose what to do. Then they are not only anxious about what the best choice would be (it would be a *mistake* to pick the wrong activity), but they also become anxious that the time will go by and not be well spent. Following is a good homework assignment for this situation.

1. Every time you say to yourself, at home or at work, "If I ever have a few hours (or a few minutes), I want to _____," make a note. This activity can be anything at all—take a bath, plant a garden, organize photos, clean the garage, organize your tools, reorganize your files, clean out desk drawers, and so on.

2. Transfer your note to a running list that you keep in your mobile device or the old-fashioned way on paper. Divide this list into:
   - Things that take 30 minutes
   - Things that take an hour
   - Things that take three hours
   - Things that take a day

3. Carry the list with you, and whenever you are faced with the dreaded unexpected "free" time, select something from the list that fits the available time. You will be certain that you wanted to do it, you will be able to select something quickly, and that anxiety will be relieved.

4. As you complete tasks, cross them off and add more to the list from your notes. This is *very* satisfying for people with TMA.

If you are not a TMA person yourself and are helping someone with TMA, don't underestimate how often this kind of problem—having unexpected free time—occurs and increases their anxiety. It is quite possible that the person with TMA doesn't recognize these situations for what they are. Be on the alert for hearing about them. This simple fix of planning is truly that: a simple fix for a frequent and completely manageable exacerbation of anxiety in the highly active person.

Counter Perfectionism

When people who are anxious seem like perfectionists, they often don't see themselves as such. They don't feel wedded to everything being perfect, as if order and correctness are goals in themselves. Rather, perfectionism for them is a way to ward off anxiety, and they may not realize it. They just believe that if they have done it perfectly, there is no need to feel anxious! What others see from the outside is not what is going on inside.

People with TMA try to handle anxiety by eliminating reasons to worry, and a good way to eliminate reasons to worry is to make *no* mistakes. The fewer mistakes people with TMA make, the less they feel they will have to worry. And that attempt to control mistakes becomes perfectionism. It sets them up to review their work repeatedly, double-check for errors, work extra hours, and do work themselves rather than entrust it to others. I could see it in 11-year-old Emma, who did her homework three times each evening. Her mother worried it might be obsessive-compulsive disorder. But when we delved into it, Emma was a burgeoning TMA trying to avoid anxiety about her grades by making sure her work was perfectly readable and correct, so she redid it three times and then felt relief of anxiety. Emma agreed that she would do it one time and then take a break by doing something fun for an hour. Then she would allow her mom to read the homework, and if her mom could read it, she would accept that the teacher could read it too. This relieved the anxiety that was driving the triple-checking perfectionism.

Perfectionism shows up in social ways, too. The perfectionist may monopolize a committee he or she is on or refuse to let other people handle obligations such as planning a party. Younger perfectionists may not trust others on a school project to do their share. In all these cases, the underlying impulse is to take control of a situation and get it "done right." This affects relationships with other people, who see the perfectionist as controlling.

What these perfectionists do not realize is that they are going to worry no matter how hard they work. They just find other things to worry about, and their heightened stress makes them more hypervigilant and uptight. They also overlook the consequences of working that hard: no one helps them anymore, they end up with more work, they start to believe they can do it all, and—*wham!*—their anxiety level climbs even higher. It becomes a vicious circle of looking for potential problems to avert, finding them, being convinced that they have been handled, and continuing to look for more. Perfectionists fall prey to quantity stress and may encounter a phenomenon my clients call "brain freeze." When they are in this high-drive mode, if something blocks their plan, they cannot easily figure out what to. Their ACC is not just stuck but frozen. They really need help then to put in the clutch and shift gears to a new position.

Jenny, an event planner (what a perfect job for her anxiety!), described it like this:

> When someone asks me to take on a project, I feel as if I can see the way it will go, like dominoes falling. I can see the whole outcome if it goes right, or, if one thing or another goes wrong, which way the dominoes will fall. And I can plan to avoid every one of the places where trouble could occur. That means if I am careful enough, nothing will go wrong. I like being able to anticipate trouble, so that I can know things will go perfectly and everyone will be happy about it.

When I asked why she was willing to put in this level of foresight and effort to do all the planning herself, she replied:

> If I do it, then I won't have to worry about it. If I were to let other people be responsible for parts of it, then I would worry until it was done. I would know something was going to go wrong, but I wouldn't know what it would be, and I would not be able to plan how to fix it. It is not worth the worry to let someone else do the work.

But Jenny ran into trouble one day when she wasn't able to get into the venue she was decorating. She felt as if she was frozen and unable to figure out a plan. She texted me in hysterics. I knew she had two other people who were helping with this particular event, and I suggested she call voice-to-voice to hear their ideas about how to regroup. Using the benefit of someone else's prefrontal cortex (PFC) to move her own ACC along allowed her to see the problem from their perspective, and then she readily shifted gears. I sometimes refer to this need to use mentors and helpers as utilizing an "external prefrontal cortex." We suggest this for children and adolescents quite frequently (telling them to talk to their friends, their coach, their teacher, their tutor, their favorite aunt, and so on), and I think we should use this model for adults with TMA perfectionism as standard practice.

One aspect in which this anticipatory worry and perfectionism is beneficial is that perfectionists get strong positive reinforcement for being such good workers. They get promotions and praise and awards and good grades, alleviating their worry about whether they are acceptable to others. It is a part of their lives they can feel good about. On the other hand, they develop a fear that if they ever let down their perfectionistic guard, things will completely fall apart and others will blame them entirely. (Note the extreme language. This is the way the thought process goes.) In other words, they come to believe that everyone believes mistakes are intolerable and proof of their unworthiness. This is the attitude that makes stress much more stressful.

What works to alleviate this perfectionism? Identifying it is the first step. People who have this style of handling anxiety rarely see themselves as perfectionists, so calling them "perfectionists" is not useful at first. They see themselves as "careful" or "detail-oriented." Working in therapy, it is essential to make sure that the perfectionism is not serving another unconscious, psychological function and is not the outcome of a personality disorder such as obsessive-compulsive disorder. Those conditions require psychotherapeutic interventions beyond the scope of this technique. A good psychotherapy interview, such as with coherence therapy techniques, and a personality inventory can help to determine whether or not the perfectionism has deeper psychological roots. However, when it can be determined that the perfectionism developed as a tool to ward off anxiety, it can be handled with anxiety management techniques.

Identifying Perfectionism

Identifying perfectionism is fairly straightforward. Look for clues in your language about work, family, and social responsibilities.

- Do you have a strong sense of personal responsibility for the outcome of work, social, or family activities, especially when other people could reasonably be expected to do some of the work? You will see this most easily in your major areas of responsibility. For example, if you are a student, you might see it in the way you participate in a club or committee, doing all the work for the people who are supposed to do part of the planning. If you are a homemaker, you might not rely on other family members to finish their part of the laundry or cleaning or get the trash out on time. At work, there are many ways to see this. For example, as a project manager, you might assume total responsibility for the outcome of every aspect of a project.
- Is your language full of the extremes discussed earlier? This is a major indicator that the need to be perfect is connected to managing anxiety. Note self-talk such as, "This is *terrible*." "This staff *never* does things according to the manual." "No one around here *ever* does what they say they will." "I *always* end up doing all the planning." "If I don't get this done, the whole thing will be *ruined*." These kinds of attitudes and observations reinforce the importance of being watchful about your anxiety and potential perfectionism.
- Do you have a sense of the difference between "good enough" and "perfect," and can you apply it in deciding how much to do?

Once these features are observed, go on to look for a pattern.

1. First, trace the history of this behavior. Is there a time you can remember when you didn't think so hard about outcomes?
2. Next, consider what happens to your anxiety level when something goes wrong. If your perfectionism is a way to ward off anxiety, your anxiety will go off the charts when a mistake is made.
3. Then review the consequences of your mistake/anxiety. Perfectionism develops when you resolve anxiety by determining to be

more careful in the future or to take charge of more of the details personally.

4. Is there an escalating pattern in which you feel less anxiety by taking charge of situations and doing even more work, checking things more, or spending more hours on a task? If so, you are probably using perfectionism as a way to ward off anxiety.

Intervene on Perfectionism

Step 1. *Find the negative consequences of perfectionism.* This way of avoiding anxiety can be helpful and can contribute to self-esteem, so before you eliminate perfectionism completely as a defense against anxiety, you will want to be sure it has very negative consequences. Look for consequences like:

- Being blamed (unfairly) for being controlling rather than being seen as helpful or careful
- Taking on extra work that no one asks you to do and feeling overworked
- Feeling the stress of doing the work; feeling the pressure of having no time for anything else, including time to have fun, which you firmly believe you would have if you could only find the time to stop working
- A lack of pleasure and fun, even at activities that should be fun, due to feeling so responsible for the outcome of the activity
- Feeling completely exhausted and not knowing how or when you will recover
- Failing to prevent your anxiety

The last item is an especially important point. You would not be trying to control anxiety if your perfectionism was working well to manage your anxiety. Why not work less and figure out another way to let go of anxiety?

The belief that getting rid of extreme perfectionism is going to help anxiety levels in the long run must be reinforced. Learning to handle anxiety symptoms with other techniques will be reassuring and will reinforce your willingness to change the pattern.

Step 2. *Look for procrastination as a cover for perfectionism and set boundaries on the time utilized.* Some with TMA perfectionism don't start projects until they can do them perfectly. Some will simply not try: "I won't go to baking class because I don't know how to bake," or, "I won't go to the ice-skating birthday party because I have to take skating lessons first." Others plan to do it—later—when they have time to do it right. This is often seen regarding household projects. And many say, "I work best under pressure," limiting the amount of time their perfectionism can suck up by limiting the amount of time they have available at all. They feel stressed, worrying if they will finally press the deadline too close, but since they have practiced procrastinating this way, they mostly get away with this. If this is the case for you, it may be necessary to learn to anticipate the necessary amount of time and hold yourself accountable. This is another place where borrowing an "external prefrontal cortex" (someone who can give advice about how much time to spend) could really help.

An ironic outcome of this perfectionism-covering procrastination is that your environment may reflect chaos as you wait to have enough time to organize perfectly. When the world around you is untidy or disorganized to the extent that it gets in the way of your feeling good or being efficient, some organizational help is in order. Think about your environment and its impact on you to decide the right path out of it. Usually, clearing spaces in small steps can be the best process. You may need to hire an organizer for your work or home space. But there are also books and other resources that can help. Currently popular websites are www.flylady.net and www.tidyingup.com. I am not advocating that you purchase their products but just offering an idea of where to start if organizing your environment is a stress management skill you need in your life.

Step 3. *Stop using "all/never" language.* A slogan for anxious perfectionists should be "Perfection is impossible." You can follow this with the reminder that "If something is really impossible, then I have no obligation to try for it."

Step 4. *Plan for nonperfection.* Actually, planning a nonperfect performance of some responsibilities works better than noticing accidental imperfection. It won't be quite as anxiety-provoking because you will be doing it on purpose, and you will have made sure you can tolerate the outcome. Instructions for planning for nonperfection include:

- Decide not to take on a specific, one-time responsibility, and see whether the work gets done without you. Ask yourself in all seriousness, "How important is this?" Start small, but pick something you otherwise might have agreed to do, such as mowing the lawn for someone who says he is too busy, babysitting the grandkids, writing a report when someone else could do it, or covering someone else's shift. The goal here is to see whether the work gets done even if you don't do it and to recognize that someone else's urgency doesn't necessarily constitute importance. You may well find that when you hold back, someone else will step up. Or, if the work doesn't get done, it doesn't seem to end the world.

- Observe and evaluate how people respond to the imperfect work of others.

- Go ahead and assume some responsibility, but don't do what others are supposed to be responsible for. Observe the outcome in the attitudes of others and in your own anxiety level.

- Plan to not finish some work that you would otherwise have knocked yourself out to do. Miss a deadline by a little bit, or just don't do something at all. You may have to get advice on what you can let go, but when you identify that, do it. The kinds of situations that serve as good practice are usually minor in the eyes of others—for example, don't go out to buy the right napkins for the party; use paper towels. Or, ask if you can have a one-day extension on a project, and see what the boss or the teacher says. Or, don't prepare the agenda in writing before the staff meeting. These kinds of details that you formerly believed were major will turn out to be inconsequential most of the time.

- Mindfully observe how others react. You may note that they don't express the expected distress because you weren't perfect.

- Note that when something goes wrong unexpectedly, people (including yourself) usually cope pretty well with it.
- Finally, take note of what makes the difference between important and inconsequential things. This evaluative step will help you to make future decisions about what you can drop and what is essential. Your vision has become unclear about such distinctions and needs practice to clear it up.

Again, the way to identify perfectionism is to:

1. Look at the things you try to do perfectly and listen to the language you use. Identify the language of extremes—"always" and "never" language.
2. When procrastination is used to limit perfectionism, identify how it shows up.
3. Find the pattern of perfectionism in your work style.

To counter perfectionism, including perfectionism disguised as procrastination:

1. Identify the negative consequences of perfectionism.
2. Limit time spent on tasks.
3. Utilize an "external prefrontal cortex" to plan your time.
4. Use helpers to organize your environment.
5. Start to change the language of extremes.
6. Plan for nonperfection.
7. Pay attention to outcomes so you learn to distinguish *importance* from *urgency* and *consequential* from *inconsequential*. This will help you better evaluate your perfection tendencies.

ACHIEVE BALANCE

Balance in life is three-pronged: achieving emotional, physical, and mental health. People with TMA may get out of balance unintentionally but be unable to correct it. For example, someone might put all her effort into a hobby that becomes obsessive, like creating crafts to sell at a spring fair. Another might pour all his effort into participating in his children's activities, and still another might become so focused on her career that she gives up all social activity to spend more time at the office.

Getting out of balance can sneak up on a person. Often, one part of life assumes significance over other parts for good reason. It could be reasonable to work at your job 12 hours a day during a circumscribed period of time when, for example, you are preparing to sell your company or get your agency ready for inspection. It makes sense that someone could devote most evenings in a single year to finishing his academic career in night school.

However, shifting back to balanced activity can be a problem for the TMA person who gets used to the workload and keeps on doing it. These people easily continue on the trajectory they set while other aspects of their life fade from awareness. How often have you heard someone say, "I know I should exercise and take care of my health, but . . . ," or, "I know I *should* spend more time with my kids, but . . . ," or, "I know it would be *better* if I took time for myself every day, but . . . " These kinds of statements indicate the tension of being out of balance—of behaving in contradiction to personal values. The TMA person easily forgets that high activity is not a value in and of itself.

Identify Your Time-Related Values

The discussion of the values by which a person lives is hard to initiate. In our culture, there isn't much conversation about this, but people do live by their values even when they have not articulated those values to themselves. One way to start examining balance in life and whether it reflects your values is just to ask, "What do I do with my time?" This examination of values entails a major attitude adjustment and involves one of the four arenas of management (see Chapter 6) that reduce the impact of stress on individuals.

TMA people can be very, very good at thinking they are balanced enough, even when the significant others in their lives disagree. Keeping an objective, measurable record can end the debate by providing facts.

1. Keep track of what you are doing with your time for at least a week, every day, and if the week is not representative of your life, for two weeks.

2. Make a chart. Divide your week into hours with 15-minute time slots in each day. Fill in the chart each day—not at the end of the week—to keep from fooling yourself. Figure 10.1 shows a partially filled out example of this chart. It includes 16 hours, with the assumption of 8 hours of sleeping time.

3. List every activity. Include everything from personal hygiene, watching television, and eating to a breakdown of activities at work.

4. Total up the amount of time spent on each activity in minutes or hours and assign categories to each, like work, children, social life, etc.

5. Based on the time totals from the chart, create a pie chart like the one in Figure 10.2.

Evaluate Whether Your Use of Time Fits Your Values

What proportion of time for each activity makes sense? Is it sensible to spend eight hours at the office, two hours commuting, and six hours divided among the other parts of your life? What portion of the six hours should each of those other activities get? Making these decisions can be easy, but it can be confusing to know where to begin making changes. The least anxiety-provoking way to begin altering the balance of time is to increase time for something that you want very much to do and to take time away from something that matters very little.

How you spend your time reflects the choices you make, but it also may be in direct contradiction to what you *want* to do with your time. The biggest TMA problem is committing to activities that take away from other things that are more important. The activities may be fine in themselves, but

	Monday	Tuesday	Wednesday	Thursday	Friday	Saturday	Sunday
Hour 1	15 min bkfst 45 min shwr						
Hour 2	45 commute 15 min email						
Hour 3	15 min email 45 meetings						
Hour 4	60 meeting						
Hour 5	30 return calls 15 talk with colleague 15 got a snack						
Hour 6							
Hour 7							
Hour 8							
Hour 9							
Hour 10							
Hour 11							
Hour 12							
Hour 13							
Hour 14							
Hour 15							
Hour 16							

Figure 10.1 Keep Track of Your Time

when you commit to them without conscious intention, you may end up doing things you don't want to do while missing what is best for you. If you say yes to 10 hours a week of volunteer activity, that could be a wonderful thing, but what if it is half of your available time to spend with your children? This is when looking at your values can help.

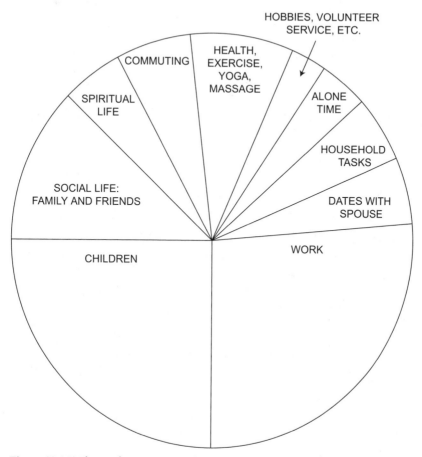

Figure 10.2 Is There Balance In Your Life?

Examine Your Values

Your values are the considerations most important to you when you make decisions. Several methods exist for looking at values. Learning what is important to you, or "values clarification" (Simon, Howe, & Kirschenbaum, 1995), can be done by thinking about how you make choices in specific situations. To understand how your values affect your decisions—in any situation in which you have a choice to make—try the following exercise:

1. Identify the situation. It could be taking a new job, buying a house, or going to school, for example.

2. Make a list of every important aspect of the situation that will affect your decision. These may be things like commute, family time, hobby time, spouse time, time to volunteer, money, and so on. Don't forget less tangible aspects such as intellectual stimulation, pride, a chance for making business connections, and using your skills.

3. Sort the list. Establish a hierarchy of which items are most significant. Sometimes you can just number your list because it's easy to see what is important, but sometimes it's not so clear. You can clarify your values by comparing one value at a time to each of the other values on your list and deciding if each of the others is more or less important. You can do this very tangibly by writing down each value on a separate piece of paper or index card. Then, select one value—"money," for example—and go through the cards for the others. Whenever you come to a value that is less important than money, put the card under the money card. You will be left with a stack of cards with considerations more important than money. Then compare again against a consideration from the "more important" pile. That card goes on top of money.

4. Let's say you selected "time with spouse" as more important than money. You then compare, deciding which considerations are more or less important than time with spouse. Repeat this process until all the "more important" considerations have been compared and put in order. Your stack of cards will now have shifted and will be in order of importance from high to low.

5. Now you can review the decision you have to make by going through your values and seeing how the decision will reflect what is important to you.

6. The ideal outcome of reflecting on what is important is that you will be able to answer these two questions:

- What qualities of life make it worth living?
- What is the value of work, leisure, and family/social activity?

The person with TMA typically is out of balance with work or tasks and spends too little time on the things that make life worth living. Recognizing how you are actually spending your time, and whether or not you are in balance with what is most important to you, you might find the fight to spend less time at work less anxiety-provoking.

Being busy may just be the way your brain is made. Your high drive—both your cognitive and physical energy—is affected by levels of norepinephrine, dopamine, and glutamate and the ways those are active even when you're not stressed out. Even if you work a little less, you are likely to be just as active, but the added activities should create some balance in your life. Remember, the goal of balance is for overall well-being. You may even discover what efficiency experts have proven—that taking breaks to relax can help you be even more productive.

Again, to achieve balance in your life:

1. Make a record of what you do with your time.
2. Examine your actual use of time.
3. Examine your values and how your time use reflects your values.
4. Add time for the thing you most want/need/wish to do, and take some time away from what you least enjoy or what is least important.
5. Evaluate how the change feels after a few weeks, and rebalance again if necessary to achieve well-being.

REDIRECT TMA TO HAVE SOME FUN

All the focus on perfectionism and the tendency to get out of balance causes people with TMA to be overworked and underrelaxed. When worriers are so preoccupied with preventing bad things from happening or making sure everyone else is okay, they don't enjoy the relaxation they could get during their leisure time. They think that maybe they could have fun if there were a time when everything else was done and fun wouldn't mean missing any work. They don't direct their high activity to their own benefit by using it for balance, rejuvenation, or relaxation. Rather, they just use their energy as a counterweight to worry.

One client of mine, Betty, described it well. Although she said she liked to entertain, she also said she could never remember much about what happened at a party because she was so busy checking food and beverages and being alert to guests who needed to be drawn into a conversation or activity. She was a nonstop perfect hostess, and her parties were a great success. She realized the only part she really liked was the knowledge that people enjoyed her hospitality. Her "fun" was hearing from guests about what they enjoyed as they thanked her for the invitation. The rest of it was work. This was classic TMA—too much work related to the activity blotted out the fun.

Laughter Is a Good Start

Laughing is a great way to increase good feelings while discharging physical energy. Remember how you felt the last time you laughed hard and long? You might have held your stomach and breathed, feeling tired yet energized from the pleasant expenditure of energy. Fun and laughter are vital to building a life that is worth living (Berk & Tan, 1989; Sobel & Ornstein, 1996). Humor activates your reward pathway and just makes you feel better (Mobbs, D., Greicius, M., Abdel-Azim, E., Menon, V., & Reiss, A., 2003). The problem for people with TMA is that constantly being on the lookout for mistakes (NE-driven vigilance) and their solutions causes them to gradually take everyday life so seriously that they stop experiencing the humor in it. Their time is spent watching for potential problems rather than for potential delight. They become so accustomed to worrying that they can barely recall any other mental attitude.

If you recognize yourself in this scenario, take the time to remember what life was like before you were consumed with worry. Re-creating fun and getting relief with laughter will be serious therapy for you. Ask, "What makes me laugh?" Time with friends playing board games? Going to a slapstick movie? Hearing a comedian? Playing with a small child? Make a plan to do whatever it takes to get that laugh.

Find Relaxation and Fun in Small Things

The rebalancing that fun stimulates can start with small things that give pleasure. But often those with TMA think too hard about whether there is time to do these small things, or whether they will lead to trouble. Will it cost too much money? Will it inconvenience someone? Could something productive be done instead? (Hear the perfectionist-minded attempt to prevent anxiety in these questions?) At times, rebalancing can be as simple as following a wish to do something without first considering who else needs to be taken care of.

A favorite story of mine about how a small thing can help someone get a sense of balance—and how taking just a small time-out can provide relief—came out of a homework assignment I gave a client named Anna. Anna was a perfectionist and hard-working woman. I instructed her to do one thing she wanted to do over the weekend that involved *no work whatsoever*—she was to do it just because she felt like it at the moment. In other words, it was to be something just for fun. She was not to turn it into a family outing or do anything that required her to work first, like invite the neighbors for a barbecue. When she came back the next week to report on the outcome of that activity, she was still smiling. In the middle of her errands, she thought an ice cream cone would really taste good. It was, after all, a homework assignment. She pulled her car into the nearest ice cream store, did not call home to see if anyone there wanted a cone, ordered her favorite flavor, and stayed there to eat it, tasting every bite, before she continued with her errands.

Being immersed in eating the cone was delightful to her, and to her amazement, no one got mad or hurt or felt upset because she did it. It was just fun. Her good mood lasted and made other parts of her day better. She reflected that balance for her was not necessarily about taking a *lot* of time, but about the *quality* of the time. That gave her pause to think about how often she denied herself the moments that would make life more worth living. She commented on how often she wouldn't take 10 minutes to watch the sun set, or enjoy her coffee with a few minutes of reading, because she felt pressure to keep moving. She resolved to keep trying to take a few minutes for small fun, knowing the effect on her mood for the rest of the day would be entirely worth it.

Busy Fun Is Still Fun

People with TMA will probably never embrace the lie-in-the-hammock version of time off. For them, balance is usually better found in busy activity, as long as doing the activity is not a way to avoid anxiety but a way to use some energy in a fun way. Whether it is a day of gardening, a 40-mile bike ride, or hitting every garage sale in town on a Saturday morning, high-energy people usually want their fun time to be busy, not leisurely. Discharging energy is good for TMA people. The high energy level needs to be discharged, and using it for active nonwork activities is beneficial for anxiety relief and for calming the stress response. That said, the person with TMA needs to distinguish between the pleasure of accomplishment and pleasure just for the sake of pleasure. The actual *doing* of the activity—not just accomplishing it—should be pleasurable.

Pay Attention to Whether Fun Feels Like Fun

Preoccupation with worry causes people not to notice fun when they are having it. Their minds are in the future or the past but not in the moment. Not paying attention to fun robs it of its usefulness. Over time, you can get totally out of touch with what you enjoy. Your thoughts about doing something for fun may go something like, "Oh, I *have to go* out to dinner with my best friend," or, "Oh, no, Friday is the night I *have to go* to the ballgame." Again, the emphasis should be on figuring out what is *pleasurable*.

When you pick what side of the fence an activity falls on—*pleasurable* or *unpleasurable*—don't use all the caveats that rob activities of fun. For example, if you played games with the family on a Friday night and have to choose whether the experience was pleasurable or unpleasurable, you can't say, "Well, it *would have been pleasurable* if I had done better." If you are forced to pick, the statement becomes, "It was pleasurable." If you have to go on to modify the pleasure, use the word "and"—for example, "It was pleasurable, *and* I wanted to do better." Then you can examine more readily how you are interrupting your pleasure and how you can change that interrupting.

Noticing pleasure and positive experiences is a huge challenge for over-active people who are vigilantly looking out for mistakes in what they do. Their difficulty in shifting their thoughts away from worry and their on-the-go-no-time-to-stop-to-reflect activity level interfere with noticing pleasure. But you can learn to pay attention to what pleasure feels like—first by exploring it in retrospect and then by paying attention on purpose when it happens. This requires some brain power—you must use your prefrontal cortex to make a decision to turn off your vigilance and deliberately shift the gears of your ACC, and then consciously block the resulting anxiety. It also requires energy from the prefrontal cortex to hold your attention. If those things are just too hard to accomplish, you will first need to acquire mental tools to interfere with preoccupation and then come back to exploring positive experiences.

Pay attention to activities you do during the week that are not work related and should be fun. Right after doing them, decide if the activity was pleasurable or unpleasurable. Then write, draw, or talk with someone about how the fun felt. Talking about what was pleasurable will expand the experience of pleasure and make it easier to find similar opportunities to have fun.

Positive psychology researchers have demonstrated that enhancing positive experiences is a necessary part of recovering from anxiety. Barbara Fredrickson (2001, 2009, 2013), a prolific researcher and valuable contributor to the field of positive psychology, has researched the impact of positive emotions. She has described how to increase the benefit of positive experiences by careful attention to the experience and rehearsing it mentally. She calls this "broaden and build." This method helps people fully appreciate what positive activity does for their entire self and teaches them how to bring more balance into their lives when they are short on fun and relaxation. In short, the method entails recalling a positive situation, event, or interaction in full detail, remembering the feeling from each of the senses. Next, you repeat the experience or create a similar experience. Then you notice how the new experience is similar or different from the previous positive experience. This can build upon the positive experience and cause you to be on the lookout for other positive experiences.

In sum:

1. Find opportunities to laugh. It is a great way to discharge tension.
2. Follow an impulse to do something small just because it is fun.
3. Notice whether the quality of the fun activity affects how balanced you feel or how much anxiety you feel about other parts of your day.
4. Look for fun activities that require physical energy output.
5. Identify what is pleasurable or unpleasurable and pay attention to pleasurable experiences.
6. Expand your awareness of positive experiences with the intentional recollecting and reexperiencing of a similar event.

TMA AT DIFFERENT AGES AND IN SPECIAL CIRCUMSTANCES

These methods to counter TMA can be used at all ages and with good success. Even though TMA seems to be more of a problem for adults in their working years, a few comments about other ages are useful.

We don't often worry about children being too busy, especially whether they are too busy to relax. Therefore, it should be a warning sign when you encounter a child who is very tense and who is constantly busy. First, look for whether the parents (or you, if you are the parent) have set up too much activity because of their own anxiety about not giving their kids the advantage of doing every activity humanly possible during their childhood. These are children who are going to become anxious, who will not learn self-soothing because they don't sit still long enough to calm themselves, and who are going to hardwire their brains to need constant stimulation. Later in life, they will have great difficulty finding balance.

We don't often worry about children being able to have fun, but when you encounter a child who is very tense, it is wise to look for reasons at home, such as abuse in their household or some other family secret that keeps them vigilant. Also, there might be other mental health reasons, such as obsessive-compulsive disorder. However, children and adolescents may be troubled by *specific* anxiety about their social skills. Children are not good reporters of how they are getting along with others. They may do very well one-on-one with a peer but not be able to handle the stimulation or pressure of group activities. They may fear being teased for poor performance and stay out of activities that would otherwise be fun. Contact teachers about how they do when they are in class or free time to assess their ability to have some fun.

Adolescents who are tense and not relaxing may have anxiety that keeps them perfectionistic or guarded against mistakes. Also, any teen with social anxiety is in rough territory when at school. Their peers are very hard on them, and they have very little power to control classroom demands for public performance. With adolescents, looking for the causes of this tension is essential, because there is no way for them to relax and have fun if they can't escape peer or authority situations that keep them tense. In these cases, anxiety management involves specific problem-solving geared toward interactions with peers or classroom demands.

Sometimes the teen with high drive from basal ganglia overactivity will be busy every moment with optional activities but not really relaxing while participating in sports or clubs or extracurricular activities. Help them get into activities that they do not direct (they tend to be team captains or club presidents) and that are pleasurable but not graded or scored, such as bike riding, to open the door to the stress relief of active fun.

Elderly adults usually have the fewest demands for performance, but as people with TMA age, they may face problems in managing their anxiety when their activity is limited by health and mobility. Knowing one's purpose in life can be a great benefit in choosing how to stay active as levels of energy and mobility change (Alim et al., 2008).

Aging TMAs may not recognize the connection between slowing down and their anxiety revving up. They may need help to see that connection if they want to correct the anxiety level. Plans may be very pragmatic. A study with tremendous implications for dealing with changing life circumstances—

such as when TMAs retire or, at any age, are forced to slow down—had to do with how to make life more meaningful by creating routines and patterns (Heintzelman, Trent, & King, 2015). It might be as simple as keeping an office tidy or scheduling a regular dinner with friends or watching a favorite program at regular times. Going to synagogue, church, or mosque or a regular book study can contribute to creating a sense of meaning and purpose in life—a counteracting force to the anxiety of a TMA who is not as active as previously. But learning to consistently plan to participate in enjoyable activities counteracts the depression that may emerge when TMAs cannot be as active as they have been (Catalino, 2015). In fact, a skill for all TMAs may be to learn to find alternative ways to be happy. If you want to be happier in general, it is important to look at your choices. When you can't have what you want, rather than settling for the second best option, pick something entirely different (Huh, Vosgerau & Morewedge, 2016). That might mean that if your knees won't let you continue to run marathons, continue to get exercise, of course, but maybe all that extra time you spent training could be spent volunteering to push children's wheelchairs on a hospital unit.

When people are aging, it is important to take mobility, declining faculties, and changes in social structure very seriously as underlying causes of anxiety and then plan to manage those. For example, a newfound problem with vision could be an obstacle to playing cards or reading or driving to activities. Such a problem can cause anxiety to skyrocket, and advice about how to cope with it may be needed. This would be a good opportunity to transfer worry to organizations that help. For example, associations for vision-impaired individuals have many ideas for coping with vision loss, and occupational therapists may have ideas for the assists that will get a person with temporary or permanent impairments in mobility out and about.

A final caveat about handling TMA is to remember that there are people whose time off of work is also work. Some people work two jobs, so time without work is minimal. People who work a job and then come home to work for six more hours (cooking, cleaning, caring for children or elderly parents, etc.) are not going to have time to relax or have fun to relieve TMA. They suffer burnout from too much work. They need relief, but careful thought must precede changes to get the most self-care and balance back into their lives. This may involve finding connections to social services that could help them. It may involve problem-solving to make their work hours more efficient or their minimal relaxation time more useful. All of the options cannot be identified here, but practical support can often be a great anxiety and worry reliever, and help from mental health practitioners at this practical level can be very powerful.

CONCLUSION

Finding every practical and delightful measure to reduce the impact of TMA and get some relief requires people to value their leisure as restorative and productive. The mind and body that have had time to play will be more productive and creative. Remember this as you begin to manage your anxious behavior and direct your energy to fun and relaxation.

ELEVEN

Technique #9

Talk Yourself Into Changing Behavior

This technique reflects how changing your mind and changing your behavior go hand-in-glove. A great deal of the behavior of anxiety is avoidance behavior. People with panic avoid situations in which they might panic, and if they can avoid them, they may feel fairly comfortable. The most obvious avoidance is that of the person with blushing, quaking body symptoms who tries to avoid being observed. These people talk themselves into feeling anxious when others are observing them. And this is no surprise; it's brain function that leads people to overestimate how anxious they will feel in these situations and how avoidance will help. This avoidance can also manifest as mental avoidance, whereby worriers try to avoid their worried thoughts.

Managing your anxious mind depends on changing your self-talk, which is how the anxious mind creates anxious behavior. Change your anxious mind with more positive self-talk, and you'll change your anxious behavior.

DON'T DELAY SEEKING HELP

People with social anxiety suffer from some of the worst problems with avoidance. Children with this type of anxiety may hold themselves back from achieving in social and academic ways because they will not put themselves in positions where others might observe them and they might fail (Eisen, Kearney, & Schaefer, 1995). One client told me that when he was a boy, he couldn't even go through the grocery store line with a gallon of milk without suffering; he blushed, sweated, and trembled at having to speak to the cashier, give money, and take change. He would avoid every situation in which people looked at him. As a small child, he hid behind his mother. As he got older, he stayed quiet in school, had one friend at a time, and didn't participate in any activity that required him to talk. His talent for and love of sports eventually took him into the spotlight in the comfort of being part of a team, and he gradually improved his ability to tolerate being looked at. He believes that without the desensitizing impact of his sports activities, he never would have developed the courage to go away to college and achieve the level of success he did. There can't be a better reason for people who suffer from this kind of anxiety to get help as soon as possible to achieve their full potential socially, educationally, and financially.

CHANGE YOUR SELF-TALK

The problems of social anxiety are the most important ones to address with changes in self-talk. Self-talk isn't necessarily ruminative like worry, and it isn't much like the fear of being afraid, as in a panic attack; rather, it has the quality of stating truth. People believe that what they say to themselves is true. Because they have probably been shy as children (Eisen, Kearney & Schaefer, 1995) their self-talk reflects beliefs that a social situation is cause for fear (Gazzaniga, 2012). This fear reinforces the need to continue avoiding. "If people see that I look nervous, they will laugh at me. Therefore, I will avoid having people see me." The outcome of negative experience is learning negative self-appraisal.

Alternately, having a rewarding experience and recognizing it as such leads to willingness to repeat that effort (Anderman & Gray, 2015). The neurological basis of that is in the reward pathway. When an intention to act (glutamate is involved) results in a positive outcome (dopamine is released), motivation follows. The goal of treatment is to encourage intentional, attainable goals that will result in success and thus increase motivation. Thus, the two therapy goals—to decrease fear and increase motivation—can be prepared for with self-talk.

THE PRECURSOR TO CHANGE:
GET EDUCATED ABOUT ANXIETY

Changing your behavior starts with the conviction that behavior change is necessary to accomplish being less afraid and more able to cope with social circumstances. Even though it will be necessary to practice in real-life situations, there are some mental changes that come first. To put that effort forth, people need to believe their effort will pay off.

Education can be obtained by reading (reading this book, for instance!) or by working with others in a group setting, like a clinic or self-help group. It can also be provided to individuals in psychotherapy or other kinds of settings. Education is an essential component of therapy because it creates the willingness to practice the self-talk strategies. People with panic symptoms benefit from knowing that they are not alone; that they are not dying, going crazy, or losing control; and that methods to calm their anxious body really work. People who worry too much need to learn that persistence in stopping worry will lead to less worry. And people with social fears must learn that their fear is caused by their *imagination* about the outcome of an interaction with someone else.

Psychoeducation teaches people *how* changing their behavior works to change the way they feel. The most important component of this is memory reconsolidation. Research during the last several years (Dahlitz & Hall, 2015; Kredlow & Otto, 2015; Oyarzun et al., 2012; Phelps, 2010; Phelps, Delgado, Nearing & Ledoux, 2004; Schiller et al., 2010; Schiller, Raio, & Phelps, 2012) has brought important information to light about how to change your behavior in order to change how you feel so that you can diminish or eliminate your panic and social anxiety.

MEMORY RECONSOLIDATION

It was once thought that memory could be extinguished—that if it were not retrieved, it would disappear. We discussed in several chapters how the brain can erase the traces of worry when worry highways are traveled less. Changing memory is different. Memory may fade, but when circumstances are again similar, it will reemerge (Chhatwal, Stanek-Rattiner, Davis, & Ressler, 2006), often with as strong a feeling attached to it as previously—and that is a real problem when a person has memories of panic or humiliation that reemerge in particular social or performance situations.

When a bad experience occurs, a person may mark it so strongly in his or her amygdala that whenever the situation is similar, that bad memory reemerges. It is now clear that bad memories can be changed by a process called reconsolidation. When you want to change the bad memory, the best way to do it is to bring it back on purpose by reentering a similar situation prepared to succeed. The two situations are then woven together, changing the memory.

For example, if a student is humiliated in front of a classroom when giving a speech, the memory of humiliation is consolidated with all the specifics, including how her body felt. It is likely that the student will remember and feel the same humiliation the next time she has to stand in front of the class. This may generalize to every time she feels she is being observed and judged in school—even just in answering questions aloud. The memory affects her; she become more vigilant to the potential for failure, and this, in addition to the activation of fear she experiences when exposed to that threat, interferes with her performing such tasks successfully.

So how does a consolidated memory change? It must be evoked in order to be changed. Reconsolidation requires that the memory be active, including the affective and cognitive aspects of it, and then the person must have a "mismatch," that is, a positive outcome that is the opposite of the prior failure to succeed (Ecker, Ticic, & Hulley, 2012). So, for the student who was humiliated in class to change the outcome of speaking publicly from negative to positive, she needs to have a success in speaking. The situation must be similar to the first one—giving a speech or a report in front of the class—so that the whole sense of the experience is likely to occur. The hippocampus will help retrieve the memory and the details of it. The insula will help create the physical sensations that were occurring, prompted by the amygdala recognizing the danger for humiliation. And the prefrontal cortex will have thoughts about the prior experience, including fearful thoughts of whether it could happen again. That is the affective arousal—the memory of the event—just as it was when the first humiliation occurred.

For that memory of the original scene to become malleable—that is, able to be reconsolidated—there is a time element. To be changed, the memory must be activated for at least 10 minutes but not more than six hours. And within that six-hour window, if there is a mismatch—a success even in the face of the prior outcome—the memory is changed at the cellular level. It is *reconsolidated* with the new information, "I succeeded!" Then, if the student rehearses the positive outcome—she validates the success and can benefit from others noticing and validating it too—it will ensure the best outcome of the reconsolidation.

This student needs three abilities to pull off memory reconsolidation: she has to be calm, competent, and confident. Competence and confidence will be discussed in Chapter 12, but here we will take on the first necessary condition to pull off a successful memory reconsolidation: calm. Calm is necessarily about physical calm but is also about thinking calmly.

WHAT ARE YOU TELLING YOURSELF?

To do any exposure to a feared situation, you want to be sure that you can breathe to calm down and relax your body. That means learning those skills first. But changing self-talk is a part of getting calm enough to pull off an exposure. It will take some time to accept the idea that fear is unnecessary. People trying to change their anxious behavior need to develop new self-talk that will help them try something new. They need to believe that their anxious bodies are *unnecessarily* trying to protect them. They will have to commit to ignoring their body by changing the way they talk to themselves about their fear. And they will also need to:

- Learn to tolerate uncomfortable sensations
- Take control of their negative self-talk

- Act in direct opposition to their false beliefs
- Practice repeatedly so that their amygdala can relearn anxiety cues

Again, making an intellectual decision to try to overcome emotional reactions uses the executive decision-making power of the left prefrontal cortex (PFC) to override the emotional demand of the limbic system. If people with social fears believe the explanation of how they became anxious and how they can control it, they will be more likely to plan and carry out exposures (practice sessions) even though they may be uncomfortable. The exposures for memory reconsolidation sessions are the ultimate goal, because they allow the amygdala to relearn what to react to and get comfortable doing it. By going out in real life prepared to succeed, the goal of calming the amygdala and the limbic system is achieved.

Remember:

- Anxiety symptoms are usually not happening because of any real risk. It is biochemistry.
- Panic, worry, and social fears can be changed by changing thoughts and behaviors.
- Social anxiety is not specifically fear of danger, but rather fear of exposure (the fear that others will observe you looking embarrassed). It is the autonomic response to being exposed with a risk of humiliation. All of that is the result of negative self-talk.
- Changing self-talk and beliefs is a key component of changing behavior. Beliefs drive action.
- Practicing new behavior to achieve memory reconsolidation is the ultimate way to change the anxious brain.

FIND THE SELF-TALK

Beliefs about the self, the world, and other people are reflected in the choices people make, and their impact is revealed in self-talk—that internal dialogue of which many are unaware. Every small thought that creates anxiety must be identified and corrected.

Ask Your Yourself, "So What?"

People can be unaware of how they talk to themselves in self-sabotaging ways. To hear your own voice, start out by being a detective in your own life. As you go through experiences, try to notice exactly what happens and what you are saying to yourself. Then write those observations down. You will be more likely to find your internal dialogue if you start by noticing times when you are uncomfortable and then writing down *what* is making you uncomfortable. For example, if you have to speak up at a work meeting, you might write, "I am sitting in the meeting, knowing I have to read this short report. My heart is pounding because I know I have to speak. I can feel the heat in my face, and I am afraid of my voice shaking when I have to speak." Then ask yourself, "So what? So what if my heart pounds or my face reddens?" This question will reveal your inner dialogue. The answer might be, "So what? I could look stupid! People will think I don't know what I'm doing because my voice is shaky. Or they might look away and my nervousness could make them uncomfortable, so they won't like me."

Use the Three-Column Method

Sometimes people are aware of what they are saying to themselves, and they know they keep up a negative inner dialogue that stops them from trying things. The task here is to identify situations in which you are holding yourself back and to identify the entire list of negative thoughts you might produce about the situation. This two-column list can then be expanded into three columns to counter the negative self-talk.

First, start by making three columns on a piece of paper. In the first column, put down the goals, actions, or intentions that raise anxiety. In the second column, write down your first thought about the situation. If this thought is negative, think about the impact of such negativity on achieving your goal or intention. The third column will be completed as you plan the direction of change for your self-talk.

Figure 11.1 shows how this worked for Guy, a 22-year-old who wanted to go back to college after he had dropped out due to anxiety. He knew he

Goals, Actions, Intentions That Raise Anxiety	First Thought	Opposite of First Thought
Start school in 6 weeks	I may not be able to meet that timeline. I always miss deadlines.	
Talk to admissions about getting credits accepted	I don't know where to go and I don't know who to talk to there. It might not even be worth it—I bet they won't transfer credits from the junior college.	

Figure 11.1 Finding Self-Talk With the Three-Column Method

had the intelligence to go to school, and it bothered him that he was working in a gas station when he could be in school. First, he listed his intentions:

- I want to start school again in six weeks.
- I want to talk to the admissions office about getting all of my other credits accepted.
- I want to be able to talk to other students about the classes.
- I want to attend every class and not leave at any time due to nervousness.
- I want to finish school completely in two and a half years.

Then he began to fill these intentions into the chart, and as he thought about each, he wrote in his first reaction, planning to talk about his reactions in therapy before he filled out the third column.

By writing down his reactions, Guy began to reveal his negative self-talk. This was the first step in figuring out how to challenge this self-talk (discussed later in this chapter).

Use the "A" and "B" Parts of the ABCD Method

Another way of identifying your inner dialogue is to use the ABCD method, created by psychologist Albert Ellis. The "A" and "B" parts of this method are the ones pertinent to the discussion here. (To see the whole method, read

The Practice of Rational Emotive Therapy by Windy Dryden and Albert Ellis, 1987, pp. 52–53). The "A" and "B" parts of Ellis's method stand for the *activating* event and the *belief* that a person holds about himself, others, and the situation.

A: The activating event. Describe the situation that contributed to the anxiety. (In Guy's case, this was deciding to go back to school and asking the admissions office about getting his credits from the junior college accepted.)

B: The belief a person holds about:

- himself (like Guy saying to himself, "I have never managed this before, and I probably won't be able to do it now")
- others ("The admissions people will see me as a failure and won't be interested in helping me")
- the situation ("I shouldn't get my hopes up because college works out better for other people than it does for me")

Try to especially notice beliefs that start with:

- "should" ("I/You should . . .")
- "must" ("I/You must . . .")
- "have to" ("I/You have to . . .")
- "It would be awful if . . ."

These are essentially *demands* that people make on themselves or others, whether they realize it or not. People with social anxiety become more aware than most people about the little rules they set for themselves to make situations safe or to reassure themselves that they followed the rules. Then they can feel less perturbed about how they performed or how they met expectations.

To recap, the best way to identify your negative self-talk is to:

1. Ask yourself, "So what?" and then list the answers to that question.
2. Use the first two columns of the three-column list for identifying negative thoughts about specific situations.

3. Use the ABCD approach.

4. Try not to reinforce the beliefs. Rather, go on to discuss and counter the negative self-talk that you identify.

CHALLENGE THE NEGATIVE SELF-TALK

It is logical to think that the minute you find a negative, you can apply a positive to counteract to it. However, this doesn't always work in practice. Finding the negative self-talk can be harder than one would think; therefore, just getting as far as finding the self-talk might be a reasonable goal for someone who is not always able to self-appraise.

It is also important to note here that changing self-talk engages your negative internal dialogue directly rather than trying to stop or contain the resulting behavior. (See Chapters 7 through 9 for techniques for addressing panic and worry.) Changing self-talk is not about ignoring it, stopping it, or putting it aside. It is about getting a very clear picture of the negative aspects of it and then deliberately changing it whenever it shows up in your inner dialogue.

Challenging negative self-talk is a part of the process needed to change the sensitivity of the amygdala. That sensitivity, which sets off anxiety in social situations, can only be relaxed via new experiences that are well tolerated. Without challenging negative self-talk, people will be reluctant to have new experiences in which they can succeed and calm their amygdala.

Plan the Counter-Cognitions for the Three-Column List

Using the three-column list you began earlier, evaluate your thoughts one at a time and find their opposite. Write down this positive opposite in the third column. Figure 11.2 shows how Guy filled out the third column in his chart.

The action of making a list of counter-thoughts directly confronts the negative with a positive alternative. Talking about positive alternatives also engages the prefrontal cortex, which helps those new thoughts to be more readily remembered. With the stronger etching of the new thought in conscious awareness, it is more likely that it will be able to replace the negative

Goals, Actions, Intentions	First Thought	Opposite of First Thought
Start school in 6 weeks	I may not be able to meet that timeline. I always miss deadlines.	I have filled out applications before and I know I have time to do this. I will use my support system to encourage me.
Talk to admissions about getting credits accepted	I don't know where to go and I don't know who to talk to there. It might not even be worth it—I bet they won't transfer credits from the junior college.	I can call ahead to get the information about who to see and where to go. Other students figure it out, so I can too. I can't know what they will accept if I do not ask. It is worth it financially to make this effort, even if I don't like it.
Talk to other students	I will make a fool of myself. I am no good at talking to strangers.	Everyone in the class will be strangers to each other. Talking about class does not require me to be witty or tell jokes—just to talk, which I can do.
Attend every class and not leave because I am nervous	I have always run out of class.	Even if I am nervous, I can stay. I have practiced skills to stay.
Finish school completely in 2 1/2 years	I will never finish school. I don't think I have ever stayed long enough to get enough credits.	Things are different today. I have a goal, and I can stay in school even if it is hard.

Figure 11.2 Identifying Counter-Cognitions with the Three-Column Method

consistently. Rereading the list frequently then strengthens the memory of what to look for and what to change.

Use the "C" and "D" Parts of the ABCD Method

Ellis's ABCD method is one of the clearest ways to challenge negative self-talk. Because it identifies a very specific event that activates anxiety and the subsequent avoidance behavior, specific self-talk is required to challenge it as well. After you have identified the beliefs regarding the activating event, you can address and confront the reality of the behavior. This is done by using the "C" and "D" parts of the method. "C" stands for the *consequences* of A and B. "D" stands for the *demands* you place on yourself, others, or the situation.

Adrienne was a client in her thirties who felt she was heading for career trouble. She had a boss who was moody, and she was sure he was mad at her and about to fire her whenever he came through the office without greeting her pleasantly. This was disturbing to her, and every time it happened, Adrienne would spend the whole day using self-talk about how she wasn't good enough, would never get promoted, and even might get fired. This was not like the ruminative worry that a plan could settle. It was only triggered on days when the boss didn't sound pleasant enough. On other days, Adrienne was not at all troubled by thoughts of being fired. However, a promotion opportunity was coming up, and she hesitated to put her name in for it because she would have to ask her boss to give her a recommendation, and she was sure he would never recommend her. She couldn't bring herself to talk with him for fear that he would "look at her funny" or hesitate to offer the recommendation. Then she would blush, stammer, and need to walk out.

I decided to use the ABCD method with Adrienne to identify and challenge her negative self-talk. Naming the *activating event* was very easy for her: "I have to ask my boss for a recommendation for a promotion." Next, Adrienne identified the beliefs she held about herself, others, and the situation, noting especially those that started with "should," "must," "have to," and "it would be awful if." "I must be completely calm when asking about the new job or he won't recommend me," she said. "He must be in a perfect mood or he will never listen to me. I have to present every one of my reasons to apply in perfect order or he won't agree to recommend me. It will be awful if he is rude or impatient and doesn't make me feel good about applying. I think I would just run out of his office and never show my face again."

We then moved onto the "C" and "D" parts of the method.

C: *What are the consequences of A and B?* What are you likely to do, or what did you do if you are thinking about this activating event? (Adrienne responded, "I guess I won't ask him for the recommendation. I don't know if he will ever be in a perfect mood, but I sure know I will never manage to ask him perfectly.")

D: *Look at the demands you place on yourself, others, or the situation.* Question them, and question the ratings you make for situations. For example, ask yourself, "How do I know that _____?" "Why must she always _____?" "Who ever promised that _____?" "Why do I think this is the worst _____?" You get the most effect out of this if you write out the question and the answer as well as talk them over.

Adrienne realized she was attempting to mind-read when she assumed she knew what her boss would act like and why it was awful. "How do I know?" was an important question for her. She realized that her only evidence that he would be rejecting was that he was grumpy on some mornings, so we took it a bit farther: "How do you know that he is grumpy?" "How do you know that you are the cause of his grumpiness?" Maybe he was just tired; maybe he was being cheerful in his own way; maybe his whole day would turn around when he saw her.

Adrienne wrote:

> I place a demand on myself to be perfect because I think that will make my boss listen. But actually, I have no idea what makes him listen, because I have no idea what makes him grumpy on some days. I also don't know that I will run out of the office if he is impatient, and I don't even know that it will be awful. I won't like it all, but I could stick it out, I guess.

Adrienne then wrote counter-messages to herself to dispute the beliefs she held and the demands she had made:

- "I must be completely calm when asking about the new job or he won't recommend me" was countered with "He knows my work. Whether I am calm while asking will not change his assessment of my work."
- "He must be in a perfect mood or he will never listen to me, and I have to present every one of my reasons to apply in perfect order or he won't agree to recommend me" was countered with:

"There is no need to be perfect, because there is no way to know what perfect is in this situation. I can be prepared, and I will be."

- "It will be awful if he is rude or impatient and doesn't make me feel good about applying; I think I would just run out of his office and never show my face again" was countered with:
"Who said he should make me feel good about applying for a promotion? His feelings don't have to affect me. There is no need to run if he is rude or impatient. I have talked to him many times when he was impatient, and I can do it again."

Once the challenge is set—countering negative self-talk—it is necessary to review the results often. The new messages can be written down in a notebook or on a card, placed on the refrigerator door—anyplace they will be visible and accessible on a daily basis to counter the negative self-talk.

Recite Affirmations

Saying affirmations is a way to form and ingrain new thought habits and establish new, positive self-talk. An affirmation is a positive statement about yourself, said aloud as if it were already true. The idea behind affirmations is that we create the reality we believe. If we believe we will fail, we will. Our chances of success are much better if we imagine ourselves succeeding and see ourselves doing something right. By affirming what we want to be true (about our lives, our situations, our character, our attitudes, and so on), we create the conditions for that truth and make it manifest, even as we speak. For example, if I want to become more comfortable talking at meetings, an affirmation I might say would be, "I am confident and competent when I express myself at staff meetings." I say the affirmation as if the attitude and action were true right now.

Self-affirmation is a positive reflection of what you can do and increases your confidence to do what is difficult (Cascio et al., 2015). You can affirm that you have had successes in past similar experiences or affirm that you have prepared well and can perform your best. You can affirm that you will survive any negative outcome. The affirmation of your competence and confidence can help buoy you when you feel a bit nervous about going into a challenging situation.

Another way to use affirmations is to direct your attention to what you want to become true, even if in this moment it hasn't happened yet. This type of affirmation does not differentiate past, present, and future (Evers, 1989), but rather affirms that what you hope for is already happening. For example, you can affirm, "My new job is coming to me." It is a way of inviting the positives you want into your life. That said, affirmations need to be grounded in reality. Star, a client who wanted to design movie sets although she had no training or experience, wanted to affirm that she could move to Hollywood and be employed as a set designer. This could only be a setup for disappointment. Reality suggests that one needs some verifiable skills to get that kind of job. After some work, she realized that a more realistic affirmation was, "I can learn the skills I will need to achieve my goals."

To summarize, you can challenge negative self-talk by:

1. Filling out the third column on the three-column list
2. Carrying the list with you, using the new self-talk thoughts to replace the old, negative ones
3. In a specific situation, analyzing the effects of your beliefs with the ABCD method
4. Reviewing your new, positive self-talk messages at least daily
5. Reciting affirmations about being confident and competent in the situation, even when you don't feel confident or competent, and inviting positives into your life

CHANGE THE FILTERS ON EXPERIENCE

People fulfill their own expectations. If they expect to panic when they get in a car, they will panic. If they worry about whether a party will go as they planned, it will not go as planned. If they expect to be rejected or expect to appear nervous, they will look nervous and spot someone who appears to be rejecting. People create what they fear. More importantly, they will notice things that fulfill their expectations. They will note when things were less than perfect, and they will filter new experiences for evidence that they are being rejected or nervous. They especially notice bad experiences and don't notice positive ones. They begin to make inaccurate generalizations about their experiences ("I will obviously panic whenever I get into a car") and don't draw good conclusions about the experience ("I know I didn't really panic, but I felt like I might at any moment, so that is just as bad"). And they begin to see risk in situations where none exists.

People with social fear have expectations of being socially humiliated or of being unassertive, ignored, embarrassed, or flustered, and often those anticipated fears will be fulfilled. They will stop seeing the moments when others responded warmly to them or when they succeeded socially. Behavioral avoidance is when individuals avoid these situations and rationalize their avoidance with self-talk. But this self-talk isn't necessarily accurate. It reflects specific kinds of mental errors that are common to social anxiety, and these errors are not challenged because the fearful person avoids the very situations that could contradict the error. These mental errors get reinforced by experiences that seem to prove them true.

The following beliefs are common to all people with anxiety, and especially to those with social anxiety or panic:

- Overestimation that what you fear will occur. If you have had panic, you believe you *will* panic. If you are worried about something, you believe it definitely *will* happen. If you fear others will notice you and reject you, you are *certain* that will come true.
- Catastrophic expectations. You believe that no matter what happens, it will be the worst.
- Underestimation of your capacity to tolerate negative experience. You believe you can't tolerate anxious feelings or any negative thing you fear might happen.
- Belief that feelings are not controllable.
- Belief that outcomes are up to others and that you can't influence your own actions and feelings if you feel anxiety.

Giving control over to anxiety is debilitating. Of course, *total* control is not realistic, but nor is it necessary. Control over one's *emotional* reaction to situations is, however, an achievable goal. A place to start is to search for situations that disprove these false beliefs. This will help you change your filters on experiences.

Kristen needed to examine her thoughts and her behavior in response to her thoughts to see that she had quite a distorted picture of what was happening at work. Kristin had recently been promoted, and her boss told her that she should ask for help to learn a computer program that she was going to need to generate reports. About three weeks into the new job, Kristen told me in tears that she was going to get fired because the boss was too busy to train her on the program. When I asked about how she knew the boss was too busy, she replied, "Every time I go to knock on his door, he is busy." When I asked what she did, she said she didn't knock, went back to her office, and tried to find an opportunity later to seek help. Kristen never asked for help, assumed the boss didn't want to help, and, as a consequence, didn't get the training she needed. But she didn't see how this might be under her control or at least under her influence in that she might be able to get help by asking for it. She was not being rejected; she just feared she would be.

1. If you have social anxiety, look for and write down situations in which you did *not* experience rejection or humiliation. If you have generalized anxiety, look for and write down times when the thing you were worried about did *not* ever come to pass. If you suffer from panic, note the situations in which you could have panicked but did *not* panic.

2. Bring these notes into therapy for discussion or write about them to enhance your awareness of positive situations. People with social anxiety should pay special attention here; even though you might have *felt* embarrassed, did others *actually* humiliate you? It doesn't count to say that the other person probably was thinking negative thoughts about you. You can only record actual spoken words and specific actions, so if the person remained engaged in

conversation and pleasant, it must be noticed as a positive. (This is helping the amygdala with new learning.)

3. Keep up this search for positives as a regular part of your life. Unlearning a lifetime of negative filtering takes some time.

CHANGING SELF-TALK IN CHILDREN

Children may develop negative self-talk at a young age, prompting them to withdraw from social interactions or successes in school. They can become solemn and overwhelmed by anxious thoughts and engage in behavior that is self-defeating unless corrected. It is highly effective for parents and children to watch for and correct the negative self-talk that occurs as children tell stories about their social experience (Rapee, 2002). Parents can talk with children to help them identify and reinforce positive corrections for catastrophizing, overestimating that the worst will occur, fearing that they cannot handle bad experiences, or believing they cannot control their own feelings. These positive corrections include:

- "Things happen. Everyone has a bad experience once in a while."
- "Even if you feel scared, you can go ahead and do things anyway. That's what 'brave' means."
- "Bad things happen to good people. Lots of bad experiences are not your fault."
- "If you actually did something wrong, you can correct it."
- "Focus on the good things that happen to you. Thinking about bad things that happened only teaches you how to do things wrong again."

CONCLUSION

Learning positive self-talk strategies is a crucial aspect of effectively managing the anxious mind. Once you get the right self-talk down, behavioral change—the next chapter of this book—is much easier to implement. The self-talk is the cognitive part of calm, the first element necessary for creating memory reconsolidation. A person who hasn't exercised for years can't get up and run a marathon tomorrow; no one would expect her to. She would need to start with a short walk—practiced, repeated, and extended to be longer and faster—before she could ever expect to make a long run. Every small step of progress is necessary, even if it's not sufficient for the final goal to be met. This is true of changing anxious behavior by changing self-talk. Changing self-talk is like taking walks before beginning the marathon of behavior change.

TWELVE

Technique #10

Implement a Plan and Practice the Three Cs

This technique is about mastering the three Cs of behavior change and memory reconsolidation: calm, competence, and confidence. In this chapter, I focus on how you may acquire competence and confidence—the two steps that follow staying calm to achieve success in social engagement. If you have had a prior bad experience, whether due to previous panic or to social anxiety, you will want to focus on the goal of memory reconsolidation. That process definitely requires all three of the Cs of a successful exposure.

Calm, competence, and confidence are the major behavioral goal for people with the social anxiety symptoms of appearing very nervous in situations where they will be observed. The only possible way to achieve competence and confidence is through experiences that expand or strengthen knowledge and skill. Technique #10 shows you how to develop competence and confidence for managing anxiety in work and social settings. To devise a plan and carry it out, you will need to build on other techniques, because part of confidence is the knowledge that if anxiety occurs, you will be able to manage it.

THE BRAIN LEARNS AND UNLEARNS FEAR

Expectations of being anxious will cause anxiety to happen. It is probable that an enlarged amygdala (the part of the brain that warns of trouble) causes people to be overly sensitive to faces. When they detect even the slightest shift on a face, the amygdala interprets the shift as negative, causing them to believe they are being judged as failures or will be rejected. They then develop expectations such as, "I can't speak in public without shaking and embarrassing myself," or, "If anyone notices me eating, I will humiliate myself somehow by spilling food or making a mistake," or, "I just know I will panic if I have to wait for a long time to get seated at the restaurant." The die is cast. If they go into those situations, they will panic or feel humiliated. Their expectations create their future reality.

Fortunately, the amygdala that warns of danger also has a function to unlearn fear. I described this process, called memory reconsolidation, in Chapter 11. The amygdala can only unlearn fear when it is in a situation that previously created fear and now does *not* create fear. The appraisal process of the cortex, in concert with the insula and hippocampus, forms a new memory, and the amygdala recognizes future exposure to the situation as safe. Once you unlearn the fear, you can behave competently and confidently and can do it again in a similar situation.

Unless new learning is planned for, there is no chance for the amygdala to unlearn fear. Without a plan, you will be filled with the same old intense fear—the thinking brain will be busy noticing how scary the situation is. Change requires a deliberate decision to behave as if the situation is not frightening. With specific planning and preparation, the amygdala has a chance for new learning.

THREE DEEP BREATHS AND GOOD PREPARATION

When I was in high school, I was stricken with vicious stage fright, which I now know was an outcome of having panic attacks that attached themselves to a variety of situations as well as to my acting. Waiting in the wings to go onstage, I would pray to God to make me fall over dead before I had to go out and sing. Dying would not have been a particularly useful avoidance behavior, to be sure, but it was about the only excuse the rest of the cast and crew would accept for missing my cue. My drama coach taught me one of the best anxiety management ideas I would ever learn: to breathe slowly and deeply. She also gave me a mental framework for handling the anxiety. "All you need to go out there without fear is three deep breaths and good preparation." Her "three deep breaths and good preparation" has become my model for getting rid of anxious behavior in any anxiety-producing situation and setting the stage for the three Cs.

"Three deep breaths" stands for the ability to remain physiologically *calm* while waiting for the practice to start. People who are going to go out into the real world and do something new—order in a restaurant, speak at a staff meeting, sit in the middle of a theater, drive on the highway—need to stay as calm as possible so that it is harder to trigger their anxious reactions. Keeping the body calm with breathing and muscle relaxation is a choice a person can make, a prefrontal cortex activity that has effects on physiology and on brain function.

Begin one-breath relaxation or your favorite breathing method the moment you know a situation could stir anxiety. If you have planned your practice, you will know ahead of time that you need it. For example, if you are going to speak up at a staff meeting, deliberately breathe and loosen up throughout the day before the meeting. Prevent getting tense and uptight. Once you are in the room for the meeting, use one-breath relaxation to stay physically calm until it's time for you to speak. In this way, your body remains as quiet as possible—your sympathetic nervous system is quieter—so your symptoms will not be as easily triggered. Even if you feel somewhat nervous, you won't be as uptight when you start speaking and will manage anxiety successfully, which is the desired outcome of practice. In every planned practice, staying calm is part of the plan. Once you've learned that, it is time to move on to the heart of technique #10—developing competence (skills to do the task) and confidence by implementing a plan and practicing in real life.

"Good preparation" stands for competence and confidence—the stages of learning the skills you need for the particular situation you face and practicing before you get to the real-life opportunity for new learning (memory reconsolidation) to occur. Preparation includes mental readiness, such as technique #9 for changing self-talk, which establishes the mental bridge to practicing management of anxious behavior. Good preparation also includes finding the right motivation.

One aspect of preparation involves finding the motivation necessary to go ahead with all this skill building and practicing you are about to do.

Think about my willingness to sing. (It is the same process as your fear of speaking in front of a group, introducing yourself at a conference, giving a book report, or any type of performance.) Why in the world, when I wanted to die rather than sing a solo in front of an audience, would I go out to sing more than one time? Motivation. Once I got in front of the audience without dying, I enjoyed the act of singing. I had practiced it and I could do it well. Serotonin gave my brain a sense of satisfaction at a job well done. And then there was the applause. My brain liked the dopamine flowing as people applauded the performance. With enough motivation, a person will face fear. Once fear is faced, it is diminished; that is the benefit of the three Cs. I went on to major in speech and drama in college with my anxiety for performing well under control!

IMPLEMENT A PLAN

Knowing precisely what you want in life and going after it is harder than most people realize. Take some time to figure out what you desire and then follow this process.

Set Goals

The first part of making a plan is setting a goal. It is goal-setting that gets you in touch with motivation to do what scares you. Keeping motivation in front of you will help you face the things that cause fear and be able to relax about them. Know exactly what you want to do. People want to achieve myriad goals, some very specific and some more general:

- "Order in a restaurant without breaking into a sweat."
- "Speak to my boss without a quavering voice."
- "Stay in class this semester."
- "Start interviewing for jobs."

The best plans start with getting very specific about what you want to accomplish.

Assess What Makes You Anxious and What Skills You Need

After the goal is identified, it is time to assess what skills are needed to meet the goal. This is the competence part of the process. If you are preparing to attend social functions for work, assess your ability to comfortably greet people and initiate conversation. If the goal is to go to a job interview, assess your ability to field interview questions. If you want to begin dating again, assess what opportunities are available for meeting people via email, by phone, and in person and what communication skills you need.

Accurately assessing what makes you anxious and what skills you might need requires a careful review of your history. This is very hard for a person to do on his or her own. Working with a therapist for this whole technique is not only helpful but also probably necessary. Review your life experiences in the following areas to assess what is needed.

Social Skills

Do you have the need or desire to go out socially with friends or to date? Pockets of social uncertainty can crop up unexpectedly, and sometimes otherwise highly functioning people will have surprising insecurities about social events. Specifically assess whether you have developed social skills for everything you want to do. Do you need to learn assertiveness? Can you introduce yourself to new acquaintances? How about being able to enter a meeting room and choose where to sit or how to greet a colleague? Can you talk to your child's teachers or the parents of your child's friends in person and by phone? Can you ask for a date or invite a new acquaintance to a social gathering?

Personal Business Skills

Do you have the ability and willingness to do the social aspects of personal business, such as disputing an inaccurate bill with the cable company or talking with retail personnel? Can you ask questions to purchase, return, or exchange goods? Can you talk with medical personnel and clarify information about medical conditions and treatments? Can you talk to your child's coaches or tutors and make appointments and financial arrangements for lessons with ease?

Work and Career Skills

This is not so much about actual work skills but rather the more social components of a job: asking questions of a supervisor, talking with a coworker at break, talking with a coworker about a work situation, and so on. Are work-related and presentation skills developed? Can you interview for a job? Do you know how to make a presentation in a meeting? Do you know how to offer comments during a committee meeting? Do you have skills to handle discussions with managers or supervisors regarding work?

Assertiveness is a skill that may be needed for any of these areas of functioning. Assertiveness means knowing and being willing to ask that your needs be considered and met in any situation. This is usually a relevant concern in situations that may involve a hint of conflict, such as returning retail items to a store, objecting to inaccurate charges on a bill, asking a repairman to clarify appointments or bills, asking for changes in a work schedule or requesting a vacation date, or telling a manager that a work assignment is too much.

Build Skills

Once the assessment is done, creating the plan to build the skills and develop a practice routine comes next. When a person is missing skills, even skills that are very easy to learn, he or she probably doesn't know what skills are necessary or where to get them. That must be specifically planned.

There are so many ways to learn skills. Consider using workbooks for social skills and assertiveness training. You can learn skills in group therapy for assertiveness, social interaction, conflict management, anger management, and so on. You can go to Toastmasters for developing speaking skills. There are a wide range of books on how to talk and act in business settings. In *Anxiety Busters*, I wrote a chapter of tips on handling difficult situations, such as going to funerals or being at family gatherings where there is tension. A recent book—*There Is No Good Card for This* by Kelsey Crowe and Terry McDowell—tells you what to say in all kinds of "scary, awful and unfair" situations. Adult education departments at community colleges often offer free or inexpensive classes for topics like public speaking, flirting, interviewing, etiquette, Internet communication, and the like. You can even consider an improvisation class—they are great for developing confidence in handling the spontaneity of conversation!

Develop Confidence—Practice in Private

Trying out the skills is very important to achieving confidence that you can have success. You will want to make the steps small enough to be done successfully. Your brain needs the successes to achieve memory reconsolidation. If you felt the fear from the memory of a prior failure or embarrassment and then were able to do well, you will have literally changed the memory and be able to go on to a more difficult step with confidence.

Your brain knows if you are not competent and will generate anxiety if you move too fast. Again, breaking every goal into small steps is the best approach. Finding the right teacher, usually a psychotherapist, is critical to success. Trying new skills requires the right amount of encouragement to get the practice done. If you are working from a workbook, you should review to make sure that you have the right idea and aren't working too fast, and a therapist can be an asset in making sure you are on track. Mastering each level of skill will increase your confidence that you can do what it takes. If your amygdala is going to unlearn fear and if your memory is going to be reconsolidated, it is essential that you don't rush into trying something until you're sure you can do it. For example, if you want to learn to interview for jobs without looking nervous, you might break it down into smaller steps, like these:

- Learning to shake hands while making eye contact and practicing this
- Making a list of questions and referring to it casually while practicing asking the questions
- Constructing some information about your work history, your strengths, and your job skills and practicing describing this verbally

- Learning to pause and think if a question requires it without appearing nervous
- Conducting a practice job interview with a therapist, friend, or colleague

With a therapist, people can "act as if." In other words, they can practice skills as if they are in a real-life situation while still feeling safe. That practice will help their amygdala to unlearn some of their fear before they go to practice in real life. In a therapy session, a person can try out skills that the therapist has taught or skills that are being learned from workbooks. Skills classes are another way to practice in private before going out into real life.

Many people resist practicing in private because they're embarrassed. That is exactly why it is necessary. Not practicing before the real event is akin to learning a part in a play and then saying you don't want to rehearse it before going onstage for the first performance in front of an audience. It's important to practice what you will say to a server in a restaurant, what you will say if you run into your new boss in the hallway, what you will do if you must use the restroom during the middle of a movie, what you will say to your teacher if you're feeling you can't join a study group, and so on.

Find someone to practice with—a parent, a therapist, a spouse, a friend—or speak your part out loud on your own. Your lips will remember better what to do if they've said the words before. When you practice, your brain is getting a workout directed by your prefrontal cortex, and all the parts of your brain are involved—the amygdala, motor cortex, limbic system, anterior cingulate cortex, orbitofrontal cortex, and prefrontal cortex. The more often you practice, the better you will remember. You literally form pathways of connections in your brain that will make it easier to remember what you have practiced when you are under pressure.

To summarize:

1. Set a clear goal.
2. Assess what makes you anxious.

3. Build skills by reading and using workbooks, attending classes, etc.
4. Break your goal into manageable steps and accomplish them one by one.
5. Practice in private.

DESENSITIZATION OF TRAUMA

Desensitization can't be taught here but must be mentioned on behalf of those who have a history of trauma that blocks their being able to go back to an experience. When people have been traumatized, just imagining a similar situation may activate their peripheral nervous system. In these cases, psychotherapy is necessary to desensitize the memory of that trauma. Desensitization can occur with memory reconsolidation using a variety of therapy techniques, including systematic desensitization, eye movement desensitization and reprocessing (EMDR) (Shapiro, 2012), or energy tapping in one of its many versions. Each of these methods requires working with a therapist who is specialized in it.

- *Systematic desensitization.* In this method, the therapist begins by teaching the client relaxation and then creating a hierarchy of anxious elements of a situation. Starting with the element that produces the lowest level of anxiety, the client imagines the element until he can relax fully. The therapist then guides the client up the hierarchy, one step at a time, until all elements are desensitized.
- *Energy therapy.* With this method, the client identifies the thoughts that stimulate negative feelings and identifies the exact nature of the negative feeling (anxiety, embarrassment, phobia, etc.). She then notices the level of negative physical arousal and rates it. Next, she taps on acupressure points that correspond with the physical arousal and rates the feeling again until the negative feeling has dissipated.

- *EMDR.* Eye movement desensitization and reprocessing is the most versatile, profound, and challenging method for a therapist, but it often produces results that may be unattainable with any other method for traumatic experience, especially shame trauma for people with social anxiety.

Memory reconsolidation science makes it clear why several other models of working to resolve painful life experiences may produce profound and lasting change. Coherence therapy (Ecker & Hulley, 2013) and focusing (Cornell, 2013) are two such models that may be extremely beneficial, and these also must be done working with a therapist trained in the modality.

Similarly, panic causes a rapid association between panic and details of a situation. Panic attacks cause people to make the mistake of believing the situation *caused* the panic, and then their brains automatically assume panic will occur whenever they are in the situation. People who have panicked in a social setting will need help desensitizing before they can reenter a similar setting, just as those with social anxiety symptoms need help to recover from shame trauma for situations in which they were intensely nervous and were humiliated for it.

REAL-LIFE EXPOSURE (PRACTICE)

Exposure—practice in real life as opposed to in private—is done in small steps that gradually increase the length of time in the situation to allow a person to leave the situation while still feeling calm. The competence achieved by learning skills and the confidence acquired in practice before entering the real-life situation are necessary for achieving the success that will make memory reconsolidation occur. The steps should also move from "low stakes" to "high stakes"—high stakes are for the final stages, not the beginning. For instance, if you fear sitting in the middle of a theater and are practicing going to the movies, don't start real-life practice by arriving late, when most of the seats are occupied, and staying for the duration of the entire movie. Don't go to the opening night of a blockbuster movie when every seat will be taken. Don't ask a first date to go along on a practice run when the consequence of bolting from the theater in embarrassment might be humiliation in the eyes of your new romantic partner. Instead, break the situation down into steps of increasing exposure, like this:

1. Decide if any skills are necessary, such as buying tickets without embarrassment.
2. Plan how long the exposure should be based on your level of fear and prior experience. Should you allow yourself to leave when the lights are dimmed and when people are still coming and taking seats, or can you stay for the previews and then leave as if you need more popcorn before the show starts? Can you sit through the entirety of a short film if you are by the door?
3. Plan whether you need a support person, like a good friend or a spouse, or if it is better (less embarrassing) to try this alone.
4. Make the steps as large as possible but reasonably achievable. Arrive early to a show that has been out for several weeks. Sit next to the aisle by the door and stay as long as you planned and no longer. Leave while feeling competent so that you will be more confident for the next level of exposure.

The most difficult part of this technique is getting exactly the right degree of exposure to build competence without the risk of diminishing confidence, which will give you the best chance for memory reconsolidation.

Cooperation for Real-Life Exposure

Getting the cooperation of people who are in a position to make the exposure go better is not just a good idea but also necessary. This is particularly true with children who have school-related anxieties. Various staff, such as the principal, the school nurse, teachers, and the counselor, all need to know what the goals of exposure are so that accidental escape or—worse—accidental humiliation is avoided.

Parents play a key role with younger children. Ten-year-old Madison had been nervous about school and was a shy child but had friends and was liked by her teacher. After she had a substitute teacher twice in a week, she started asking to stay home, saying she felt sick in the mornings. (The stomach is a good indicator of how nervous a person is—the peripheral nervous system in action!) Her parents allowed her to stay home "just until her stomach settled down enough to go to school." It took only about three days to notice that Madison's upset stomach always seemed to get better around 3 p.m., when school was over for the day and she wouldn't have to go. Her parents needed to get her back into the classroom despite knowing she would cry, so they contacted the office to make a plan.

The plan was that Madison would go to school the next day, but she would be able to leave early, right after the first two classes, which she enjoyed. The next day she would stay longer, through lunch so she could sit with her best friend, and then leave while she felt good about that. On the third day she would stay all day. Madison's parents told her the plan and made sure she understood it. They also made sure she remembered what they had taught her about how to breathe and stay calm.

The following day, the plan was begun. Madison's parents brought her into the classroom before other students started arriving and were met by the nurse and the teacher. They explained that the nurse would not be calling her parents even if she felt sick, and that she would stay in the classroom without going to the nurse even if she cried. As they left the classroom, her parents reminded her that they would be there to pick her up after her second class. Madison cried, but as there were no other students around yet and her parents were not there, her avoidance behavior was not reinforced. She found that after she was in the classroom and distracted by the day's activities, she did not feel sick. It was easier for both the parents and Madison to return to school the next day.

Another example is that of Meagan, who was a freshman in high school. Meagan had always been timid. Although she did well in most subjects, she felt out of her league in geometry. After she developed a string of reasons to skip class, go home before class, and get sick just before class, the teacher spoke to her and her counselor about it. Meagan revealed that speaking in math class was unbearably anxiety-provoking. She couldn't stand the fear that she might be called on, get the answer wrong, and be humiliated. Together with her parents, the counselor, and the teacher, a plan was hammered out:

1. Meagan was taught one-breath relaxation to stay calm in class.
2. Meagan's parents continually reviewed the homework with her so she could practice saying answers out loud.
3. The first real-life practice would occur the next day in class. Meagan would raise her hand if she knew the answer. Her task was to do that at least once, preferably at the beginning of the class. (This was the "do the worst first" method of worry management.)
4. The teacher would immediately call on her if her hand was up and would not call on her if it was not.
5. As Meagan successfully accomplished each step, she would review with her parents and the counselor her successes and then go into class knowing the next step. This would validate her success and increase the chances for memory reconsolidation to occur.

The next stages of practice would take place as soon as Meagan felt competent to raise her hand and get called on immediately:

1. Meagan would raise her hand, and the teacher might or might not call on her so that she could get used to the "surprise" if she was called on.
2. She would practice one-breath relaxation while she waited.
3. After she felt competent to wait without anxiety, the next level would be tried.
4. The teacher would call on her no more than one time in a class when her hand was up.
5. After Meagan could do that without fear, the final stage would be to solve a homework problem on the board. The teacher would tell her ahead of time which problem he would call on her for. She would undoubtedly feel all the bad feelings of being humiliated when in front of the class, and this would be necessary for the memory reconsolidation to work effectively.

Practice Without a Support Person

An adult may have social goals that will not necessarily require cooperation with others, but when adults live with others, there is usually someone who is running interference for them on things they need to avoid. If a spouse or parent is involved, make sure he or she knows the plan and doesn't inadvertently foil it.

Jerrold had just been appointed as project manager for a contract his firm was beginning. He was now responsible for giving regular reports in meetings he had not previously had to attend. Although he wasn't worried about talking with his team—they knew him well and it felt more like a conversation—the thought of participating in the meetings with the boss and other directors was nerve-racking. When Jerrold made his plan, the goal was obvious—to be able to speak in the meetings with his superiors without turning red and sweating. His skill set for regular conversation was good enough; however, he had avoided speaking in front of a group so often that he had no idea what it would take to handle the stress. He had been in more meetings than he could count and had listened to lots of reports, but he had always been so focused on his own discomfort and avoidance tactics that he never especially noticed how people handled their own behavior when they interjected comments or gave reports. An assessment of what went on in meetings and what he feared would trigger his anxiety was necessary.

1. Jerrold's first step was to observe the meetings—how people said hello, got coffee, and settled into their places. He was to observe the protocol for people responding to someone giving a report. How did people get acknowledged, called on, or responded to? He planned to get into the room before others arrived so that he could see how people entered, how they greeted each other, and how the meetings progressed. His assignment was to observe others speaking.

2. Jerrold's second step was to list those observations and identify his self-talk for each one. He found that he had a series of nega-

tive self-statements, such as, "I can never be as relaxed as Morgan," "No one will listen to me because I'm not charismatic like Frank," and "I will turn red the minute anyone looks at me and my credibility will be shot."

3. He then made a list of counter-cognitions to help prepare himself mentally.

4. Finally, he made a list of steps he wanted to practice before he gave his first full report.

Jerrold followed the principles we had identified to increase the intensity of exposure a little at a time. In this case, the relevant exposure was being looked at without feeling on the spot. He realized that his avoidance behavior had been to *always* be the first one in the room before a meeting. He had thus avoided coping with being looked at when he entered a meeting.

1. Jerrold decided to practice entering the room later and later until he could enter just before it started without discomfort. He was able to do that over the course of a couple of weeks.

2. When he reviewed his progress, he noted that he had overestimated how much people were noticing him. That made him feel safer.

3. Next, he wanted to practice volunteering some comments when he would otherwise have kept quiet. He decided to start with short comments that indicated he agreed with a statement so that there would be no complication of feeling nervous that he was starting a conflict.

4. When he evaluated how he had done, he was able to notice that people were polite to him and accepted his comments.

5. His next and final practice was to find a topic that was being debated and make a comment supporting one side of the debate. To his surprise, he had no trouble finding an opportunity because in every meeting there was back-and-forth conversation.

6. In evaluating his success, Jerrold realized that he was expecting others to jump on him if he stated an opinion, but that in reality

everyone else was expressing opinions and no one appeared to be shocked when he did.

7. He was ready to prepare and give his first report, which he practiced out loud a couple of times to make sure he knew what he wanted to say.

Jerrold followed the principles of good real-life practice:

- Make a list of small, achievable steps.
- Increase the intensity of the steps and the duration of exposure. That means increasing the length of time you stay in a situation, how long you speak, how many people you interact with, and so on.

What If I Fail a Step?

The point of breaking a plan down into small steps is to maximize your chances of success. However, there may be times when you fail in trying to achieve a step. Don't despair or give up when this happens! Remember:

- The real-life process reveals what else you need to know. If something goes wrong, the good news is that you now know what you have to plan for.
- Everyone makes mistakes. No one is exempt. You are human.
- Failing to achieve what you wanted in the step is no big deal—you have been scared or embarrassed before and you lived through it. Your brain is accustomed to it. It will be possible to try again with a better plan.

Help From Medication

Although all of these techniques are intended to be done without medication, a brief word is necessary here. This situation—real-life practice—is the only one in which using medication to stay calm can be a definite aid to learning. When people are overwhelmed by fear, they are not going to learn anything new. It is important to keep the degree of nervousness or fear in manageable proportions while practicing. Because panic and flushing, sweating, and shaking are so hard to completely prevent, it can be very useful to have medication as a backup to reduce the level of fear during practice.

When trying to do something new, many of my clients make a plan with their MD to use their anti-anxiety medications on an as-needed basis. They still feel nervousness, but much less of it, and they are much more likely to succeed at managing the nervousness and performing their step successfully. This helps the amygdala unlearn fear in that situation, and confidence is built that the next step will also work. Before moving to the next step, one trial without medication is a good idea. You can then use it again for the first trial of the subsequent small step.

To recap the steps of real-life exposure:

1. Remember the three Cs. This will help you calm your mind and body, get skills, and plan a practice to develop confidence.
2. Make a list of all the possible small steps and then pick the largest small step that can be done successfully.
3. Enlist the assistance of everyone who can help or inadvertently hinder the steps to be sure they understand the plan and will do their part to help you succeed and not rescue you.
4. Decide whether to use medication; if you do, plan to use it for the first trials of the graduated steps.
5. Begin planned, graduated real-life practice steps—specific small steps that can be prepared for and for which your success is assured.
6. Review your success and select the next step, increasing the duration of exposure but making sure the step can be achieved so new learning can occur.
7. Evaluate any failures to achieve the steps and make course corrections for practice.
8. Continue each step with preparation until the whole goal is met. At every stage, the new learning (or unlearning of fear) lays

groundwork for the next step to occur safely. It isn't until the whole goal is met that the safe experience will completely turn off the warning signal for that specific situation in the future.

CONCLUSION

Practice means exactly that—making trial runs to do things you haven't been able to do before. Nothing works better to develop confidence in your competence. And no one goes out on a practice run without preparation and without the skills to do it. If you are preparing for an athletic event, you learn skills, you try them out, you see what works and what doesn't, you get advice about how to do those skills, and then you try them out again before the competition. If you will be running a marathon, you go through months of preparation, starting with short runs and working up gradually to the long run. If you are going to act in a play, you practice by using a script and staying within marks on the floor of a room to show where the stage is. Then you practice on the stage without the script, and finally you have a dress rehearsal with all the parts in place before an audience sees you. The same is true for real-life practice. Become able to take those three deep breaths, calm down, learn the skills to prepare well and become competent, and get ready to confidently go out into real life. Practice makes possible.

References

Alim, T., Feder., A., . . . & Charney, D. (2008). Trauma, resilience and recovery in a high risk African-American population. *American Journal of Psychiatry, 165*, 1556–1575.

Alsene, K., Deckert, J., Sand, P., & de Wit, H. (2003). Association between A2a receptor gene polymorphisms and caffeine-induced anxiety. *Neuropsychopharmacology, 28*(9), 1694–1702.

Amen, D. (2003). *Healing anxiety and depression*. New York: Penguin.

Amen, D. (2015). *Change your brain, change your life, revised edition*. New York: Harmony.

Anderman, E., & Gray, D. (2016) Motivation, learning, and instruction. In J. Wright (Ed.) International Encyclopedia of the social and behavioral sciences (2nd ed., pp. 928-935). Waltham, MA: Elsevier.

Aron, E. (1997). *The highly sensitive person*. New York: Broadway Books.

Aron, E., & Jaeger, B. (2003) *Making work work for the highly sensitive person*. New York: McGraw-Hill.

Bartholomew, J. B. (2005). Brief aerobic exercise may improve mood, well-being in major depression. *Medicine and Science in Sports and Exercise, 37*, 2032–2037.

Beck, J., & Beck, A. (2011) *Cognitive Behavior Therapy, second Edition: basics and beyond*. New York: Guilford Press.

Beck, A., & Dozois, D. (2011). Cognitive therapy: Current status and future directions. *Annual Review of Medicine, 62*, 397–409.

Benson, H. (1996). *Timeless healing: The power and biology of belief*. New York: Fireside.

Benson, H. (2015) *The Mind-body effect*. New York: Simon & Schuster.

Benson, H. and Proctor, W. (2004) *The breakout principle*. New York: Scribner.

Benson, H. & Klipper, M. (2000) *The relaxation response*. New York: William Morrow Paperbacks.

Bidonde, J., Busch, A., . . .Foulds, H. (2017) Aerobic exercise training for adults with fibromyalgia. *Cochrane Database of Systematic Reviews*, 2017, Issue 6. Art. No.: CD012700. DOI: 10.1002/14651858.CD012700

Blaylock, R. (2004). *Connection between MS and aspartame*. Retrieved from www.wnho.net/ms_and_aspartame.html

Brown, R., Gerbarg, P., & Muskin, P. (2012) *How to use herbs, nutrients and yoga in mental health treatment*. New York: W. W. Norton.

Brown, L. (2015) Good and Cheap: Eat Well on $4/Day. New York: Workman Publishing Co.

Busch, A., Ciccolo, J. Puspitasari, A., & Stults-Kohlemainen. (2015) Preferences for exercise as a treatment for depression. *Mental Health and Physical Activity (2015)* http://dx.doi.org./10.16/j.mhpa.2015.12.004

Cascio, C., O'Donnell, M., Tinney, F., Lieberman, M., Taylor, S. Strecher, V., and Falk, E. (2015). Self-affirmation activates brain systems associated with self-related processing and reward and is reinforced by future orientation. *Journal of the Society for Cognitive and Affective Neuroscience, 11(4),* 621–629.

Catalino, L. (2015) A better way to pursue happiness. *Greater Good Magazine. July 13, 2015.* Greater Good Science Center at UC Berkeley.

Chen, Z., Williams, K., Fitness, J., & Newton, N. (2008) When Hurt Will Not Heal: Exploring the Capacity to Relive Social and Physical Pain. *Association for Psychological Science, 19(8), 789-795.*

Charney, D. (2004). Psychobiological mechanisms of resilience and vulnerability: Implications for successful adaptation to extreme stress. *American Journal of Psychiatry, 161,* 195–216.

Charney, D., Sklar, P., Buxbaum, J., and Nestler, E., Eds. (2013) *The neurobiology of mental illness,* 4th Ed. New York: Oxford University Press.

Chhatwal, J., Stanek-Rattiner, L., Davis, M., & Ressler, K. (2006). Amygdala BDNF signaling is required for consolidation but not encoding of extinction. *Nature Neuroscience, 9,* 870-872.

Childre, D., Rozman, D. (2008) *Transforming anxiety: The heartmath solution for overcoming fear and worry and creating serenity.* New Harbinger Publications: CA

Chisea, A., Calati, R., Serretti, A. (2011). Does mindfulness training improve cognitive abilities? A systematic review of neuropsychological findings. *Clinical Psychology Review, Apr:31(3): 449-464.*

Cirelli, C. & Tononi, C. (2015) Sleep and Synaptic homeostasis. *Sleep, 2015, Jan 1;38(1). 161-162. Doi: 10:5665/sleep.4348.*

Cornell, A. W. (2013). *Focusing in clinical practice.* Oakland, CA: New Harbinger.

Craft, L. (2005, March). Exercise and clinical depression: Examining two psychological mechanisms. *Psychology of Sport and Exercise, 6*(2), 151–171.

Crowe, K. & McDowell, E. (2017) There is no good card for this: What to say and do when life is scary, awful, and unfair to people you love. New York: Harper One.

Cynkar, A. (2007, June). A prescription for exercise. Monitor on Psychology, pp. 42–43.

Ecker, B. Ticic, R., Kushner, E., Lasser, K. Greenwald, R., Feinstein, D. (2015) Memory reconsolidation in psychotherapy: The neuropsychotherapist Special Issue Jan 2015, Vol 1.

Dahlitz, M. & Hall, G. (Eds.) (2015). Memory Reconsolidation in Psychotherapy. P.O. Box 1030, Park Ridge, QLD, Australia: The Neuropsychotherapist.

Davidson, R., & McEwen, B. (2012). Social influences on neuroplasticity: Stress and interventions to promote well-being. *Nature Neuroscience, 15,* 689–695.

Delgado, P. L., Price, L. H., Miller, H. L., Salomon, R. M., Aghajanian, G. K., Heninger, G. R., & Charney, D. S. (1994). Serotonin and the neurobiology of depression: Effects of tryptophan depletion in drug-free depressed patients. *Archives of General Psychiatry, 51,* 865–874.

Demos, J. (2004). *Getting started with neurofeedback.* New York: Norton.

DesMaisons, K. (1998). *Potatoes not prozac.* New York: Simon & Schuster.

Drabant, E. M., Ramel, W., Edge, M. D., Hyde, L. W., Kuo, J. R., Golding, P. R., . . . Gross, J. J. (2012). Neural mechanisms underlying 5_HTTPLR-related sensitivity to acute stress. *American Journal of Psychiatry, 169,* 397–405.

Duman, R. S., & Monteggia, L (2006). A neurotrophic model for stress-related mood disorders. *Biological Psychiatry, 59,* 1116–1127.

Dunn, A., Trivedi, M., Kampert, J., Clark, C., & Chambliss, H. (2005). Exercise treatment for depression: Efficacy and dose response. *American Journal of Preventive Medicine, 28*(1), 1–8.

Ecker, B., & Hulley, L. (2013, July/August). Unlocking the emotional brain. *Psychotherapy Networker.*

Ecker, B., Ticic, R, & Hulley, L. (2012) Unlocking the emotional brain: Eliminating symptoms at their roots using memory reconsolidation. New York: Routledge.

Eisen, A., Kearney, C., & Schaefer, C. (1995) Clinical Handbook of Anxiety disorders in children and adolescents. New York: Jason Aronson, Inc.

Epstein, R. (2011, September/October). Fight the frazzled mind. Scientific American Mind. Retrieved April 20, 2012, from http://www.scientificamerican.com/article.cfm?id=fight-the-frazzled-mind

Evans, G. W., & Johnson, D. (2000). Stress and open-office noise. *Journal of Applied Psychology, 85*(5), 779–783.

Evers, A. (1989). *Affirmations: Your passport to happiness.* North Vancouver, BC, Canada: Affirmations-International Publishing Company.

Farchione, T., Fairholme, C., Ellard, K., Boisseau, C., Thompson-Hollands, J., Carl, J., . . . Barlow, D. (2012). Unified protocol for transdiagnostic treatment of emotional disorders: A randomized controlled trial. *Behavioral Therapy, 43*(3), 666–678. doi: 10.1016/j.beth.2012.01.001

Field, T. (2002). Massage for fibromyalgia. *Journal of Clinical Rheumatology, 8*(2), 72–76.

Fisone, G., Borgkvist, A., & Usiello, A. (2004). Caffeine as a psychomotor stimulant: Mechanism of action. *Cell and Molecular Life Science, 61*(7–8), 857–872.

Fredholm, B., Bättig, K., Holmén, J., Nehlig, A., & Zvartau, E. (1999). Actions of caffeine in the brain with special reference to factors that contribute to its widespread use. *Pharmacology Review, 51*(1), 83–133.

Fredrickson. B. (2001). The role of positive emotions in positive psychology: The broaden-and-build theory of positive emotions. *American Psychologist, 56,* 218–226.

Fredrickson, B. (2009). *Positivity.* New York: Crown.

Fredrickson, B. (2013). *Love 2.0: How our supreme emotion affects everything we feel, think and do.* London: Hudson Street Press.

Gallo, F. (2000). *Energy diagnostic and treatment methods.* New York: Norton.

Garrison,K., Zeffiro, T., Scheinost, D., Constable, R. & Brewer, J. (2015) Meditation leads to reduced default mode network activity beyond an active task. *Cognitive Affective Behavioral Neuroscience. 15(3).* 712-720.

Gazzaniga, M. (2012) *Free will and the science of the brain.* Reprint edition. New York: Ecco.

Gendlin, E. (1998). *Focusing-oriented psychotherapy.* New York: Guilford Press.

Goldberg, J. (1997). Can we boost neurotransmitter precursors? [On-line]. *Medscape Psychiatry & Mental Health eJournal 2*(1). Available:www.medscape.com/viewarticle/431512.

Goldstein-Piekarski, A, Greer, S., Saletin, J., & Walker, M. (2015). Sleep deprivation impairs the human central and peripheral nervous system discrimination of social threat. *Journal of Neuroscience, 35*(28), 10135–10145.

Greenwood, B. N., Foley, T. E., Day, H. E. W., Campisi, J., Hammack, S. H., Campeau, S., . . . Fleshner, M. (2003). Freewheel running prevents learned helplessness/ behavioral depression: Role of dorsal raphe serotoninergic neurons. *Journal of Neuroscience, 23,* 2889–2898.

Grillon, C. Quispe-Escudero, D., Mathur, A. & Ernst, M. (2015) Mental fatigue impairs emotion regulation. *Emotion 15(3).* 383-389.

Hanson, R. (2016). *Hard-wiring happiness.* New York: Harmony.

Hariri, A. R., Drabant, E. M., Munoz, K. E., Kolachana, B. S., Mattay, V. S., Egan, M. F., & Weinberger, D. R. (2005). A susceptibility gene for affective disorders and the response of the human amygdala. *Archives of General Psychiatry, 62,* 146–152.

Harvey, B. H., & Shahid, M. (2012). Metabotropic and ionotropic glutamate receptors as neurobiological targets in anxiety and stress-related disorders; focus on pharmacology and preclinical translational models. *Pharmacology Biochemistry in Behavior, 100,* 775–800.

Haskell, W. L., Lee, I. M., Pate, R. R., Powell, K. E., Blair, S. N., Franklin, B. A., . . . Bauman, A. (2007). Physical activity and public health: Updated recommendation for adults from the American College of Sports Medicine and the American Heart Association. *Circulation, 116.* Retrieved from www.circ.ahajournals.org/cgi/content/abstract/circulationaha.107.185649

Hayes, S., Strosahl, K., & Wilson, K. (2016). *Acceptance and commitment therapy.* New York: Guilford Press.

Heintzelman, S., Trent, J., & King, L (2015). Revisiting desirable response bias in well-being reports. *Journal of Positive Psychology,* 10, 167-178.

Heinz, A., & Smolka, M. N. (2006). The effects of catechol O- methyltransferase genotype on brain activation elicited by affective stimuli and cognitive tasks. *Reviews in the Neurosciences, 17,* 359–367.

Huh, Y., Vosgerau, J. & Morewedge, C. (2016). More similar but less satisfying: Comparing the efficacy of within- and cross-category substitute for food. *Psychological Science,* 27(6), 894-903.

Immordino-Yang, M., Christodolou, J. & Singh, V. (2012). Rest is not idleness: implications of the brain's default mode for human development and education. *Perspectives on Psychological Science, 2012, 7(4).* 352-64.

Jabr, F. (2016). Why a rested brain is more creative. *Scientific American Mind.* September, 2016.

Jabr, F. (2016). Take that vacation: Why time off makes you a better worker. *Scientific American Mind.* September, 2016.

Kabat-Zinn, J. (2013). *Full catastrophe living,* Revised Edition. New York: Bantam Books.

Karg, K., Burmeister, M., Shedden, K., & Sen, S. (2011). The serotonin transporter promoter variant (5-HTTLPR), stress, and depression meta-analysis revisited: Evidence of genetic moderation. *Archives of General Psychiatry, 68,* 444–454.

Keefe, J., Webb, C., & DeRubeis, R. (2015). In cognitive therapy for depression, early focus on maladaptive beliefs may be especially efficacious for patients with personality disorders. *Journal of Consulting and Clinical Psychology,* advance online publication. Retrieved from https://dx.doi.org/10.1037/ccp0000071.

Kiive, E., Maaroos, J., Shlik, J., Toru, I., & Harro, J. (2004). Growth hormone, cortisol and prolactin responses to physical exercise: Higher prolactin response in depressed patients. *Progress in Neuro-Psychopharmacology and Biological Psychiatry, 28*(6), 1007–1013.

Kim, J.-M., Stewart, R., Kim, S.-W., Yang, S.-J., Shin, I.-S., Kim, Y.-H., & Yoon, J.-S. (2007). Interactions between life stressors and susceptibility genes (5-HTTLPR and BDNF) on depression in Korean elders. *Biological Psychiatry, 62,* 423–428.

Kim, Y., Chu, Y., et.al., (2014). Central Terminal Sensitization of TRPV1 by Descending Serotonergic Facilitation Modulates Chronic Pain. *Neuron, 81(4), 873-887*

Kosfeld, M., Heinrichs, M., Zak, P., Fischbacher, V., & Fehr, E. (2005). Oxytocin increases trust in humans. *Nature, 435*(2), 673–676.

Kredlow, M., & Otto, M. (2015). Interference with the reconsolidation of trauma-related memories in adults. *Depression and Anxiety, 32,* 32–37. DOI: 10.1002/da.22343

Kroenke, K. (2007). Anxiety disorders in primary care: Prevalence, impairment, comorbidity, and detection. *Annals of Internal Medicine, 146,* 317–325.

Kross, E., Berman, M., Mischel, W., Smith, E., & Wager, T. (2011) Social rejection shares somatosensory representations with physical pain. *Proceedings of the National Academy of Sciences of the United States of America, 108 (15), 6270-6275.*

Kumar, S., Singh, R. K., & Bhardwaj, T. R. (2017). Therapeutic role of nitric oxide as emerging molecule. *Biomedicine and Pharmacotherapy, 85,* 182–201.

Laber-Warren, E. (2015). Out of sync: How modern lifestyles scramble the body's inner clock. *Scientific American Mind*, 26(5) 62-65.

Larson, E. (2006). Moderate amounts of regular exercise might delay Alzheimer's disease in older adults. *Annals of Internal Medicine, 144,* 73–81.

Lonigan, C., & Phillips, B. (2001). Temperamental influence on the development of anxiety disorders. In M. W. Vasey & M. R. Dadds, Mark R. (Eds.), *The developmental psychopathology of anxiety* (pp. 60–91). New York: Oxford.

Macdonald, C., Lepage, K., Eden, U. & Eichenbaum, H. (2011) Hippocampal "time cells: bridge the gap in memory for discontiguous events. *Neuron, 71, 737-749. Doi: 10/106/j.neuron.2011.07.012*

Mahan, M., Ressler, K. (2012). Fear conditioning, synaptic plasticity and the amygdala: implication for posttraumatic stress disorder. *Trends in Neuroscience. 2012 Jan; 35(1):24-35.* doi: 10.1016/j.tins.2011.06.007. Epub 2011 Jul 26.

McDonald, G., & Leary, M. (2005). Why does social exclusion hurt? The relationship between social and physical pain. *Psychological Bulletin, 131*(2), 202–223.

McMullin, R. (2001). *The new handbook of cognitive behavioral therapy.* New York: W.W. Norton.

McNally, R. J. (2002). Anxiety sensitivity and panic disorder. *Biological Psychiatry, 52,* 938–946.

Mobbs, D., Greicius, M., Abdel-Azim, E., Menon, V., & Reiss, A. (2003). Humor modulates the mesolimbic reward centers. *Neuroscience, 40,* 1041–1048.

Muller, T., Peterson, S., Sonnewald, U., & Unsgard, G. (1995). Effects of aspartame on Ca+ influx and LDH leakage from nerve cells in culture. *Neuropharmacology and Neurotoxicology Rapid Communications of Oxford Ltd., 6,* 318–320.

Myers, H., Wyatt, G., Ullman, J., Loeb, T., Chin, D., Pause, N., & Liu, H. (2015). Cumulative burden of lifetime adversities: Trauma and mental health in low-SES African Americans and Latino/as. *Psychological Trauma: Theory, Research, Practice and Policy, 7,* 243–251.

Nardi, A., Valença, A., Lopes, F., de-Melo-Neto, V., Freire, R., Veras, A., ... Zin., W. (2007). Caffeine and 35% carbon dioxide challenge tests in panic disorder. *Human Psychopharmacology: Clinical and Experimental, 22*(4), 231–240.

Nelson, M. E., Rejeski, W. J., Blair, S. N., Duncan, P. W., Judge, J. O., King, A. C., . . . Castaneda-Sceppa, C. (2007). Physical activity and public health in older adults. *Circulation, 116.* Retrieved from www.circ.ahajournals.org/cgi/content/abstract/circulationaha.107.185650.

Newberg, A. and Waldman, M.R. (2010). *How God Changes Your Brain.* New York: Ballantine Books.

Northrup, C. (2016). *Goddesses never age: The secret prescription for radiance, vitality and well-being.* New York: Hay House.

O'Riordan, M. (2007). *ACSM/AHA updates physical activity recommendations, including guidelines for older adults.* Retrieved from www.medscape.com/viewarticle/561102

O'Riordan, M. (2007). *ACSM/AHA updates physical activity recommendations, including guidelines for older adults.* Retrieved from http://www.medscape.com/viewarticle/789499

Otto, B., Misra, S., Prasad, A., & McRae, K. (2014). Functional overlap of top-down emotion regulation and generation: An fMRI study identifying common neural substrates between cognitive reappraisal and cognitively generated emotions. *Journal of the Society for Cognitive and Affective Neuroscience, 14*(3), 923–938.

Oyarzun, J., Lopez-Barroso, D., Fuenetemilla, L., Cucurell, D., Pedraza, C., . . .de Diego-Balaguer, R. (2012). Updating fearful memories with extinction training during reconsolidation: A human study using auditory aversive stimuli. *PLOS One, 7,* e38849. doi.org/10.1371/journal.pone.0038849

Paruthi, S., Brooks, L., D'Ambrosio, C, Hall, W., Kotagal, S., . . . Wise, M. (2016) Recommended amount of sleep for pediatric populations: a consensus statement of the American academy of sleep medicine. *Journal of Clinical Sleep Medicine, 2016, 12(6),* 785-786.

Penedo, F. J., & Dahn, J. R. (2005). Exercise and well-being: A review of mental and physical health benefits associated with physical activity. *Current Opinion in Psychiatry, 18*(2), 189–193.

Phelps, E. Making the paper. (2010). *Nature.* 463(8). http://dx.doi.org/10.1038/7277008a.

Phelps, E., Delgado, M., Nearing, K. & LeDoux, J. (2004). Extinction learning in humans; role of the amygdala and vmPFC. *Neuron, 43,* 897-905, doi:10.1016./j.neuron2004.08.042.

Pliszka, S. R. (2003). *Neuroscience for the mental health clinician.* New York, NY: Guilford.

Poe, G. (2017) Sleep is for forgetting. *The journal of neuroscience.* Jan 18, 2017, 37(3):464-473.

Rapee, R. (2002). The development and modification of temperamental risk for anxiety disorders: Prevention of a lifetime of anxiety. *Biological Psychiatry, 52,* 947–957.

Ratey, J. & Hagerman, E. (2013). *Spark. The revolutionary new science of exercise and the brain.* New York: Little Brown and Company.

Schaubroeck, J., & Ganster, D. (1993). Chronic demands and responsivity to challenge. *Journal of Applied Psychology, 78*(1), 73–85.

Schiller, D., Monfils, M., Raio, C., Johnson, D., LeDoux, J., & Phelps, E. (2010). Preventing the return of fear in humans using reconsolidation update mechanisms. *Nature, 463,* 49–53.

Schiller, D., Raio, C., & Phelps, E. A. (2012). Extinction training during the reconciliation window prevents recovery of fear. *Journal of Visualized Experiments, 66,* e389.

Schlichting, M. & Preston, A. (2015). Memory integration: neural mechanisms and implications for behavior. *Current Opinion in Behavioral Science,* 2015 Feb:1: 1-8.

Schmidt, K., Beck, R., Rivkin, W., & Diestel, S. (2016). Self-control demands at work and psychological strain: The moderating role of physical fitness. *International Journal of Stress Management. Feb 14, 2016.*

Schousboe, A., & Waagepetersen, H. S. (2009). Gamma-aminobutyric acid. *Encyclopedia of Science.* doi: 10.1016/B978-008045046-9.00685-9

Schwartz, J., & Gladding, R. (2011). *You are not your brain.* New York: Avery.

Schwartz, J. M., Gulliford, E. Z., Stier, J., & Thienemann, M. (2005). Mindful awareness and self-directed neuroplasticity: Integrating psychospiritual and biological approaches to mental health with a focus on obsessive-compulsive disorder. In S. G. Mijares & G. S. Khalsa (Eds.), *The psychospiritual clinician's handbook: Alternative methods for understanding and treating mental disorders* (pp. 281–300). New York, NY: Haworth.

Schwartz, T., Azhar, N., Husain, J., Nihalani, N., Simionescu, M., Coovert, D., . . . Tirmazi, S. (2005). An open-label study of Tiagabine as augmentation therapy for anxiety. *Annals of Clinical Psychiatry, 17*(3), 167–172.

Shapiro, F. (2012). *Getting past your past.* Rodale: New York.

Siegel, R., (2007). *The Mindfulness Solution.* New York: Guilford Press.

Simon, S., Howe, L. & Kirchenbaum, H. (1995). *Values clarification.* New York: Grand Central Publishing.

Sobel, D., & Ornstein, R. (1996). Good humor good health. *Mind/Body Newsletter, 6*(1), 3–6.

Stahl, B. & Goldstein, E. (2010). *Mindfulness-based stress reduction workbook.* Oakland, CA: New Harbinger.

Steckler, T., & Risbrough, V. (2012). *Pharmacological treatment of PTSD: Established and new approaches. Neuropharmacology, 62,* 617–627.

Taliaz, D., Loya, A., Gersner, R., Haramati, S., Chen, A., & Zangen, A. (2011). Resilience to chronic stress is mediated by hippocampal brain-derived neurotrophic factor. *Journal of Neuroscience, 31,* 4475–4483.

Talbott, S. (2007) *The cortisol connection: why stress makes you fat and ruins your health and what you can do about it.* New York: Hunter House.

Teding van Berkhout, E., & Malouff, J. M. (2016). The efficacy of empathy training: A meta-analysis of randomized controlled trials. *Journal of Counseling Psychology,* advance online publication. Retrieved from http://dx.doi.org/10.1037/cou0000093

Vai, B., Bulgarelli, C., Godlewska, B., Cowen, P., Benedetti, F., & Harmer, C. (2016). Fronto-limbic effective connectivity as possible predictor of antidepressant response to SSRI administration. *European Neuropsychopharmacology,* 26, 2000 – 2010.

Walton, R. (1998). The possible role of aspartame in seizure induction. *Proceedings of the First International Meeting on Dietary Phenylalanine and Brain Function, Washington, DC, May 8–10, 1987.* Reprinted in *Dietary phenylalanine and brain function,* pp. 159–162. Boston, MA: Birkhauser.

Weil, A. (2004). *Natural health, natural medicine: A comprehensive manual for wellness and self care.* Boston: Mariner Books.

Weil, A. (2007). *8 weeks to optimum health.* New York: Ballantine.

Weil, A. (2017). *Mind over meds*. New York: Little, Brown and Co.

Weintraub, A. (2012). *Yoga skills for therapists:effective practices for mood management*. New York: W. W. Norton.

Whitehurst, L., Cellini, N., McDevitt, E., Duggan, K., & Mednick, S. (2016). Autonomic activity during sleep predicts memory consolidation in humans. *Proceedings of the National Academy of Sciences of the United States of America (PNAS)*. June 28, 2016, *113(26)*. doi: 10:1073/pnas.1518202113.

Williams, M., Teasdale, J., Segal, Z., & Kabat-Zinn, J. (2007). *The mindful way through depression*. New York: Guilford Press.

Wilson, R. (2016). *Stopping the noise in your head*. Deerfield Park, FL: HCI.

Wolfersdorf, M., Maier, V., Froscher, W., Laage, M., & Straub, R. (1993). Folic acid deficiency in patients hospitalized with depression. A pilot study of clinical relevance. *Nervenharzt, 64,* 269–272.

Xie, L., Kang, H., . . .& Nedergaard, M. (2013). Sleep drives metabolite clearance from the adult brain. *Science*, 2013, Oct 18, 342(6156): doi: 10:1126/science.1241224.

Zahl, T., Steinsbekk, S. & Wichstrøm, L. (2017) Physical activity, sedentary behavior and symptoms of major depression in middle childhood. *American Academy of Pediatrics*. doi:10.1542/pds.2016-1711

Zhou, Z., Zhu, G., Hariri, A. R., Enoch, M.-A., Scott, D., . . . Goldman, D. (2008). Genetic variation human *NPY* expression affects stress response and emotions. *Nature, 452,* 991–1001.

Resources

Options for excellent information obtainable over the Internet abound. They also change frequently; new resources are added at a remarkable pace. Therefore, the lists here are subject to change, but at least they are a place to start:

APPS FOR MOBILE DEVICES

- The Anxiety Depression Association of America (www.adaa.org) provides a review of new mobile apps that you might find helpful.
- An excellent resource from Northwestern University is IntelliCare—a review of mental health apps for all conditions. Their website (https://intellicare.cbits. northwestern.edu/) explains: "IntelliCare is a suite of apps that work together to target common causes of depression and anxiety like sleep problems, social isolation, lack of activity, and obsessive thinking. These apps are part of a nationwide research study funded by the National Institutes of Health. Download individual apps or the whole IntelliCare suite from the Google Play Store."

Here are some apps I like that have been around a while.

Breathing:

- Breathe2Relax
- MyCalmBeat
- Relax Lite

Worry:

- MindShift
- SamApp
- Breathing Bubbles

Meditation:

- Calm
- Headspace
- Simply Being

Sleep:

- CBT-i Coach

WEBSITES

Several helpful websites contain mental health resources, including those of the major universities and treatment facilities where research and training occur.

National Websites Related to Mental Health:

- Anxiety and Depression Association of America: www.adaa.org
- American Psychiatric Association: www.psychiatry.org
- American Psychological Association: www.apa.org
- National Library of Medicine: www.medlineplus.gov
- National Alliance for the Mentally Ill: www.nami.org
- National Institute of Mental Health: www.nimh.nih.gov
- Substance Abuse and Mental Health Services Administration: www.samhsa.gov

Websites for Psychotherapy:

- Aaron Beck offers tools and resources for cognitive therapy: www.beckinstitute.org
- David Burns focuses on depression as well as anxiety and has many resources: www.feelinggood.com
- For more about Albert Ellis and rational emotive behavior therapy (REBT): www.rebt.org
- For links to many websites with information about REBT and national organizations for REBT, including addiction work: www.rebtnetwork.org/links.html
- Mindfulness is one of the most rapidly growing arenas of help for all forms of psychological healing. Jon Kabat-Zinn is a leading developer of a program called Mindfulness-Based Stress Reduction (MBSR) at the University of Massachusetts Medical Center: www.umassmed.edu/cfm
- Daniel Siegel is a major contributor to teaching therapists the benefits and techniques of using mindfulness for healing: www.drdansiegel.com

Websites for Sleeping Better:

- The website of the American Academy of Sleep Medicine has significant information about sleep disorders: www.aasmnet.org

- If you want ideas for sleeping better, consult www.sleepeducation.com, which is sponsored by the American Academy of Sleep Medicine.

HERBAL MEDICINES AND SUPPLEMENTS

Several excellent commercial websites offer good information about herbs and supplements (the Bibliography also includes books on the topic). The American Botanical Council has one such website (http://abc.herbalgram.org), which describes the organization's mission as follows: "At the American Botanical Council, we are passionate about helping people live healthier lives through the responsible use of herbs, medicinal plants. We are an independent, nonprofit research and education organization dedicated to providing accurate and reliable information for consumers, healthcare practitioners, researchers, educators, industry and the media."

GUIDED IMAGERY AND RELAXATION

YouTube provides an endless array of choices for guided meditation and relaxation. You can also check out some of the authors who offer guided meditation: Barbara Frederickson (www.pusuit-of-happiness.org), Jon Kabat-Zinn (JKZ Series of Apps for Meditation in your Apps store), Kristin Neff (www.self-compassion.org), Daniel Siegel (www.drdansiegel.com).

OTHER THERAPIES

EMDR:

The "EMDR International Association (EMDRIA) is a professional association . . . committed to assuring that therapists are knowledgeable and skilled in the methodology of EMDR . . . [Their] website provides information and services to the greater EMDR community including clinicians, researchers, and the public that our members serve" (www.emdria.org).

Energy Therapies:

- Emotional Freedom Techniques: www.emofree.com
- Fred Gallo and Harry Vincenzi and energy tapping: www.energypsych.com
- George Pratt and Peter Lambrou and Instant Emotional Healing: www.instantemotionalhealing.com

Rapid Resolution Therapy:

Founded by Jon Connelly, Rapid Resolution Therapy utilizes precise hypnotic communication therapy techniques to resolve trauma: www.rapidresolutiontherapy.com

Index